Waste and the City

Waste and the City:

The Crisis of Sanitation and the Right to Citylife

Colin McFarlane

VERSO

London • New York

First published by Verso 2023

1 3 5 7 9 10 8 6 4 2

Verso
UK: 6 Meard Street, London W1F 0EG
US: 388 Atlantic Avenue, Brooklyn, NY 11217
versobooks.com

Verso is the imprint of New Left Books

ISBN-13: 978-1-83976-054-9
ISBN-13: 978-1-83976-073-0 (UK EBK)
ISBN-13: 978-1-83976-074-7 (US EBK)

British Library Cataloguing in Publication Data
A catalogue record for this book is available from the British Library

Library of Congress Cataloging-in-Publication Data

Names: McFarlane, Colin, author.
Title: Waste and the city : the crisis of sanitation and the right to
  citylife / Colin McFarlane.
Description: London ; New York : Verso, 2023. | Includes bibliographical
  references and index.
Identifiers: LCCN 2023015014 (print) |
LCCN 2023015015 (ebook) | ISBN
  9781839760549 (trade paperback) | ISBN 9781839760747 (ebook)
Subjects: LCSH: Urban sanitation—Popular
works. | Urban health—Popular
  works. | Right to sanitation—Popular works. | Sanitary
  engineering—Popular works. | Medical policy—Popular works.
Classification: LCC RA567 .M385 2023 (print)
| LCC RA567 (ebook) | DDC
  363.7209173/2—dc23/eng/20230420
LC record available at https://lccn.loc.gov/2023015014
LC ebook record available at https://lccn.loc.gov/2023015015

Typeset in Sabon by Biblichor Ltd, Scotland
Printed and bound by CPI Group (UK) Ltd, Croydon CR0 4YY

Contents

The average person goes to the bathroom six to eight times a day. You do the math.

Lezlie Lowe, *No Place to Go*

It is not about toilets in my opinion.

Municipal official, City of Cape Town

The mistake is to treat bodily margins in isolation from all other margins.

Mary Douglas, *Purity and Danger*

1

The Right to Citylife

At first glance, the building looked more like a large house than a toilet block. In the midday Mumbai sun, it gleamed bright white, the painted brickwork decorated with red plants. A local social worker explained that the community structure contained forty-six toilets, split centrally into male and female, and a children's area. On the second floor there was a water tank and a caretaker's room. Here, in one of the poorest neighbourhoods in the city, community groups had organised the construction, fed into design plans, managed the contractor, raised funds, and even contributed some of their own money. Community toilets in the city often lack a water supply and electricity, and many are badly neglected.[1] This one was a source of local pride.

The social worker interrupted our conversation to call over a woman who was passing. She explained that she was one of the organising committee members for the toilet block. 'It must have been a huge amount of work to manage a project on this scale,' I said. 'Actually,' interrupted the social worker, 'she demanded it. We want to help them realise their aspiration.' The woman smiled and added that the government should be doing this work. People were fed up waiting, she continued, especially local women. Each household that used the facility was contributing twenty rupees per month, from which the caretaker and much of the maintenance was funded.

This was to a recurring story in the research I was doing at the time: people in some of the poorest neighbourhoods having to develop and maintain their own sanitation systems, often with limited resources and capacity.

A man saw us talking and wandered over. He looked up to the toilet. 'Do you like it?' he asked. 'Very impressive.' We stood quietly looking at the block. 'We call it the White House,' he smiled, 'because it, too, is full of shit!' He barked out a big warm laugh and strolled off. It was not the first time I'd heard this kind of humour around sanitation. Nor was it the first time I'd heard people complain about waiting. Waiting in line outside defunct community toilets, waiting for the government, waiting for change. If smiles and jokes were rarely far from people's lips, so too were frustration and dismay. Mumbai is one of the most unequal cities in the world, and people are acutely aware of it. More than half of the city's residents live in low-income neighbourhoods, often toiling in poverty in the informal economy while living squeezed into just 8 percent of the land in India's richest city and financial centre. Beneath the smiles and jokes were stories of daily struggle just to make ends meet and to satisfy the body's most basic needs.

I was conducting doctoral research on housing and infrastructure in the city, but I was becoming increasingly concerned with sanitation. Whenever I asked people about housing or infrastructure, the conversation seemed very often to turn into long discussions about water and sanitation. Residents and activists often took me to look at the local toilet facilities, and unlike the case above, they were typically ashamed of the condition the toilets were in. In addition to the poor and dysfunctional state of toilets, there were horrific stories of injury and even death, including of children and adults falling into broken septic tanks or into contaminated watercourses. Some of the toilets were little more than wood and metal latrines hanging precariously over drains or streams.

There were never enough toilets. People complained of illness, including diseases like malaria and dengue from mosquitoes drawn to pools of stagnant waste and water, and outbreaks of cholera and tuberculosis. They often missed school and work due to poor health, and the capacities to play or move around the city had diminished. It was impossible to keep things clean and to adequately care for sick family members. Talking to an activist one day, he stopped trying to explain how people cope without reliable toilets and instead pointed to the open garbage ground on the edge of the neighbourhood. An old man was squatting. 'Look around and see how many children use toilets, or wash their hands,' he added, 'there is nothing available. What is here comes mainly from the labours of the people themselves.'

With all this on my mind, wondering how to focus my research, I attended a conference on the enticing and bold theme of the 'future of the city in India'. During one talk on sanitation by a city activist, she stopped, looked up from her script, and asked the room in an exasperated voice: 'How, really, can we talk about a world-class city when there's nowhere to shit?' The event brought together activists, academics, and urban practitioners working in planning and development from across India. The discussions were wide ranging – how to plan for future urban growth, how to develop 'world class' infrastructure, how to solve the housing crisis, and so on.

She had put the problem in its simplest and starkest way. Not only had her question focused minds, she connected toilets to the larger issue of urban inequality and to what residents have the right to expect of their city. She wasn't being rhetorical: she wanted to know how a moment had arrived where people can develop and preach elaborate fantasises of digitally controlled cities, while at the same time millions of people in that very city did not have access to a decent or reliable toilet. And not just at home. If you are a working-class woman in Mumbai, she went on, try finding a decent toilet much anywhere in the city. I had not set out to study sanitation in my doctoral research, but by the end of my field research in urban India it had become the focus of my work.

All of this happened two decades ago. Since then, I have returned to sanitation again and again in my research.[2] I have become convinced that urban sanitation is one of the most urgent and pressing crises on the planet, one that is worsening year after year. The impetus for this book, which I have wanted to write since not long after those encounters two decades ago, is to understand the growing urban sanitation crisis and how to respond to it.

It is such a dry word, 'sanitation', curiously itself empty of the messy lived realities of human waste and the tragedies that surround it. Even now, when I say the term my mind sometimes goes to images of clean and functional pipes and facilities, to engineering and hardware, before people, lives, gender, class, health, disease, work, school, dignity, sociality, aspiration – all the struggles and possibilities tied up with sanitation in the city. I ask students to think about sanitation as a fundamentally *networked* problem.

By this I mean that sanitation is always spilling over into all kinds of other issues, always more than toilets alone, and it needs to be understood and addressed as such. It is an approach that most research and too much policy has failed to meaning-fully grapple with. Sanitation is fundamental to poverty, inequality, and life in the city. At stake in this idea of networked sanitation, and the central contribution of this book, is not just more toilets, but the very right to citylife and all that comes with that.

A global turning point?

There was another moment two decades ago, around the same time, one that helped shape the larger world of research and debate on cities, poverty, and inequality. In 2003, the United Nations Human Settlements Programme (UN-Habitat) pub-lished a highly influential report, *The Challenge of Slums*. For the late urban critic Mike Davis, whose book *Planet of Slums* was in part inspired by the report, it was 'the first truly global audit of urban poverty'.[3] It was to global urban poverty what the Intergovernmental Panel on Climate Change (IPCC) reports are for climate, and it was significant in shifting attention onto the growth of 'slums' and their production through deepening inequality. Above all else, the report made two key contributions that significantly advanced global thinking and debate on urban poverty.

First, it provided an operational definition of slums, described their production, provided a breakdown of their different kinds, and looked to learn from best practices on how to improve them. The definition was suitably broad and vitally important, because it brought together a range of data and research and provided a framework for policy, practice, and study. Slums were defined at a UN Expert Group Meeting in Nairobi in October 2002 as combining key characteristics: inadequate access to safe water, sanitation, and other infrastructure; poor-quality housing; and insecure residential status.

Slums, then, were spaces that lacked key fundamentals of urban living: basic services, satisfactory housing, healthy and safe conditions, and so on. The report was at pains to show how slums are places where people develop solutions to these challenges, either through routinised learning in building and maintaining housing or infrastructure, or in forming organisations and alliances that innovate new models of housing, financing, and the provision of basic needs ranging from food to livelihood and mobility.

Second, the report drew the attention of national and global policy and development actors, thinkers, educators, and activists to the sheer scale of the challenge ahead. It estimated that 924 million people lived in slums in 2001 – a third of the global urban population at that time and getting on for 80 percent in some of the poorest countries – and predicted that it would grow to 2 billion by around 2030, mostly in cities with 5 million inhabitants or less (indeed, we are well on the way to meeting and exceeding this projection). It found, too, that the global geography of slums was highly varied. While Asia had most of the world's slum residents, sub-Saharan Africa had the largest proportion of its residents living in slums – 72 percent – followed by south-central Asia at 58 percent.

The position that *Challenge* took was that urbanisation had sped up and gone beyond the capacity of local and national governments to respond. For the authors, this was nothing short of a 'new urban revolution'. Rural economies were struggling, and inequality in cities was growing due to unfettered market processes and poor (or absent) state decision-making, creating 'housing deficits' in cities that led to new or growing slums. There was a generalised 'apathy and lack of political will' in many countries. People were forced to build their own homes – a process that some have called 'autoconstruction', 'peripheral urbanisation', or 'makeshift urbanism' – or to informally rent from one another or sometimes unscrupulous and typically unaccountable landowners.[4] While this was largely beyond the capacity of many states, the report suggested, there were countries that had allocated national annual budgets to successful housing programmes without breaking the bank, including Singapore, China, and South Africa.

Challenge also took issue with the structural adjustment programmes that international actors like the World Bank and International Monetary Fund (IMF) had promoted and steered through the 1980s and 1990s, arguing that these austerity programmes had reduced the scope of the state. In *Planet of Slums*, which was itself to become highly visible and influential, Davis went much further. He pointed to how such policies had devastated farming communities and served the interests of powerful agricultural actors, driving landless or impoverished villagers to towns and cities, where they then met social and political stigmatisation alongside profound everyday struggle, hardship, and labour exploitation in precarious informal economies.

What, then, was to be done? For the authors of *Challenge*, a big part of the answer was security of tenure. This was, the report argued, more important than home ownership or land titles. There are different forms of tenure security, but the report emphasised that what matters most is not just the legal documentation, important though that often is, but recognition and legitimacy from the state that assures people they won't be dispossessed of their homes and that they can invest in those homes and access rights using their address. The challenges are huge here, and particular models – different kinds of rental, individual, or collective ownership, and so forth – work better in different cities. The key starting point is protection from eviction.

In addition, *Challenge* argued that some of the best examples of urban development in slums are participatory in nature – that is, they involve genuine dialogue with residents about their needs and aspirations and build interventions from those positions. Policies, the report went on, should seek to support livelihoods in place, enabling informal economies rather than limiting or destroying them. A vital thread running through the whole report was the view that solutions are often already bubbling away in poor neighbourhoods among residents, community organisers, and practitioners, and states should learn from and work with those actors and forms of knowledge. In the world of mainstream urban development debate at the time, this was bold stuff.

The report was essential. The first systematic attempt to define, measure, and describe the key spatial expression of contemporary urban poverty on a global scale, it demonstrated how slums work and what can be learned from efforts to address their challenges. And yet it is striking that there is remarkably little of substance on sanitation across its 300 pages. While sanitation is frequently mentioned, especially its links to health, infrastructure, and mortality, it appears only in the most general and fleeting way. It is positioned as a minimum requirement for cities, but by the end of the report the reader is left with scant understanding of the scope of the problem, how to think about it, or what to do going forward.

Instead, sanitation was the feature of a separate UN-Habitat report published the same year, *Water and Sanitation in the World's Cities: Local Action for Global Goals.*[5] This report echoed much of the arguments of *Challenge*, including the call for solutions that worked for residents and in ways that reflected their needs and local environments. Like *Challenge*, it was the first UN-led effort to bring together data to globally analyse a key urban concern. *Water and Sanitation* argued that the global water and sanitation challenge was under-reported, underestimated, and not given anywhere near the attention it deserved by governments and international agencies. The report contributed to the debate about how to meet the water and sanitation targets in the Millennium Development Goals (MDGs), which included halving the numbers without basic sanitation by 2015. Major progress in sanitation was impossible, the report argued, without a new policy and budgetary prioritisation by governments and international agencies.

Taken together, *Challenge* and *Water and Sanitation* had a major impact on me. They provided a context into which I could situate the work I was doing at the time in urban India, and the knowledge resources through which to understand the scale of the challenges and how we might begin to respond. At the same time, it seemed unfortunate that while *Water and Sanitation* argued that sanitation should be positioned more centrally in urban policy and spending, *Challenge* seemed to largely skirt the issue, giving it only cursory treatment. This approach to water and especially sanitation as separate and specialised is a problem that has stubbornly pervaded urban research, policy, and practice in the years since. Even if today sanitation is less often, as *Water and Sanitation* described it, forgotten and ignored in global urban development debates, neither does it receive the attention, focus and funding it so desperately needs.

This book, produced twenty years later, is not, of course, a UN report, nor does it try to be. I aim to bring sanitation and the city firmly together, to ask what difference one makes to the other, and in so doing to place sanitation into a network of concerns ranging across people, infrastructure, and protest movements; animals, microbes, and climate change; and institutions, land, and housing. And while both reports focused, understandably, on the Global South, in this book I will also examine the urban dimensions of the sanitation crisis in the Global North, which is significant and growing.

In the intervening time since the publication of the *Challenge* and *Water and Sanitation* reports, there has been an explosion of writing on cities, poverty, and inequality, and here Davis's bracing *Planet of Slums* was an important catalyst.[6] This growing tide of popular and influential urban writing reflects a larger understanding that we now live in an 'urban age', both in demographic terms – the shift to more than half of humanity living in cities probably happened soon after *Challenge* was published – and in the central importance of cities and urbanisation for economic, environmental, and social conditions in the world. These writings have included a focus on the profoundly and increasingly unequal conditions in housing, land, and economy, including questions of tenure security for those living in so-called slum neighbourhoods. More and more often now, too, we wrestle with the impact of climate change and how we must adapt to or mitigate it.

While a significant body of research has focused specifically on sanitation, that work has remained peripheral to the cut and thrust of this new urban debate and to city thinking, imaginaries, and politics across the world. Yet issues like land, housing, economy, and climate are intimately connected to sanitation. Sanitation seems to get oddly pushed offstage. That problem has intensified with the more recent fixation on building 'smart cities' and other discourses of digital boosterism. For many urban progressives, including in much policy, urban development, and public debate, sanitation continues to be a marginal concern.

A word on terminology is due here. Both the UN *Challenge* report and Davis's book had 'slum' in their titles, and used the term on almost every page. This reflects a wider use of the term in mainstream policy and international development practice, as well as in radical scholarship. At the same time, there is often an uneasiness in using the term, and one that I share. Indeed, the *Challenge* report itself described the term 'slum' as 'loose and deprecatory' while nonetheless using the term on the basis that in some countries it has a more neutral valence.

In truth, the term carries weighty connotations in much of the world, and it was not a helpful decision to popularise it further through the report. This includes the idea that they are places *apart* from the rest of the city that are dangerous, criminal, dark, threatening, and replete with despair.[7] The term does imaginative work, and that work can prevent us from seeing places for what they are: neighbourhoods. Places where people live all kinds of lives, ups and downs, struggles and ventures. Places of urban culture, politics, and sociality – in short, of citylife. I prefer to describe such places, typically on the economic margins of the urban world, as low-income neighbourhoods where urban majorities increasingly live.

A deepening crisis

Why a book on sanitation now? First, because of the growth in the urban sanitation crisis, which is enormous and far deeper than I understood it to be two decades ago. More than half of the global urban population is forced to live without safely managed sanitation. More than a billion people are forced to regularly defecate in the open and hidden spaces of the city, under bridges, at garbage grounds, by railway tracks, along riverbanks and shorelines. In 2016 alone, diarrhoea led to the entirely preventable deaths of more than 1.5 million people, over a quarter of whom were children under five. As the world continues to urbanise, it is the poorest neighbourhoods that are growing fastest, and it is here that the sanitation crisis is at its most acute. Cities are expected to grow by another 2.5 billion people by 2050, placing huge demands on already woefully insufficient sanitation, water, and waste systems.[8]

Sanitation in the city is far more than simply the safe removal and containment of human waste; more, too, than managing the supply and demand of technologies. It is about governance and provisioning, but it is also about bodies and their wastes, broken and inadequate toilets and pipes, municipal officers and activists, places and political economies, cultural politics and people, microbes and legal rights. Sanitation erodes health, deepens the exploitation of especially women and girls, limits people's ability to move around the city, keeps children out of school, stops adults getting to work, reflects and exacerbates local tensions around religion, race, or ethnicity, stunts bodily growth, curtails the nutritional value of food, acts as a vehicle of disease, becomes a fulcrum for urban protest and resistance – and so on.[9]

If the world's poor had access to decent water and sanitation tomorrow, at least 10 percent of global health concerns and their social and economic consequences could turn the corner.[10] Unsafe sanitation costs an estimated US$223 billion a year as health costs and lost productivity and wages.[11] In one estimate, Nigeria loses US$191 million per year in the health costs to treat waterborne diseases and US$13 million per year from children missing school.[12] Lost productivity due to improper sanitation can cost as much as 7 percent of the GDP of poorer countries, yet every dollar invested in sanitation generates economic returns of US$5.50 to US$9.00.[13] The cost of providing basic sanitation, water, and hygiene provisions for all could be as much as US$114 billion per year over a fifteen-year period: a huge figure, to be sure, yet more than a hundred billion less per year than the estimated health and labour losses alone.[14]

But this is a profoundly human crisis, and it would be a mistake to view it through economic costs alone. Sanitation is central to everyday life and is intimately connected to inequalities in health, gender, caste, religion, education, and work. It spills across multiple domains of life, habitation, and mobility in the city and cannot be seen as an isolated issue. It prescribes people's ability to realise opportunities, socialise, and plan – in short, to live fully in the city.

Climate change is intensifying the sanitation crisis in cities, particularly through flooding and drought. When poorly maintained waste pipes or septic tanks burst, as they routinely do in cities across the world, wastes spill into homes and streets. Clogged drains and waste-polluted rivers and streams surge around neighbourhoods. Human, solid, and industrial wastes form toxic mixtures that seep into basements, lanes, and food supplies. Public health provisions that might alleviate sanitation concerns, ranging from medical infrastructure to emergency care or vaccination delivery, are disrupted.

When the rains come in Nairobi, for example, rivers flood streets and burst sewer lines, and many people must wade through contaminated waters to get to school or work. In Dar es Salaam, fruit seller Hadija Menato described some of the impacts: 'We not only suffer from intestinal diseases but fungus attacks on legs as we have to wade through faecal-laced water every day. In dry months, clean water supply becomes scarce and most of us suffer from diseases like jaundice and diarrhoea.' Climate change could cause more than 316,000 additional annual deaths related to diarrhoeal diseases by 2050, and it will be the poorest, typically living in the most vulnerable locations, who are hardest hit. Yet less than a third of the total investments needed in water and sanitation are being made.[15]

It is not only economically poorer countries that face such challenges. In richer countries, climate change is rapidly exposing ageing infrastructure and years of disinvestment. In November 2021, the Canadian city of Merritt was ordered to evacuate following the flooding of a wastewater treatment plant. The water system was contaminated by sewage and deemed undrinkable even if boiled. In recent years, this part of British Columbia has suffered not just from flooding but from record-breaking heat waves, droughts, and evacuations due to forest fires. Cities are increasingly forced to prepare for a multi-hazard confluence of climate-sanitation crises, with short- and longer-term impacts on livelihoods, homes, neighbourhoods, and ecology.

The impact is devastating for both people and environment. Like many cities in the United States, Philadelphia has a 'combined' sewer system. This means that the sewer collects rainwater and sewage in the same pipe, unlike more modern systems where they are separate. When there is higher rainfall, which is increasingly common, sewage spills into the environment. As much as 11 billion gallons of sewage per year can end up, untreated, in the city's local waterways. The Environmental Protection Agency states that cities with combined sewer systems increasingly violate the federal Clean Water Act.[16] Untreated waste exposes people and food supplies to pathogens, and damages local waterways, plants, animals, and habitats, both within and downstream of the city. In Britain, the Environment Agency has said that not a single river, lake, or stream is known to be in 'good status', and public concern over untreated sewage spilling into rivers, waterways, and coastlines has grown in recent years.

If the sanitation crisis is also a climate crisis, it intersects, too, with other health crises. The COVID-19 pandemic shone a glaring light on the profound inequalities in sanitation in cities across the world, including in access to the toilets, soap, and water that are important for reducing the spread of infection. During the pandemic, residents in Nigeria, Ethiopia, and Congo accounted for a third of those in sub-Saharan Africa lacking soap and water at home, while a third of all school-age children across the region lacked basic handwashing facilities at school. Half of the world's health care facilities, used by almost 700 million people, lack basic hygiene provisions like soap or alcohol gels.[17] Many countries don't have reliable data, so the scale of the challenge is likely underestimated.

These conditions meant people were far more exposed and vulnerable to COVID-19, particularly in poor and dense urban environments, and less able to contain it, just as they are with other disease outbreaks. Yet the pandemic has not catalysed new urgency on sanitation. If lessons are not learnt, these will become the conditions of the next global outbreak. Sanitation, climate change, and disease constitute a profoundly damaging and dangerous nexus of intersecting crises. The health of the body, the city, and the climate are not isolated but thoroughly entangled. A politics of one is also a politics of the other. Good quality sanitation is a network of issues. It connects toilets in the home and public toilets in the city centre to waste treatment on urban peripheries and hygiene provisions in health settings, and it brings the city, public health, and environment into the same framework.

There is, to be sure, a history of interventions that are welfarist and enabling, addressing sanitation poverty and inequality with ongoing commitment. We can think of these as instances of *affirmative sanitation*. I'll mention just a few examples. In Salvador, Brazil, 2,000 kilometres of small sewer pipes were built between 1996 and 2004 through state investment, connecting 300,000 homes. In Karachi, Pakistan, the Orangi Pilot Project of civil society organisations built a network of small sewer pipes, improving public health and local environmental conditions. In Kampala, Uganda, between 2003 and 2015 the government worked with civil society organisations to increase the amount of human waste being treated by thirty times.[18] In South Africa, the eThekwini municipality cross-subsidised water costs for the urban poor and provided more than 80,000 households with toilets.[19] Ethiopia reduced the numbers of people answering the call of nature in open spaces by more than half by 2015, following government prioritisation of public health. Across the urban world there have been thousands of small-scale interventions led by residents, activists, and practitioners, from toilet blocks that double up as community centres to eco-sanitation initiatives that generate fertiliser for growing food while reducing water use.

But there is another politics, one that operates with a very different sanitation logic. This is a politics bent on 'cleaning up' the city by displacing the poor, often violently. We can think of this as *destructive sanitation*. In 2021, for example, the government of Pakistan embarked on a campaign of bulldozing homes and evicting residents who live along the city's narrow waterways ('nullahs'). The government, with the support of the Supreme Court, has argued that clogged nullahs are the cause of floods during the monsoon rains. Activists have countered that the main impetus for the evictions is to clear the way for new roads, and they called on the World Bank, which is funding water and sewage work in the city, to condemn the acts and remove support. Some accused the Bank of effectively enabling the evictions.

Thousands of homes were destroyed and many more people made homeless. The promised financial compensation did not reach many residents – not that it was anywhere near enough to move to a new house even if it did. Children were out of school, many adults could not get to work, and residents suffered mental and physical health consequences, including reduced access to decent sanitation.[20] As is too often the case the world over, 'sanitising' urban space here becomes an ugly politics of removing the most marginalised rather than supporting communities with a fundament of everyday life.

Discourses and representations that portray particular places *as* waste play on the very real crisis *of* waste, but too often in ways that seek to stigmatise, demolish, or evict rather than support and restore. If sanitation has long been connected to powerful representations of urban misery, collapse, or dystopia, from Charles Dickens's *Bleak House* to Danny Boyle's *Slumdog Millionaire*, it is in the city's poor and poor places that these representations most acutely register. At the same time, this history shows that the urban poor are incorporated for their labour or votes even as they are stigmatised and denied provisions. As Jacob Doherty has shown in his research on garbage in Kampala, this twinning of inclusion and exclusion is very often what 'disposability' is really about. Disposable bodies are also sources of cheap labour, including in the work of cleaning and sanitising the city.[21]

Destructive sanitation can also take the form of state abandonment. In 2015–16 in Flint, Michigan, water contamination created a public health crisis caused by lead leaching into the water supply from ageing pipes. Budget cuts had led to the city shifting its source of drinking water from treated water via the Detroit Water and Sewerage Department to the Flint River.

The river was known to possess high quantities of corrosive chemicals from its industrial past, which exacerbated the leaching of lead in water pipes. Lead poisoning can cause reduced mental capacity and increase the risk of Alzheimer's disease; children are especially vulnerable.

An outbreak of Legionnaires' disease, which killed twelve people around the same time, may have been caused by the poor water quality. The disease causes fever, diarrhoea, vomiting, pains, and shortness of breath. Flint's population is mainly lower-income Black residents, and the impact of the poisoning was shaped by a long history of racial and economic inequality. This is a deeply racially divided town in which housing and infrastructural neglect and abandonment are ongoing and structural.[22] By the summer of 2021, over 10,000 lead pipes had been replaced, but the effects will unfold over the coming decades and residents have expressed continuing concerns over water quality.

If the case from Pakistan seems to be an active bout of spontaneous destruction and Flint one of a slower unfolding of neglect, both are shaped by wider societal and environmental inequalities and a failure to prioritise sanitation to support citylife. The global urban sanitation crisis has been in the making for generations. We see this in the histories of underfunding of basic infrastructure and services, from water and sewage to drainage and treatment, or in the lack of priority given to decent toilets across the public spaces of our cities. Climate change and health crises like COVID-19 hugely intensify the sanitation crisis. In response, a politics that places sanitation at the centre of the urban agenda – and connects it to the body, the city, and the environment – is vital.

But the ways in which those connections are made is itself an intensely political realm. In addition to affirmative and destructive sanitation, for instance, there is *market sanitation* – another theme I will return to throughout the book. At its worst, this is a form of sanitation that relies on the private sector for solutions. In those situations, sanitation systems can become prohibitively expensive for the poorest in marginal neighbour-hoods. I have seen gleaming toilet blocks in poor neighbourhoods across the world that are unaffordable to those who need them most, especially to larger families in which costs are higher, and particularly when people in the family have an illness – which can be a frequent occurrence – that demands frequent use.

At the same time, it would be at best unwise – and at worst downright damaging for the urban poor – to not see the role that small businesses, often those that are community run, have in establishing and maintaining provisions. The larger question here is: how are the various systems in place providing for *all* residents, including the poorest, in ways that reflect their needs and aspirations?

Finally, there is one other form of sanitation that is important to spotlight. This is, depressingly, an argument I have heard in all kinds of places, typically by people on the political right. It is the position that sanitation should not be provided to the urban poor because it encourages people to move from rural areas to poor urban neighbourhoods. This argument needs calling out wherever it is aired, not just because it is hopeless and wilfully withholds fundamental provisions to the urban poor, but because it makes no sense even in its own terms. Even if people did move for sanitation provisions, and there is little evidence that they do – in truth, people end up living where they live due to all kinds of structural, land, and housing processes, and personal connections and calculations – so what if they do? Wouldn't you? What kind of judgement is the 'you're just after a better life' position? It is a politics to nowhere, and it's usually driven by prejudice towards those most in need.

In contrast, affirmative sanitation, the demand of sanitation for all, begins from the position that sanitation is a fundamen-tal right and that it underpins the wider experience of living in the city. Affirmative sanitation promises to take the statement 'sanitation for all' – such an important universal rallying cry to hold on to – and commit to it through place-based solutions rooted in the different needs and aspirations of residents themselves. The aim is universal, but the form is radically multiple. To meet this promise, however, we must do much more than is espoused in the current global discourses and approaches to sanitation captured in the UN's Sustainable Development Goals (SDGs).

At the global scale, the United Nations General Assembly recognised the right to water and sanitation in 2010, and Article 25 of the Universal Declaration of Human Rights calls for the right to an adequate standard of health and well-being. But the key provision is the sanitation SDG, which aims to provide sanitation for all by 2030. This aim is a vital one. While there have been global commitments made before, such as in the 1976 UN Habitat 1 conference in Vancouver, which called for greater coordinated planning and investment in living standards and for governments to set sanitation targets (although sanitation was largely grouped under the broad category of 'infrastructure and services', rather than directly discussed), having a specific global goal is significant.

There was no firm sanitation target in the Millennium Development Goals until one was hastily added in 2002. The MDGs had initially included halving the numbers of people without access to safe drinking water and achieving significant improvement in the lives of at least 100 million residents of slums, including in relation to sanitation. Shortly later, in response to the relative lack of attention to sanitation in the MDGs, the World Summit on Sustainable Development added the target to halve the proportion of people who lack access to basic sanitation by 2015. But by the summer of 2014, UN Deputy Secretary-General Jan Eliasson described the sanitation target as the 'most lagging' of the MDGs, and data revealed that one in three people lacked improved sanitation facilities. There had been progress, to be sure, and greater talk globally about sanitation. But the failure to meet a target that would, had it been met, still have left half the world's population without access to basic sanitation, tells us a great deal about whether sanitation has been adequately prioritised.

The SDG sanitation goal matters, not least because it is far more ambitious than the previous MDG version. The goal focuses minds, helps generate momentum, and gives people a target to measure progress and pressure governments. Yet, consider how 'sanitation for all' is understood here. The key category used is that of 'improved' sanitation. This is the measure of progress mobilised by the JMP – the WHO-UNICEF Joint Monitoring Programme for Water Supply, Sanitation and Hygiene – the leading group tasked with monitoring global water and sanitation. But 'improved facilities' includes quite a range of conditions, such as 'self-provisioned drains that remove untreated human waste from the household or plot but dispose of untreated waste in nearby waterways'. The JMP characterises 'improved facilities' in three ways: limited, basic, and safely managed.[23] 'Limited' facilities are decent toilets shared between two or more households, while the next rung up the sanitation ladder – 'basic' – are those that aren't shared. The top rung is 'safely managed', and this refers to basic facilities where waste is safely disposed of either in situ or off-site.

This results in inconsistencies and questionable measures of progress. Globally, around a third of people who have access to sanitation defined as 'improved' by the JMP have connections to sewerage systems with no waste treatment. Only 6 percent of Nigeria's urban homes have their own toilet connected to a sewer, yet 39 percent of provisions are deemed 'improved' – even if that includes shared facilities that are not safely managed and lack decent provisions of water, hygiene care, or menstrual supplies. 'Improved facilities' also includes, as the JMP acknowledges, a diverse array of toilets and septic tank systems, including septic tanks that, as one JMP report notes, are not watertight and which are effectively 'cesspools'.[24]

At the same time, the definition of improved sanitation has a built-in bias against shared toilets, especially those shared with more than two households. On the face of it, this is an understandable position to take, but it leaves even very well-functioning community-based toilet blocks as 'limited' at best, when in practice some – if only as short-term solutions – are healthier options than many rudimentary individual toilets in or outside the home.[25] Ethiopia's success in improving sanitation conditions has largely been through shared toilet structures. Research in Bangladesh, Ghana, and Kenya has found that shared toilets work well provided that certain quality standards are met, namely: no more than three households per toilet; well-maintained toilets with good handwashing facilities, where wastes can be flushed away, and which are closely located, accessible, and available when needed; and toilets with good levels of safety, security, and privacy, especially for women and girls.[26]

A more reasonable position for the JMP would be to adopt its top tier of 'improved sanitation' – 'safely managed' sanitation – as its only definition of 'improved sanitation', and to allow for the possibility that in some cases, in the short term, shared toilets of two or three households might be much better than poorly built toilets in the home.

The JMP is tasked with creating definitions that work across different locations and forms of data collection, and so it is understandable that the categories at work are broad. However, in lumping together such markedly different forms of sanitation under the threefold category of 'improved', the definition may do more harm than good. At worst, it implies that what are in practice profoundly unreliable and unhealthy provisions are acceptable. And yet even by this broad and low-standard definition, the JMP estimated that before the COVID-19 pandemic, eighty-nine countries were *not* on track to meet universal basic sanitation by 2030.[27] The pandemic then set conditions back further still.

The right to citylife

Not only do we lack the right answers to the global sanitation crisis in cities, we are not even asking the right questions. How big a problem is sanitation in today's cities? How does it relate to poverty, inequality, and the climate crisis? What does the sanitation crisis mean for the urban experience? And what might be done about it? My response in this book is to place sanitation in the context of *citylife*. By using this couplet, connecting 'city' and 'life' together, my intention is to keep in view the ways in which urban sanitation is always already about life itself. This includes living and dying, living healthily or just about struggling through, surviving and thriving, and life in all its guises – from human bodies and wastes to the microbial world and wider ecologies that compose and are impacted by sanitation.

When we think of 'citylife', we typically imagine bustles of people in busy city centres, surrounded by tall buildings and shunting traffic. We often think of the noise, density, busyness, and sights of people thrown together in a small footprint of space, going to work or out for the evening, or moving to and from shops, markets, cafés, bars, theatres, and squares. What people often don't think of is the poor neighbourhood. Usually, though not always, located on the spatial and economic margins of the city, the poor neighbourhood is an urban phenomenon very often described in pejorative terms: the 'slum', the 'ghetto', the 'barrio', and so on.

These spaces, tremendously varied in their physical, economic, and social form, tend to be seen as *apart* from citylife. Now, cities *are* sharply divided, to be sure, and this is increasingly expressed spatially. They are fragmenting spatially and economically, carved up by growing disparities in land and housing costs, and more and more residents find themselves unable to live in the vast majority of city spaces, struggling to meet the costs of basic services and infrastructure.

In the past few decades, extreme poverty has fallen globally, but housing has often become prohibitively expensive and exclusive, and cities are increasingly divided into richer and poorer areas. The numbers of people living in so called 'slums' is estimated at one in every three or four people living in cities. It rose to around 880 million people by 2014, even as it reduced as a proportion of the urban population from 46 percent to 30 percent over the previous quarter century. Income gaps have widened, especially in larger cities, with the top 10 percent increasing their share almost everywhere decade after decade.[28] For all the allure of cities and the opportunities they generate, increasing numbers are finding that citylife is very often about exclusion, struggle, uncertainty, vulnerability, and hardship.

Think, for instance, of photographer Tuca Vieira's famous image of São Paulo, which shows the Paraisópolis favela next to the wealthy neighbourhood of Morumbi. To the right, Morumbi's tennis courts and tower blocks with swimming pools and rich, verdant green space. To the left, a dense mixture of ramshackle housing, almost devoid of public and green space. For Vieira, the image captured the 'brutal' inequalities of the city.[29] But to say that these deepening urban inequalities are spatialised is to say not just that we can visibly *see* inequalities in the city as we move around it from place to place. It is to say, too, that spatial inequality is woven through the very process of urbanisation itself. Spatial inequality manifests not only in the unconnected sewer pipe or water connection, or in the neglected neighbourhood or cosseted gated enclave, but in policy documents, legal regulations, investment and spending decisions, and the economic transformations that a city experiences.

So yes, in these ways poor neighbourhoods are very often set apart. Yet the poor neighbourhood, and its multitude of residents, are integral to citylife. They are often the toilers that reproduce the city, enabling its buses and taxis to move, its factories and shops to run, its cafés and restaurants to remain clean, its markets and roadside stalls to keep going, its medical and care provisions to operate. They very often do the work of urban sanitation: cleaning streets, collecting garbage, recycling wastes, maintaining toilets, tending to infrastructure, staffing sanitary services of all sorts, and so forth. As the COVID-19 pandemic so vividly revealed, without these often informal and poorly paid urbanites, cities would grind to a messy halt. While these neighbourhoods might be discarded from the mainstream imagination of citylife, they are part of the social and cultural life and experimentation of the city, vital to its political and environmental transformations.

Nonetheless, without decent sanitation in the home, at work and across the urban realm, the ability to participate in the city is radically reduced. Tackling sanitation poverty and inequality isn't just about better toilets. It is a much larger question of the *right to citylife*.

The idea of the right to the city has been popularised in recent decades. It is associated with French philosopher and urbanist Henri Lefebvre. In his 1967 essay, *La droit de la ville*, Lefebvre positioned the city as a site of both exploitation and tranformation, of rampant inequality and incessant possibility. For Lefebvre, the right to the city was not just a specific kind of right, such as the right to a house or a toilet or water or education, but instead something larger, a 'transformed and renewed right to urban life'.[30] It connects well with the idea of sanitation as a networked problem.

The right to the city is both a working slogan and a political ideal rooted in the historical idea of democratic control and participation over the production of the city. This includes not just decision-making on specific policies, whether on sanitation or anything else, but in the setting of planning priorities and budgetary decisions, alongside the capacity to live a full life in the city. It is fundamentally an urban and a spatial question focused on 'who gets what, where, why and how?'[31]

At the heart of the right to the city idea is a larger historical struggle for democratic control, participation, economic redistribution, and opportunity. The idea has been pursued in all kinds of ways – most notably, the 2001 Statute of the City in the Brazilian Constitution, which promoted rights to land, services, and leisure as well as the genuine participation of residents at the centre of urban planning, particularly through a committed programme of participatory budgeting that in some cases led to a redistribution of state investment into poorer neighbourhoods. It can also be found in some of the thinking of UN-Habitat, the World Social Forums, the new municipalism movement, and social movements from Occupy to the Indignados and Black Lives Matter.[32] It is a focal point around which all kinds of urban concerns can rally and a position from which we can develop a picture of what affirmative sanitation might be.

There is a long history of connecting sanitation and rights that takes us beyond the abstractions of global human rights talk and into the textures of life in the city – its schools and colleges, clinics and hospitals and transport hubs, parks and public squares, homes and neighbourhoods, and so on. We see this from colonial subjects refusing inappropriate imposed sanitation regimes or in the action of civil rights activists and sanitation workers in the postwar United States, through to struggles around caste and sanitation in India and public toilet campaigns in Britain.

In the 1970s, for example, the Committee to End Pay Toilets in America (CEPTIA), formed by a group of students, played a pivotal role in ending pay toilets across several cities. The group ran campaigns and a newsletter, *Free Toilet Paper*, and was cited as a key influence in Chicago's decision to ban pay toilets in 1973. 'Pay toilets are a disgrace and quite possibly a violation of our civil rights,' fumed the paper in the spring of that year, 'exploiting human discomfort for commercial purposes.' Gender was at the centre of CEPTIA's campaigning, given that it was cubicles, not urinals, that were charged, meaning women paid more often than men.

Move fifty years forward and switch location to India, and a group called the Right to Pee was similarly campaigning against women being charged more to use toilets. In Mumbai, Right to Pee amassed a body of data about sanitation across the city. They began by surveying 129 city toilet blocks and lobbying the state on its relative budgetary neglect of sanitation for women and girls. They launched a public signature campaign in the railway stations, calling for an improvement to the woefully inadequate and usually broken or poorly functioning toilets. Given that Mumbai's rail network is one of the busiest in the world, the provisions that do exist fall far short of need in what are very often extremely crowded stations.

What marks out campaigns like CEPTIA and Right to Pee is their commitment to changing sanitation not just in one place, but as a universal right. Right to Pee is not only about low-income neighbourhoods, but about sanitation experiences *across the city* – in town, in transit, near home, and for everyone from low-income vegetable vendors to middle-class commuters. In late 2015, the Bombay High Court agreed that public toilets in the city must have trained maintenance staff, reasonable charges, and better conditions for women and girls. But progress has been slow. One year later, Right to Pee returned an award they had been given from the city's mayor, arguing that 'nothing has changed on the ground'.[33] Still, state and public authorities do occasionally make progressive moves themselves, setting precedents to which campaigns can point. In the UK, for instance, Network Rail scrapped toilet charges at their busiest stations in 2021.

In these campaigns, the question of the toilet is one of equality. 'Today, the Right to Pee is everyone's campaign', one of its organisers has said. 'From women fruit vendors to doctors and educationists, to town planners and gender experts.'[34] Another activist in the movement, Usha Kale, has said that 'ours is a movement of sewage cleaners and sweepers, flower sellers and fishwives'.[35] One Right to Pee activist told me that the campaign had 'evolved' from 'right to pee to right to city', while another talked about the 'freedom' to participate in the city, to move around and not be stuck indoors, and repeatedly asserted that the struggle was about 'citizenship': 'It's not about facilities, it's a political statement.' If there are no facilities, she continued, then the city is saying to people: 'Shut up and stay home.' Instead, they are asking: 'How do you claim your city as a citizen?' As activists well know, this is as much about planning and culture as it is about toilets and drains.

The appeal to universal rights is a tremendously powerful one, and while it is an abstraction it is also one that is often deeply felt by residents and activists. Nonetheless, the idea and discourse of rights is not shared universally across the world, nor is it understood necessarily in the same way. Some rights are set out as citizenship provisions in constitutions and their amendments, such as in Brazil, India, or South Africa. In other cases, residents or activists might make 'claims' on the state for sanitation, which might not quite be understood as a 'right' even though the terms closely overlap.[36] The term 'rights' also has a long association with ideas of justice, equality, and equity, though it is not equivalent to them.[37] In environmental justice activism, for example, the unjust distribution of resources and hazards like water and sanitation has been shown to exacerbate inequality, poverty, risks, health, and well-being, curtailing the right to citylife.[38]

The locating of toxic facilities such as urban garbage grounds and processing plants in predominantly Black, lower-income communities, for example, has been one focal point of the environmental justice movement. For environmental justice campaigners, questions of recognition, fairness, power, and voice in political, legal, and policy processes are vitally important, as is equity across space.[39] Ideas of justice, equality, and rights are also impacted by how cities and societies change over time. In India, for example, we might consider how the urban middle classes were progressively able to insulate themselves from the health impacts of poor sanitation in other parts of the city. Susan Chaplin has described a historical shift from 'enlightened self-interest', in which the middle classes saw personal benefit in universal sanitation to control disease and illness, to a time in which the middle classes instead could protect themselves through private health provision, antibiotics, and customised local infrastructure, thereby diminishing pressure on the state to provide 'sanitation for all'.[40]

For all their differences, what is shared across these ideas of rights, equality, and justice is a concern with the recognition of different needs and aspirations, political and economic action based on that, the fair distribution of resources and safety from potential hazards, and provision and accountability of robust and relevant rules, guidelines, and laws.[41] I focus on rights rather than justice or equality because rights draw specific attention to who gets access to what where, when, and why, and because it carries with it the promise of universalism in that provision. Connecting rights to citylife, however, adds a vital urban dimension. Sanitation as the right to citylife compels us to ask what enables life in the city not only to survive but to thrive.

At a minimum, for sanitation this approach imagines a city that has five critical elements in place: a strong and coherent long-term vision for universal access to sanitation for all, catering to a range of needs, and with substantial political and budgetary commitment for both provision and maintenance; clear and meaningful opportunities for residents to shape the planning of sanitation in both the locale and the city as a whole; a commitment to maximising health and well-being for all, regardless of status, location, or background; safety and hygiene in and around the home and neighbourhood, as well as in the environment beyond; ensuring the freedom to move around the city and participate in urban life by providing good sanitation across the urban realm; and promoting the ability to go to school, college, university, and work through clear requirements on good sanitation within those spaces.

The right to citylife idea connects to two fundamental features of the urban sanitation crisis: first, that it is profoundly *networked* across multiple issues; and second, that it is made, expressed, and experienced *spatially*. As geographer Ed Soja argued, it is helpful to approach the right to the city spatially.[42] This includes who gets what access where; how the city is planned as a whole; the actions of local, regional, and national states; and whether and how meaningful opportunities to participate in urban life are realised across urban space.

The rallying slogan of the right to the city as a 'cry and demand' is an inspiring and powerful one, and connecting it to the geographies of the city is a crucial part of pursuing it into reality. With a focus on citylife, these demands are made solid in the actual lived realities of experiencing the city, in the political claims and movements that emanate from the urban margins, and as a source of expression and hope for what a better city might be.

I am arguing for the 'right to *citylife*' rather than the 'right to the city' not because the right to the city as a specific phrase is inadequate, but to signal the fundamental focus that sanitation brings to the relationship between city and life in a time of deepening urban inequalities. Sanitation systems make the city possible. They are the materialities of urban life, the stuff of urban reproduction, the exoskeletons upon which life, cultures, and economies depend. They constitute a vital political ground for the urban future and ought to be one of the most important political lines in the world today. It is a hugely demanding politics, defined by ongoing and multiplying struggle. The right to citylife is always on the horizon, and the horizon keeps expanding.

The concerns attached to sanitation often vary across streets, neighbourhoods, bus and train stations, public squares, workplaces, schools, prisons, and so on. For some, sanitation will surface as a problem primarily of gender and power; for others, it is disability, caste, race, ethnicity, or religion that matters most, or the technological challenge, or perhaps it's a question of cultures of hygiene, while others still insist on the centrality of how sanitation interventions can support livelihoods or urban agriculture.[43] The kinds of issues that come to the fore change over time, from debates on pandemic provisions, services to disabled or elderly groups, or trans rights. Climate change is placing new demands on ageing infrastructure; while for some, sanitation needs to be reinvented from a question of getting rid of waste to one of seeing waste as an energy resource.

In this changing and multiple context, the right to citylife must by necessity shift and expand, take on new directions, form new alliances, provoke new questions, and point to alternative solutions.

The right to citylife is very much not, then, a manifesto of fixed rights in the legalistic sense, even though legal and regulatory changes are often called for in the pursuit of it. If, for example, exclusion from sanitation is often about social relations of race or ethnicity, where people are denied access at work or as they move around the city on account of prejudices based on skin colour or religion, then having a legal right may not be enough to create change. The networked nature of sanitation and the stubborn insistence of cities to produce new and sometimes surprising challenges and aspirations means that we are dealing with a more dynamic sense of right than legal provisions alone. What emerges is a shifting and multiple global urban field and struggle. The urban sanitation crisis is at once a crisis of social power, health, and environmental contamination, and it requires a radical shift in how we think about, live in, and govern our cities.

2

People

Around the time I first became interested in sanitation in
Mumbai, the city municipality was involved in a large and controversial sanitation initiative, the Slum Sanitation Programme
(SSP). Funded originally by the World Bank and later by the
state, the project was huge in scale, costing almost US$300
million and aiming to provide sanitation to 1 million of the
poorest in the city. The project was to be 'demand-driven': residents were to form community organisations that would request
a toilet block, the logic being that if they asked for it, then they
would be more likely to invest time and resources in caring for
it. This is an inverse of the 'if you build it, they will come' view,
in places where there are often barely any decent toilets either in
the home or the neighbourhood. The rationality was skewed
from the start; I have yet to meet anyone who would prefer not
to have sanitation.

The SSP typically involved building large community pay-per-
use toilets, sometimes two or three storeys, in poor neighbourhoods across the city. Construction and maintenance would
create, in characteristic World Bank–speak, 'partnerships' between
the municipality, NGOs, private firms, and community groups.
The hope was that toilet blocks might become commercially
viable, in that community groups charge residents to use them
and use that money both to maintain the toilets and to generate
a surplus for other community activities. And there were many
cases where that happened. As the World Bank put it, toilet
block contracts had proven to be 'good business propositions'.[1]

The resulting picture was mixed. In the initial phases of the SSP, from the mid-1990s to the mid-2000s, there were some great successes. More than 300 community toilet blocks were built, providing over 5,000 toilet seats serving around 400,000 people.[2] But there was evidence too that some toilet blocks had been poorly built, were structurally unsound, or lacked decent water or electricity connections. A Bank-commissioned evaluation at the time concluded that there had been issues with construction quality and that there were too many cases where residents were not in fact meaningfully involved in the planning of the blocks. Women and girls sometimes felt unsafe using the structures, particularly those that were dark at night, or simply felt the toilets were mainly for the men. There were even cases of toilets collapsing, sometimes with people still in them.

In the years that followed, the SSP improved. There was greater effort to work more slowly with community organisations and to better understand the maintenance challenges.[3] But charges still excluded some of the poorest from using toilets, and community organisations often struggled to meet water or electricity costs. At the same time, there is money to be made in SSP toilet block construction and maintenance, and there have been cases of NGOs teaming up with or even setting up their own construction companies to build blocks. With land scarce in Mumbai's often dense neighbourhoods, any vacant land that becomes available might then be identified by elected officials for all kinds of purposes, including sanitation construction linked to a favoured private developer, NGO, or community group. These processes can become murky, uncertain, and occasionally violent.[4]

The SSP project remains controversial, both in its design and results. Too often, what was missing in the debate was attention to the residents themselves. How do residents experience sanitation on a daily basis? What are their priorities? How does that vary by gender or age or religion, caste, race, ethnicity, bodily ability, and so on? And what does listening to those stories mean for policy, planning, and budgeting? These are the questions that drive this chapter.

In a research project I ran with two colleagues – Renu Desai and Stephen Graham – called 'everyday sanitation', we sought to understand the experiences residents in Mumbai have with sanitation, including but not limited to the SSP toilet blocks.[5] The research revealed the day-to-day encounters and concerns that are often off the radar of city authorities. It transformed how I understood sanitation and revealed a world of labour, struggle, hope, apprehension, care, and politics that is too often swept under the carpet of state policy machinations.

Sameera was sixteen years old when she told Renu of her experience of sanitation. At the time, she was living in Rafiq Nagar in northeast Mumbai, one of the poorest neighbourhoods in the city, with her parents and six siblings. Her day, she described, started at 8 a.m. She prepared tea, washed her face, and helped with breakfast for the family before tidying the mattresses away. Then she washed the utensils at the threshold of their small house, in the same area in which the family's clothes were washed, in front of the narrow open drain that runs through the centre of their lane. 'We don't wash clothes daily,' she said. 'They pile up because of the water [shortage]' – at the time, the municipality was cutting what it identified as 'illegal' water connections. She fetched water from the local pipe each morning, and if that wasn't running – and often it wasn't – she had to buy cans of water from the relatively expensive cycle-wallahs.

The rest of the morning was taken up with cooking tiffin lunches for her siblings at school and work, and in the afternoon she helped to prepare dinner. She used the local community toilet later in the afternoon, around 3 p.m., adding that between queues and chores she did not have time in the morning. The family paid ten rupees per month towards maintenance of the local community toilet, but cleaning was intermittent. There was no water in the toilet, so she took a bucket of water from one of the lower-quality taps that she would not want to drink (the water often ran yellow from the tap). Near the toilet there was a large storm water drain, clogged with garbage, where, she said, monsoon rains led to stagnant water, mosquitoes, and illness.

Sameera felt that life would be easier if there was a bathroom in her house, but then added that 'it will smell in the house'. Like many residents around her, Sameera's family had a *mori* (washing and bathing area) in their house that they cleaned every day, a space sometimes used as a toilet by children. She contrasted her home with that of her aunt's in nearby Lotus Colony, who had a larger place with a toilet, pointing out that the arrangement works well there because there is a wall separating the toilet and living space, so 'there is no smell'.

Farida also lived in the area. She described how her husband had lost his auto rickshaw to the bank and now rents one, and she could no longer depend on his earnings: 'Some days he will give a hundred rupees, sometimes eighty rupees, sometimes a hundred eighty rupees, sometimes he won't give anything . . . I have to pay the bills, send the children to school.' To save water and money, Farida scolded her children if they wet the bed – which resulted in additional washing – and would wake her youngest at 1 a.m. to go the toilet: 'Otherwise she will wet the bed and it will stink.' She went on: 'I have a habit of keeping cleanliness but I am not able to do that because of the water situation.'

Farida and her family could not use the latrine in the house because the water shortage meant she couldn't clean it. Instead, they used the 'one-rupee toilet' per use on the main road, a block run by a private company. The block was unclean and the groundwater it used yellow, she said, but it was still cleaner than the municipal toilet and some of the other private blocks in the nearby market area. She had been using a nearer municipal toilet by the mosque, but because she had to carry a bucket on the way past the mosque she became uncomfortable. 'It is embarrassing to go to the toilet carrying a pot.'

The SSP understood and diagnosed the problem and solution of urban sanitation in a very particular way: building large toilet blocks in communities. Residents were to form groups and 'demand' structures that they would partly pay for and maintain. But when we start with the daily experiences of people like Sameera and Farida, the diagnosis changes. It is not just toilets that matter, but their specific location and the social context in which they are embedded, including questions of gender, age, or religion. It is not just toilets that matter, but local water supplies, including how that water meets – or doesn't meet – the wider repertoire of daily chores, from washing clothes and homes to cooking and clearing drains. These stories show, too, that livelihoods in marginal neighbourhoods can suddenly change, meaning water and sanitation at home, or the ability to pay for toilet block access, falls into jeopardy.

When we place sanitation into the lives of residents, in how people experience and perceive it at home, in streets and neighbourhoods, in public squares or train stations, the picture of what sanitation is all about shifts. When we 'see' sanitation from the position of the different people struggling with it – women, men, children, labourers, refugees, municipal officers, and more – then the questions of what sanitation is, of what its stakes are, and of how to make it safe and reliable, need to be understood in a different light. As a networked urban problem that connects to a larger right to citylife, sanitation is seen in diverse and sometimes actively conflicting ways. In this chapter I will focus on different angles of vision on sanitation that I regard as critical, including gender, age, disability, labour, refugee struggles, and in the work of the municipality.

Understanding sanitation from the experience and perception of different groups in the city leads to three important insights. First, sanitation is work. It is laborious. It takes time, often substantial effort, and sometimes brings little reward. It can be a source of immense anxiety, fear, and struggle. Sanitation is an investment of energy, money, labour, and hope. That investment is not distributed equally – women and girls bear the brunt of it. Second, it allows us to see some of the ways in which sanitation exists as a networked problem and why this matters in understanding it as part of the larger right to citylife. This is an instructive vantage point from which to grasp the scale and scope of the crisis in the city. Third, these different lenses on sanitation reveal the ground from which solutions to the urban sanitation crisis must emerge.

Sanitation as gendered violence

We tend to think of the stresses inadequate toilets, water, and hygiene have on the body, but in doing so we also need to recognise the consequences for mental health. There is evidence that people who need to use toilets more often, whether due to age or health or because of caring roles, often reduce the time they spend moving around the city and in some cases limit leaving their home altogether.[6] The impact of inadequate sanitation in schools can have powerful consequences for children's mental health, particularly girls, and as Farida indicated above, sanitation can become wrapped up with feelings of shame and humiliation.

In many cities across the world, women and girls suffer ongoing worries over the health of themselves or their families. There is research suggesting that sanitation-induced stress may also impact low infant birth weight and preterm births.[7] Fear of harassment and rape linked to going to outside toilets, or to using open spaces when toilets are absent or unavailable, is tragically common.[8] While this affects literally millions of women, it is women from minority groups who often report the highest rates of male harassment and violence, as do younger women. We know the problem is huge, and yet we know too that it is underestimated. Assault and harassment are under-reported, and especially so in contexts of stigma and elevated fear of retribution. It's under-reported, too, because, awful as it may sound, for many women and girls harassment and violence have simply become normalised.

A lack of sanitation can generate anxiety and depression. It can become an ongoing set of stressful calculations: will I have enough water to wash the dishes if the pipe runs dry this afternoon? Will there be recycled water to take to the toilet? Can I afford the toilet costs if we all get sickness and diarrhoea at the same time? If I join this community group and pay what they are asking, will I see a toilet block any time soon, and will I be able to access it? The mundane calculations over how much water to use or money to spend on sanitation, food or medicine are part of the everyday hum of the urban sanitation crisis.

Mumbai's poorer neighbourhoods, for example, typically receive less than half the average water supply of wealthier areas. Marginalised and, from the state's perspective, largely or entirely 'illegal' neighbourhoods such as Rafiq Nagar often get nothing or next to it, at least not legally. More than half of the residents need to pay for water, one of the biggest financial outlays for many families, and there is just one toilet for every 145 people. Across Mumbai's poorer neighbourhoods, just 5 percent of residents have access to individual water connections and around half rely on standpipes, and it is women and girls who typically fetch the water. The quantity and quality of water is often unreliable and more expensive than in middle-class neighbourhoods.[9] The gendered labour of water unfolds through a variety of ongoing and ad hoc wider negotiations: whether a neighbourhood is built on municipal land or private land (in the latter there is generally less piped water), whether the neighbourhood is legalised, or on the ethnic, caste and religious relations between residents and local politicos or landowners. The mushrooming wealthy tower blocks and shopping malls draw in huge amounts of water, while the informal labour force that cleans and maintains these spaces is denied basic services at home.

At least a quarter of children in Mumbai are underweight. Many of the city's poorest residents lack ration cards that give access to subsidised food or access to fuel. During the pandemic, public health NGO Apnalaya found that in Shivaji Nagar, over a third of the residents lacked ration cards and so could not benefit from emergency government support. There is a profound lack of adequate health services, and the areas in and around Shivaji Nagar have had the highest infant mortality rate in the city largely due to the combination of malnutrition, poor sanitation, and precarious work on the local municipal garbage grounds.[10] Even before the arrival of COVID-19, there were outbreaks of multi-drug resistant TB, alongside skin and gastrointestinal infections, frequent fevers, hypertension, and occasional outbreaks of typhoid, hepatitis, and cholera. Women and girls bear the brunt of sanitation-related illness, labour, and the ongoing mental toll of struggling to manage the costs of food, health, disease, water, and hygiene.[11]

Across the urban world, sanitation struggles deepen urban inequalities and press into the body and everyday experience. A fundamental concern here, and one that connects inequality, planning, and the body, is menstrual hygiene. Globally, one of the main reasons girls miss and drop out of school is the embarrassment of leaking rags and the paltry provisions that exist in typically underfunded schools. They are expected to quietly manage without fuss, even though research has shown that menstrual product dispensers are often broken or absent in schools. There is often a huge amount of embarrassment and discomfort that accompanies girls and younger women asking for or buying sanitary towels or tampons, or trying to hide stained clothes.[12] Too often, makeshift sanitary protection takes the form of old clothes and sheets, towels or torn mattresses, impossible to keep clean and causing infection, pain, and discomfort.

Along with pregnancy and menopause, menstruation creates profound challenges for women and girls seeking safe, healthy sanitation in the city. Without proper menstrual hygiene across the urban realm, women suffer shame, humiliation, discomfort, and pain, as well as premenstrual dysphoric disorder, polycystic ovaries, dysmenorrhea, abnormal uterine bleeding, endometriosis, and more. Even in places where sanitary pads are relatively cheap, the poorest families face impossible choices with what to spend money on every day. And in places where menstruation is taboo, women and girls often keep themselves at home, cut off from the outside world. Perimenopausal women in Ghana have listed the provisions that are needed to make menstrual hygiene safe: infrastructure that can conceal blood-stained waste from public view in busy, dense neighbourhoods, including wipeable surfaces and floors and effective soakaways and drainage; areas in public toilets where women can change and wash materials privately; adequate sanitary disposal bins, and more.[13]

Yet menstrual hygiene is often completely removed from the agendas of municipalities and states. Even well-meaning urban sanitation debates tend to overlook or ignore it. The politics of sanitation here lies not so much in how menstruation is seen as an urban issue, but in the fact that it is so often not seen at all. The city, as feminist scholars have shown, has been historically shaped as male, heteronormative, and ableist. Talk of bodies, particularly bodies that leak, has been avoided in most places most of the time across the urban world. Or, if they are discussed, the question is how to regulate bodies out of sight and out of mind.[14]

Slowly, schools and workplaces are encouraging people to talk about these issues and to ensure better provisions, but change is extremely uneven. And this is not only a concern for poorer neighbourhoods in the Global South. In 2020, for example, the Scottish Parliament passed the Period Products (Free Provision) Act following a four-year campaign to make local authorities legally obliged to provide free period products to those who need them. At the same time, urban planner Clara Greed argued that in the UK, austerity cuts to public toilets further reduced provision of toilets for women and girls.[15]

What compounds all of this, Lezlie Lowe argues, is the fact that men still dominate urban planning, governance, architecture, and design.[16] The very mention of menstruation can lead to an awkward or embarrassed exchange, while issues like gender-neutral washroom provision for transgender people, breastfeeding, and baby-changing are often not adequately prioritised. Even the basic recognition that parity in provision of toilets means there must be *more* toilets for women and girls, given that they necessarily require more time in the toilet, is missing from much planning and budgeting. Campaigning groups like the American Restroom Association have been forced to make this case time and again over the years, arguing, for example, for changes to dated building codes that mandate equal numbers of toilets rather than what's actually necessary.

This politics derives in part from the cultural politics of the female body. In India, for instance, Hindu social orders in some areas strongly connect caste and gender. Women's bodies, and specifically processes like menstruation, lactation, or ovulation, are often imaginatively linked to contamination, dirt, and pollution. Not all bodies are treated equally. Bodies are not only gendered; they are, at one and the same time, classed, racialised, and stigmatised on the basis of ability or religion and more. For example, the National Campaign on Dalit Human Rights found that 67 percent of low-caste Dalit women – often referred to as 'untouchable' – have faced some form of sexual violence, including at or near toilets.[17]

Men, in contrast, not only avoid the mental and physical hardships around poor menstrual hygiene, they are also less likely to suffer harassment or attacks. They are more likely to carve out privacy or to benefit from the distribution of sanitation resources, including the location of toilets or the provision of clean water. They are less liable to be impacted by long queues for toilets, where they often assume or receive preferential treatment, or the labour to attain and maintain sanitation. Too often, men dominate local discussions about what needs to be done to address sanitation conditions in a given place or assume the role of community 'representative'. That said, there are other particularities that mark out how men experience sanitation. Men are more likely to respond to the frustrations of ongoing health struggles and missing work caused or exacerbated by inadequate sanitation by turning to alcohol or drugs or becoming hostile to family and friends. Competition over scarce provisions in dense neighbourhoods such as clean water or reliable toilets can enflame local tensions around ethnicity, religion, or class that can lead to violence that often involves men.[18]

It is remarkable just how often sanitation provisions are delivered without engaging with women and girls in the design and implementation. Too often, interventions fail as a result. Even where toilets are in good order and women and girls feel safe to use them during the day, they often do not feel safe at night and may then turn to open areas that can be risky and difficult to get to, from railway tracks to garbage grounds. Women and girls often avoid existing facilities if they feel the provisions are inadequate. Well-meaning solutions that do not understand those concerns risk building provisions that entrench rather than reduce gendered inequalities. A radical shift is required.

Geographer Kathleen O'Reilly has called for a 'strengths-based' gender transformative approach. This involves creating space in which women and men reflect on gender relations together, identify the individual and collective values and strengths they have, and discuss changes they would like to see in the future. The approach does not, of course, do away with gendered power inequalities, but if facilitated carefully it can upend the assumption that men ought to decide. This then can become part of the daunting but crucial politics of shifting policy and spending priorities.[19]

Of course, that can only happen in a meaningful way if we both understand the vital importance of gender for sanitation *and* recognise that gender is always already connected to other social identities and urban conditions. To return to the start of the chapter, Sameera and Farida didn't just talk about toilets when they talked about sanitation. They talked about house-work and livelihood, family and relations with neighbours, drains and water pipes, anxiety and frustration, and more. When we see sanitation from the perspective and experience of women and girls, we see both that they are the single most important aspect of the sanitation debate in cities and that sanitation – as a networked process at the heart of the right to citylife – is thoroughly intersectional, connecting all kinds of identities, spaces, and concerns.[20] In what follows, I will explore the challenge that paying attention to those intersections provokes.

Figure 1. Toilets in Cape Town. Author's collection.

Home, play, and school

'In Ghana, the streets are filled with children carrying yellow buckets on their heads, on their way to a fountain.' So says Ghanaian artist Serge Attukwei Clottey. 'Every day I would see women and children pour in by the hundreds.' Clottey is discussing his photograph of a boy sitting on the ground. The boy is surrounded by yellow water buckets. Clottey continues by explaining that his photography seeks to prompt action by connecting individuals to questions of environment, justice, and the role of the state.[21] In Ghana 70 percent of illness is caused by contaminated water and poor sanitation, and it is children who are impacted the most. But as Clottey suggests, staggering though that is, it is only one part of the story. There is also all the time lost from school or play, the impact on bodily growth and development, the consequences for friendships, and the lack of safety that children too often feel just moving around their neighbourhoods.

Diarrhoea kills a child every fifteen seconds. Countries that have the highest rates of open defecation also have the highest rates of deaths of children under five. From Nairobi to Chennai, in neighbourhoods with poor levels of piped water, sanitation, drainage, and waste treatment, child mortality rates can be *twenty times higher* than better-serviced places nearby. Children suffer more than 80 percent of the world's diarrhoeal disease and worm infections, and given that more and more children live in urban areas – currently half of all children – this emergency is increasingly an urban one. In Ghana, children suffer as many as thirty-five episodes of diarrhoea and respiratory infections per year. In Kibera, one of the largest low-income neighbourhoods in Kenya, not only are younger children most vulnerable to typhoid caused by poor sanitation, with rates going up with density, but strains are now resistant to most antibiotics. Vaccination is an urgent priority, given that sanitation improvements can take time to deliver.[22]

Inadequate sanitation is closely related to child malnutrition and weaker immune systems, and therefore potentially to weaker comprehension, reasoning, memory, behavioural problems, and a set of associated impacts on mental well-being, social development and play, parental stress, health care, and school attendance.[23] Malnutrition caused by poverty and inadequate sanitation stunts growth and keeps kids out of school, while the costs a family might face to deal with the consequences of poor sanitation can mean children have to work in an often unscrupulous informal economy.

The millions of children who live in city streets, sleeping on railway platforms or under bridges or on pavements, often have no access to any form of sanitation at all. In dense neighbourhoods, open drains, landfills, garbage grounds, and contaminated rivers often double up as play areas. Parents worry about their children being hit by cars while crossing busy roads to get to toilet blocks. Little wonder Payal Tiwari has called these conditions 'toilet torture'.[24] Children can fall into or through often precarious toilet structures located at contaminated watercourses. In Mumbai, one widow Tiwari described how her husband had died in a septic tank trying to save a child who had fallen in. The World Health Organization estimates that almost 300,000 children's lives could be saved each year through better water, sanitation, and hygiene.[25]

Yet, globally, not only do few cities even have child-centred health plans, many schools lack gender-segregated toilets. In 2019, almost 40 percent of schools – around 700 million children – lacked 'basic sanitation' consisting of functioning single-sex toilets with soap and water. What's particularly depressing here is that the standards for measuring sanitation in schools are already so low. For example, the WHO-UNICEF JMP defines schools with water – but no soap – and toilets that are *not usable* as having what they call a 'limited service'. They are not technically wrong – the service is clearly limited – but it surely cannot make sense to describe such a system in terms that imply that a meaningful facility is present. And this in the same report that emphasises the importance of soap, water, and hygiene for preventing the spread of COVID-19. The report also noted that meeting universal access by 2030 would demand 'a five-fold increase in the current rate of progress', and that northern Africa and central, southern, and western Asia were the only regions to increase basic sanitation coverage in schools by more than 1 percent in the years between 2015 and 2019.[26]

This is an astounding failing of the life chances of the most vulnerable. In practice, what this means, among other hardships, is schoolgirls sometimes going the whole day without using toilets because of the risks and conditions of the existing facility, even deliberately restricting their intake of water and food. Almost a quarter of girls in Nigeria have reported missing school in 2018–19 because they can't access what they need while menstruating, and few schools have covered bins for disposing of menstrual materials or provide free sanitary products.[27]

While some countries are making progress with sanitation coverage in schools – up to 65 percent and growing in Togo – in Nicaragua, it's just 12 percent, and overall progress is slow.

In Mexico, coverage might be better than other places but it actually *decreased* between 2015 and 2019. Nearly one in five schools across the world have no sanitation service at all, and overall conditions are worse in primary schools compared to secondaries. There is evidence, too, that conditions are worse in schools that cater largely to Indigenous groups, and that few provide for children with disabilities. Even in places with toilets in all schools, such as Tajikistan, just 11 percent of schools in urban areas have dedicated toilets for children with disabilities. Urban areas tend to have better sanitation in schools than rural areas, but the coverage is lower in poorer neighbours on the peripheries of cities.[28]

It is surely unnecessary to point out that children's sanitation is a scandal that is both preventable and urgent. It demands a radical shift in focus, placing the experience and aspirations of children at the centre, whether at home, at school, or on the move in the city. To be sure, hygiene education is part of this, particularly among younger kids, but that will not make enough difference on its own. This is clearly a structural and global problem requiring committed investment. It is not sufficient to instruct kids to wash their hands when there is no soap or the water is contaminated, or to avoid playing near drains where there is little other public space and no playgrounds. Information alone is not enough, and in any case children are often very aware of, for example, the importance of soap or handwashing.

What is needed is to better understand the risks and contaminations as they occur in different urban sites, as well as asking children how they experience sanitation hazards, illnesses, and worries. On purely economic terms, the resulting savings in health and education of healthier youngsters is likely to more than recoup the costs. Responding to the crisis demands amplifying and meaningfully listening to the voices of children and young people in policy and planning, and there is a long way to go before we have the necessary amount of research, planning habits, and frameworks that might enable that. And again, these are intersectional issues. There is evidence, for instance, that if women are given more say over sanitation resource allocation in cities, then more funds are spent on sanitation facilities for children.[29]

Focusing on children's experiences and perceptions widens our understanding of what needs to be done. In one study in peri-urban Swaziland, girls were asked to photograph areas they felt were 'safe' or 'not so safe', and the researchers were surprised to find that many of the photographs consisted of toilets.[30] The toilets, the girls explained, 'were dangerous because they were too far from the school and you could be raped there', and they were in such poor condition that they offered little privacy. The teachers were equally surprised to find that the girls had fixed on toilets. The boys, in contrast, took pictures of a wider range of sites – unclean toilets, yes, but also polluted water, debris, and broken windows. Quite different views of the same landscape, demanding what the researchers called greater 'sex disaggregation when we come up with safe spaces for young people'.[31]

Solutions necessarily vary across different urban contexts. In Mozambique, a set of interventions in smaller towns focused on mixed-media techniques such as community broadcasting radio and video that were run with residents, including children. The radio was used to raise awareness and advocate to policymakers. In Abuja, Nigeria, an initiative promoted classroom debates and stories to push sanitation further up the list of school priorities. In Somalia, handwashing facilities have been installed in schools and health care clinics. In a refugee camp in Iraq, one family spoke about how they had become accustomed to walking long distances to get water they then had to carry back in heavy plastic containers, often amid arguments about how much water each person should get. On delivery of a new nearby water tank, one mother commented: 'Before we had the tank, I couldn't wash clothes or bed sheets regularly. My children could only wash every three days. Now, they have more clean water to drink and they can wash every two days. I am also able to wash our clothes and sheets more frequently, which helps keep us all healthier.'[32]

These may be piecemeal and incremental changes, but they are vital. The problem is that given the networked nature of sanitation, specific interventions such as these can be rendered less effective, or even ineffective, because of the wider conditions of sanitation inequality and exposure. In Maputo, Mozambique, for example, the construction of on-site shared toilets and septic tanks led to only limited improvement in children's health.[33] Researchers found that the new sanitation was generally more successful in reducing exposure to pathogens from waste among younger children, but less so with older children. Older kids are more mobile, and so between home, school, play, and moving around the neighbourhood and beyond, they were becoming exposed to pathogens elsewhere, undoing the benefits of the new system. Building toilets does not change the presence of open drains containing sewage and other wastes, or prevent exposure to animal wastes.[34] As we will see in Chapter 4, pathogens do not stand still. They are on the move. Solutions necessarily need to be citywide.

Ensuring that children not only survive but that they can thrive without ongoing and repeated bouts of sickness, and that they are able to go to school and play safely in their neighbourhoods and around the city, demands understanding sanitation as a network. The network is both a set of spaces – home, school, nursery, neighbourhood, forms of transit, play areas, parks, and public spaces – and a set of issues: health, nutrition, gender, privacy, protection, hygiene, fun, training, and so on, all of which are shaped by inequalities in gender, class, race, ethnicity, age, and bodily ability. The experience children have of sanitation needs to be embedded in urban governance frameworks and municipal services. The right to citylife demands investment across the urban realm, and it is an investment not just in places, infrastructure, and services, but in young lives and the future of cities.

Working sanitation

In Hyderabad, a manual scavenger emerges from a blocked drain. Squeezed into a narrow pipe, surrounded by raw sewage, he uses his bare hands to attack the blockage. In Delhi, three men are killed trying to unblock a drain underneath the Indira Gandhi National Centre for the Arts. In Chennai, two men die attempting to unblock a forty-foot deep septic tank underneath a hotel. The men, typically working without any safety gear, were killed by asphyxiation from toxic gasses. 'I have seen both my friends Deepak and Balwinder die in front of my own eyes,' Mohan from Delhi told *The Indian Express*: 'We told the contractors that the fire from the matchstick is not sustaining in the sewer but he ignored us. My friends were asphyxiated . . . They just needed some money that day, to eat.'[35] These stories of death from cleaning drains and sewers multiply in cities across the world.

The Safai Karmachari Andolan (SKA), says founder Bezwada Wilson, is 'a platform which emerged out of anguish'. SKA has been campaigning for rights for 'manual scavengers' in India since the early 1980s. Manual scavenging is the practice of unblocking and cleaning toilets and drains and is conducted by low-caste Dalits often referred to as 'untouchable'. 'We started arguing that we are scavengers not because we are ugly, dirty, or lazy,' says Wilson, 'but because we were born into a particular caste.'

SKA has mobilised workers to campaign for safety equipment, and better pay, and it has been supporting people out of manual scavenging – work that Wilson describes as 'inhuman and heinous' – into other areas of work.[36] They have run campaigns such as 'burn the basket', in which thousands of workers destroy the baskets they use to collect human waste and which, as Shomona Khanna has put it, 'represent their enslavement'.[37] Wilson's view is that 'the right to sanitation should also include the rights of sanitation workers' – which must include, too, an expansive conversation about sanitation in their homes and local environments, about water and drainage, about the

48

discrimination and exploitation of caste, and about legal provisions and governance.[38] In short, the right to sanitation is a
networked right across all spheres of life.

Former Indian prime minister Manmohan Singh may have
described scavenging as 'one of the darkest blots' on the country,
and it may be illegal, but the practice continues nonetheless – a
stark reminder, should we need it, that legal changes in themselves are often not enough. In January 2013, the Supreme Court
expressed serious concern at the inordinate delay in passing the
*Prohibition of Employment as Manual Scavengers and their
Rehabilitation* bill, which was designed to replace the 1993
*Employment of Manual Scavengers and Construction of Dry
Latrines (Prohibition) Act.* The bill promised, in conjunction
with existing legislation, rehabilitation of manual scavengers
through training and education grants. Critics argue that this
rarely happens, or that if it does the retraining is inadequate,
and that instead the emphasis has been on punishing the workers themselves.[39] 'Scavengers' are threatened with fines or up to
five years in prison. To demand rehabilitation and immediate
passage of the pending bill, hundreds of manual scavengers and
many of their family members burnt their baskets at Jantar
Mantar in Delhi.

In September 2020, against the background of a growing
number of deaths of people cleaning sewers, the government
sought to strengthen the bill. They introduced an amendment
that increased the prison term and fine amount, and sought to
fully mechanise sewer cleaning. Pragya Akhilesh, of the National
Convener of Rehabilitation Research Initiative India, was not
convinced the amendment would lead to the necessary change –
'haven't we been here before?' he asked – and that, once again, it
did not do enough to ensure training or compensation.[40] Neither, he continued, did it identify and define different forms and
contexts of manual scavenging, ranging from schools, sewage
treatment plants, and neighbourhood sites to biomedical waste.
Moreover, he said, there isn't anywhere near enough in the bill
to punish those parties perpetuating manual scavenging.

Around 1.3 million lower-caste Indians, Dalits, make a living through manual scavenging. Most of them are women paid less than the minimum wage, using boards, buckets, and baskets often carried on the head. The International Dalit Solidarity Network has been working to bring these conditions to light, through the #stopkillingus campaign as well as through state lobbying, local and regional forums, and international activities with governments and agencies. This includes working with SKA, which regularly organises protests and events across India to demand an end to scavenging and which estimates that 1,200 people die annually in the country through such work. The reason the government does not follow through on its commitment to end manual scavenging, Bezwada Wilson argues, is because of caste-based discrimination: 'Had members of other castes been involved, some solution would have surely been found.'[41] SKA remains focused on retraining, support, mechanisation, and protest.

Just as I argued in relation to women and children, the experiences that different groups have of the urban sanitation crisis are shaped by wider social and political power inequalities. Across the urban world, this is true of those doing some of the most menial and dangerous work imaginable. In Dhaka, they are 'sweepers', in Haiti *bayakou*, and in Nairobi 'froggers', almost always stigmatised, working often without gloves or appropriate clothing, cleaning out faecal sludge with their hands and buckets, struggling with injury, disease, and infection, and rarely making it to old age.[42]

The cost of not having sewer connections can be measured not just in the impact on people's health, education, livelihoods, or in the environmental consequences, but in the often horrendous conditions that millions of people around the urban world are daily subjected to in this kind of manual labour. Even where sewers are in place, blockages resulting from high usage and inadequate maintenance are sometimes resolved by sending not machines but people into the tunnels and pipes. Vulnerable and stigmatised waste workers are always implicated in what Vinay Gidwani calls a 'political history of the senses': work requires

Figure 2. Unblocking a drain, Mumbai. Source: Renu Desai
(reproduced with permission).

colossal levels of 'sensory resilience' – visual, aural, olfactory, and tactile – while at the same time being depicted as an affront to 'bourgeois senses'.[43]

Few countries have guidelines that explicitly protect the toilet cleaners and caretakers, sludge handlers and tank emptiers, waste disposers and sewage treaters that have always done the deeply defamed work so vital to how cities operate. They enter the most unspeakable sites of the city, whether in houses or schools, hotels or bus stations, doing poorly paid, insecure, and profoundly hazardous work. Illness and injury are common. They are exposed to dangerous chemicals, pathogens, and gases and suffer frequent asthma, gastroenteritis, schistosomiases, fever, fatigue, headaches, dizziness, eye burning, skin irritation, muscle and joint pain, cuts, and trauma.

On low pay, with no labour protection, and little if any social security, they often feel trapped in oppressive work with multiple hazards. One manual emptier, Inoussa Ouedraogo, from Burkina Faso described an injury while working: 'A slab caught my finger, and I had to treat the wound for 11 months. In total, the care cost me about 60,000 CFA francs . . . I continued to work while caring for the injury.' Another, a medical waste worker in Bangladesh said, 'I carry out my responsibility to clean hospital waste, but when I become sick no one will take over my work . . . I do not have any savings to pay the medical cost.'[44]

During the COVID-19 pandemic, these workers became more vital still and few of them were able to stop working or to self-isolate either at work or home. A series of reports by Water Aid found that the pandemic exacerbated existing vulnerabilities, including the lack of health insurance and the stigmatisation of workers as 'sources of contamination'. Sanitation conditions for these workers are not a lot better at home. In Bangladesh, 60 percent of sanitation workers share a toilet at their place of residence with an average of twenty-five other users. Only just over half were found to use gloves at work, and fewer still had protections for their head, eyes, feet, and bodies, meaning not only that workers are themselves more exposed to injury and pathogens but that waste particles can travel from work to home.[45]

Recognising and supporting these forms of work is a vital first step to addressing these conditions, but the central goal must be to ensure that no worker is forced to handle or encounter human waste. Rather than putting people out of a job, what's often required is proper personal protective equipment, machinery, and the formalisation of labour, alongside clear guidelines on protections and punishment for employers who flout regulations. Legislation, policy, and clear codes of practice are essential, alongside adequate budgetary support for equipment and enforcement. Training opportunities would offer routes to other forms of work, while health care provisions are transparently in need.

The well-being and personal development of sanitation workers needs to be central when we think about and manage sanitation in the city, from the International Labour Organization to the local municipal ward. This means addressing not just manual scavenging but caring for and including the people caught up in such work, including their lives at home, support for health and education, and responding to campaigns on damaging caste ideologies and cultural stigmatisation. This is a politics not only of work but of citylife that requires building interventions around the experiences and aspirations of workers themselves.

Urban refuge

In today's urban sanitation crisis, the city does not offer much refuge for those on the margins. Indeed, the city can be downright threatening to women and girls simply trying to use a toilet or go to school or work, or to stigmatised workers desperately trying to eke out a living in the worst conditions. What, then, does the city offer refugees themselves? What kinds of sanitation conditions do refugees encounter in neighbourhoods and camps? Here we find a growing problem that is increasingly pressing in the sanitation crisis. Learning from the people caught up in the crisis – listening on the ground to their concerns, struggles, and hopes – is crucial in diagnosing the issues and developing solutions.

The public perception of refugees tends to be of people living in camps displaced for a relatively short period following a crisis. In practice, the picture is very different. Between 60 and 90 percent of the world's refugees – over 70 million people – live in cities, and the average period that a person spends displaced is almost *two decades*, during which they carve out a life in the urban area. Refugee camps are rarely short-term. In the 1980s, the average duration of displacement for refugees was nine years. By the mid-2000s, it had more than doubled to twenty.[46] This means that it is a fundamental mistake to approach the relationship between sanitation and refugees as a problem of temporary emergency provisioning alone. Instead, the approach must be long-term and consolidative, with a view to supporting and enabling refugees in their right to citylife.

One in a hundred people have been forcibly displaced from their homes in recent years, often to under-resourced peripheries of already deprived urban neighbourhoods. Refugees, whether internal or moving between countries – most are 'internally displaced' or move to neighbouring countries – are increasingly dislocated due to war, inequality, and climate-induced impacts. Contrary to much of the West's mainstream media reporting, only 16 percent of refugees end up in upper-income countries, whereas a third move to the poorest. Fewer than one in five refugees have access to safely managed sanitation where they live.[47]

In refugee camps from Ethiopia and Uganda to Brazil, inadequate sanitation drives a high incidence of diarrhoeal disease and other infections, such as hepatitis. In Kenya, almost half a million refugees – many of whom have fled violence in Somalia, South Sudan, and the Democratic Republic of Congo – live in camps where life can be difficult to bear.[48] Dadaab, on the Kenyan border, is the world's largest refugee camp and has become a city in its own right. Here, sanitation remains the most important area of intervention for people's health and capacity to take part in other activities. Over time, camps often become makeshift towns or are integrated within existing urban peripheries, yet they are often left with the rudimentary toilets, septic tanks, and pits that were initially set up as temporary measures.

In Lebanon, which hosts the highest number of refugees relative to its population of any country in the world, Syrian refugees have struggled with widespread sanitation difficulties. Contamination from human waste has seeped into water supplies not just within these neighbourhoods but across the city. In Jordan, more than a million refugees fled the war in Syria and municipalities struggled to respond to the new arrivals. There was inadequate water, and the amount of solid waste being generated was growing exponentially, but there was also a shortage of waste disposal staff and equipment. Quickly improvised systems barely coped. The challenge of keeping pressured services clean caused increasingly regular outbreaks of infections, particularly for women and girls during menstrual cycles, and led to long queues and compromised privacy. In Brazil, to which large numbers have sought refuge in recent decades, from Haitians following the 2010 earthquake to economic refugees from Venezuela, refugee support centres have helped run immunisation programmes or support during pregnancy, as well as training programmes for municipal staff on how to best support refugees.[49]

In Berlin, which received almost 60,000 mainly Syrian refugees in 2015, the municipality was heavily criticised for failing to provide the newcomers with decent conditions, including housing, showers, and adequate toilets and water. Many activists rejected the municipality's claim that it was virtually impossible to keep up with the numbers arriving. More than forty lawyers filed a criminal complaint against the former head of the state refugee processing organisation and the city's social affairs senator, alleging that institutional neglect was 'causing bodily harm' through injury, illness, hunger, and homelessness.[50] There have also been cases of the far right targeting toilets catering to refugees. In 2012, for instance, a group of neo-Nazis in Berlin set a toilet block used by refugees on fire.

In his work on Turin, Michele Lancione shows how refugees and homeless migrants experience profound sanitation marginalisation. As he argues, people find that they are outside the shelter system because they lack valid documentation and because they struggle with the language skills and knowledge to navigate the city. Refugees have been cast aside to marginal spaces in the city, occupying abandoned factories and the former Olympic village, where there are barely any sanitation facilities, or indeed facilities of any sort beyond mattresses on the ground.[51] This story echoes across the urban world. If inadequate sanitation impacts people's health, dignity, and ability to work or attend school, it is compounded by the cumulative impact of exclusion from decent housing and energy, transport provisions, public spaces, and citizenship rights, including police protection.[52]

Nonetheless, there have been encouraging examples of city and national governments that are committed and able to devote the necessary resources. During the COVID-19 pandemic, there were cases of cities providing free access to health care, banning housing evictions, precluding rent increases, and so forth. São Paulo provided food support and emergency housing to refugees, while Los Angeles gave cash assistance to undocumented migrants, and many cities made personal protective equipment freely available.[53]

International agencies like the World Health Organization and UNHCR have been advocating for holistic approaches to public health and refugees, connecting sanitation and water to food, physical and mental health care, illness and disease, and housing, labour, and energy. The largest cause of death among refugees is respiratory tract infections such as TB, followed by malaria, diarrhoea, intestinal worms, and skin disease, all of which can be exacerbated by poor sanitation but which are not resolved by targeting sanitation alone.[54] Disease outbreak surveillance and preparedness is vital but typically missing. Child refugees are often particularly vulnerable due to trauma and because they have sometimes missed vaccination programmes in their own countries.

Refugees are not, however, merely the victims of displacement or of poor sanitation. There are countless examples all over the urban world of people organising themselves to protest their living conditions or to provide self-managed systems in the absence of adequate provisions. During the pandemic, for example, in the small town of Hamdallaye in Niger, refugees organised themselves to create a small non-profit 'factory' churning out soap, handwash, bleach, and water containers for free distribution. 'We are not only helping to fight this disease but are also learning new skills that will help us when we return home,' Nicole from Libya said.[55] A local NGO, with UNHCR support, provided equipment and training. The provision was vital; only a quarter of households in sub-Saharan Africa have access to handwashing facilities with soap and water.[56]

Refugees have always been and are increasingly part of citylife across the urban world. Sanitation is vital not only to their health and well-being, but to their ability to get by and get on, to flourish in the social, economic, and political life of the city. In many cities, addressing sanitation conditions for refugees requires changes to the citizenship status and legal provisions afforded to them, as well as challenging social and cultural prejudices and stigma. All of this requires an enormous amount of time and work, but the progressive responses from civil society groups, social movements, and municipalities across the world, from Beirut to São Paulo, show that alternative routes are always possible.

Sanitary municipalism

Research and policy debate on sanitation tends to pay less attention to municipal officers than to the political will of politicians. Understandably so, given the crucial role of political will in setting policy directions and budgets.[57] But as the foot soldiers and middle management of sanitation bureaucracy and delivery, municipal officers have important insight into sanitation and their work can make a significant difference. They often do the necessary work of translating policy into workable approaches. They are the key points of contact with residents, civil society groups, and the private sector, and they have a unique view of how these different actors operate and what they bring or don't bring.

Municipal officers regularly face all kinds of dilemmas on resource allocation or delivery and must adapt and respond using whatever connections, skills, and dispositions they can put to work. She or he has to operate within the political agendas and bureaucratic strictures of the municipality, which in large cities are often multiple, burdensome, and sometimes contradictory. At the same time, municipal officers bring their own concerns, aspirations, mindsets, prejudices, and networks to their jobs. In big cities like Delhi, Lagos, London, and São Paulo you are just as likely to meet those who are well schooled in international debates on sanitation research, policy, and practice as you are to meet those who seem blissfully unaware of them.

The municipal officer is *of* the state but often unable to make 'big' decisions on policy or budgets, yet they bear the brunt of complaints, anger, and the multitude of concerns that come with working on urban sanitation. Sometimes officials share the frustration that residents have with politicians but nonetheless become the face of unpopular policies. I remember speaking to one well-placed official in Mumbai's sanitation department, for example, who argued that councillors, MPs, and MLAs (members of the Maharashtra State Legislative Authority) invest vast sums of their allocated welfare spending on toilet blocks in order to shore up votes, meaning that money and votes form a mutually reinforcing cycle, and that funds are often channelled into already established or improved areas.

Politicians often attempt to associate themselves with improved water and sanitation provisions – whether it is they who provide them or not – and disassociate themselves from the removal of toilets or the cutting of water pipes. During a cholera outbreak in northeast Mumbai in which six people died, the water department decided along with a local politician to cut the plastic water pipes in the area, on the basis that plastic pipes

are more vulnerable to being broken and therefore to trans-
mitting contaminated water. Here, as Lisa Björkman argues,
politicians are in a bind: even if they want to cut the plastic
pipes, they can't be *seen* to want to.[58] Partly to shore up their
base and enhance their credibility, they want to be seen to be
both protecting the water pipes and extending others. This
system, the official I spoke to went on, serves primarily to reproduce the status quo and limits his room to manoeuvre.

The intersections between politics and religion are important
here for how infrastructure and services are delivered, maintained, and improved, and officers are not only caught up in this
relationship, they are sometimes active proponents of it. In
Mumbai, the Shiv Sena, a regional party with a long history of
ethno-religious chauvinism and anti-Muslim politicking, and
which has governed the city since 1995, plays a vital role in the
politics of patronage. In one working-class neighbourhood in
western Mumbai, for instance, the local party *shakha* (office) is
a key urban intermediary for infrastructure and services. The
local Sena municipal staff use various state programmes and
departments to provide for work needing done, from blocked
drains to accumulated waste or dysfunctional toilets. Going
through the Sena *shakha* will generally result in a complaint
being dealt with faster than if a resident approaches the relevant
department on her or his own.

One local resident told me that the *shakha* is 'an office to
buy votes' and alleged that the party treats the neighbourhood
as an opportunity to make money through what he neatly called
'political adjustment' – siphoning off money from development
projects – rather than a place where people's lives might be
improved. Some of the residents are migrant garment workers
living in rental homes who do not get a vote and who, partly as
a result, lack sanitation services. In some areas of the neighbourhood with weaker links to the Sena, and where residents
have found it difficult to pay for a cleaner for local toilets on
their own, blocks have been effectively abandoned.[59] The work
of municipal officials in providing or not providing sanitation

can be shaped as much by cultural and political power as by policy, law, and regulation.

While conducting research in 2015 with Jonathan Silver in Cape Town, I sought to better understand how municipal officers operate in these contexts of political power bases and constraint.[60] Officers we spoke to at the City of Cape Town working on the city's informal settlements and townships described obstacles to their work, including community negotiations and land claims. As one officer put it, these obstacles are not just about money or even about toilets, but about the social and political challenges of urban development in South Africa: 'If you give me a billion rand now I can't service informal settlements. There are other issues. Space, density, community, land ownership. It is not about toilets in my opinion. The question is how are we going to deal with it in relation to other constraints?'

Here, the municipal officer positioned himself as a kind of urban broker, working sanitation as a networked issue. As a broker rather than just a public service worker, he saw himself as someone who had to know the agendas and concerns of different actors and be able to negotiate something from where people where positioned, mindful too of all the targets politicians set. On community leadership, one official working on sanitation and water in informal settlements estimated that his team spent 'maybe 80 percent' of their time in different forms of community consultation: which leaders to consult when providing sanitation, who to keep happy in order to ensure systems can be maintained, and so on. In some areas, negotiations became conflictual and even violent.

Of course, the claim that dense and Black neighbourhoods are opaque or unknowable or violent itself has long colonial roots entrenched by the cultural geographies of apartheid. This is a politics not just contingently connected to the moment, but shaped too by the long histories of race, class, and segregation in the city. Gaining local support for slow sanitation improvements in a context of deep and historical inequalities of race and class is, not surprisingly, a fraught politics. And yet local support has been shown again and again to be crucial for successful sanitation, and not just in Cape Town. Globally, estimates suggest that between 30 and 70 percent of sanitation projects fail within a few years, and one reason is a lack of engagement with local people and their concerns.[61]

Another blockage identified was described as land availability and the capacity to develop informal settlements on private land. In cases where land is privately owned, municipal officers may eventually calculate that the only practical option is to buy the land in order to control service and infrastructure provision. In other cases the challenge is what officials pejoratively call 'land invasion'. The Constitution requires the municipality to provide minimum services on at least a temporary basis to residents who occupy empty land in the city, but officials insisted that this is unfair on other neighbourhoods who are 'legitimately' in the queue ahead of these 'invaded areas'. Rather than reflect on the unequal distribution of resources, here the blockage was identified in the figure of the occupying migrant.[62]

The appeal to these kinds of blockages is, to be sure, useful for municipal officials as a political tactic in that it externalises responsibility for a lack of progress. At the same time, the officials were clearly committed, cared about delivering sanitation, and wanted to improve conditions, and it would be a mistake to dismiss their way of seeing as mere politicking. Municipal officials are not equivalent to city politicians. More often than not, they are restricted to their role as 'programmers' of the changing commitments of political parties.[63] The state is not a monolith. Municipalities and their officials are far from perfect – indeed, they are often actively complicit in urban inequalities, but there will be no solution to the sanitation crisis without them.

The COVID-19 pandemic reinvigorated long-standing agendas for a stronger, better resourced local state. Movements like 'new municipalism', for example, are important here. A politically diverse body of thinking, collaborations, and interventions – with examples in cities as different as Barcelona, Preston, Rojava, Jackson, and Cleveland – new municipalism promotes strong and resourced local and regional governments, entities that have had relative success with managing COVID-19 (see, for example, the generally good performance of Kerala in India with both the Nipah virus and COVID-19).[64] New municipalism is one impetus through which an invigorated local state, working in partnership with civil society and other actors in the city, might support sanitation as part of the right to citylife. There is no off-the-shelf model or blueprint here, and local conditions and politics can stifle change and make it difficult to operate. The right to citylife is characterised by struggle and setbacks that demand being able to read the city as it is lived on the ground.

What is to be done? My answer to that question will unfold across the chapters to follow, but what I've wanted to do in this chapter is to say: start with people. Especially those most exposed to the crisis (and, as we will see, there are many more groups struggling with sanitation that I've not yet discussed). Without understanding how the crisis is lived – how it is peopled – the planning, design, and implementation of sanitation will continue to shoot in the dark and often hit the wrong target as a result. This case may seem straightforward enough, but it is, unfortunately, an argument that needs to be made again and again. Indeed, there has always been a countercurrent in discourses about sanitation in the city in which people are seen not as the solution but as the obstruction, or as somehow not worthy of sanitation support. In some quarters blame has become an increasingly important feature in the management of sanitation.

Take, for example, community-led total sanitation (CLTS) initiatives. CLTS is based on participatory mapping of neighbourhoods to understand practices of open defecation and promote self-help, and it has been widely popularised. There are positives to CLTS. It is, for a start, people-focused. It works with residents to build understanding of where sanitation problems arise, how certain practices or local sites might lead to greater illness and disease, and from there it generates collective 'buy-in' so that people are involved in the solutions. Kamal Kar, who developed CLTS in Bangladesh, has described how the creation of shock and shame generated when people visit the accumulated areas of human waste in the village or neighbourhood spurs people on to radical change, including constructing their own basic sanitation systems, alongside new practices of hygiene when handling food and water.[65]

There have been notable success stories. Ethiopia, which more than halved its rate of open defecation in the two decades between 1995 and 2015, is one of them. In 2006, an Irish NGO, VITA, introduced CLTS and the Ministry of Health rolled the technique into its significant sanitation commitments, so that by 2015 there were programmes covering 80 percent of the country.[66] This led to many districts being issued with coveted 'Open Defecation Free' certificates. The longer-term picture is mixed, with growing evidence that open defecation has re-emerged in some of those areas due to a lack of adequate technical support, materials, and maintenance, and the existence of financial constraints and weak programme implementation. Nonetheless, there is no doubt that CLTS can have a considerable impact. Malawi, too, has had significant successes using the approach since it was introduced in 2007, with more than 2 million people, mainly in urban areas, now living in 'open defecation free' places. The country has seen some of the greatest strides in reducing multidimensional poverty linked to sanitation in sub-Saharan Africa, and CLTS has certainly played a role.[67]

However, CLTS has also been criticised for encouraging a divisive set of local relations often insensitive to gender, class, and people's backgrounds. The successes of CLTS, whether in Ethiopia or anywhere else, has in part depended on 'triggers' based on shame, disgust, and fear.[68] Shaming is an important element of the approach, with children even sometimes being given whistles to blow when they spot someone defecating in the open. CLTS can create a culture of intolerance towards those who defecate in the open when toilets are available, and there have been cases where this has involved public humiliation and even violence. As critics have pointed out, such an approach encourages residents to blame one another rather than external actors and processes for their sanitation struggles.

There is also less evidence that it works well in dense urban areas.[69] In places where there is a politics or history of stigma attached to particular groups or of city governments being hostile to poorer groups, CLTS is vulnerable to being put to work along those same lines. And there is no shortage of city or state governments twisting sanitation drives into logics of violence and marginalisation. In Indore, the city's claim to be India's 'cleanest city' was built on programmes of citizen policing, gendered power, and housing demolition that connected state, male, and cultural power to practices of shaming and violence that disproportionately targeted women. CLTS straddles the domains of both affirmative and destructive sanitation I described in the book's introduction.

While realising the right to citylife demands listening to people, placing people at the centre of solutions is not to shift responsibility to residents alone. It is not to shame those struggling or to let the state off the hook. It demands a politics of care and inclusion, of kindness even, not stigma and humiliation. It is to recognise that when the experience of a problem can be so very different, solutions must be built on careful attentiveness to those differences. Cultures of social difference such as class, race, and ethnicity mean that the right to citylife must be about more than legal provisions alone. This is the slow work of tackling cultural power and changing perceptions, promoting awareness, and calling out exclusions.

Sanitation is profoundly networked and always morphing, connecting an array of issues over urban space and time. The right to citylife begins with people, but it does not end there.

3

Things

It is easy to miss the small memorial in central London to one of the city's most impactful engineers. A small bust of a serious looking Victorian man, and underneath in embossed capital letters: 'Sir Joseph Bazalgette, CB. Engineer of the London main drainage system and of this embankment'. A few metres below the memorial lies part of the sewer system that his name will be forever linked with. Built in the mid-nineteenth century, Bazalgette's system of sewers remain among the most remarkable feats of engineering in the city's history. The Metropolitan Board of Works, of which Bazalgette was chief engineer, constructed five sewers thirty-six feet beneath the surface, running parallel to the Thames. It consisted of eighty-two miles of main lines and 1,000 miles of smaller lines, 318 million bricks and 880,000 cubic yards of concrete.[1] Accounts at the time compared it with the seven wonders of the ancient world.

Today, that ageing system struggles to cope with the level of waste London generates, and millions of tonnes of raw sewage spills into the Thames every year. 'If you're considering swimming in the river,' engineer Kayla Browne said in response to a survey suggesting that more than half of Londoners view the river as safe for swimming: 'Don't do it.'[2] Another vast infrastructure project is thus underway, the Thames Tideway Tunnel, running a fifteen-mile east–west axis 200 feet under the city and following the river, at a cost approaching £5 billion. Not far from Bazalgette's memorial you can see the ongoing works on the Thames, staff in high-visibility vests and, somewhere beneath the surface, machinery busily whirring way over a century and a half after Bazalgette and his team supervised the same sites.

Much of the material of sanitation is invisible to urban residents, hidden underground or behind walls as drains, sewers, and water pipes, or in treatment plans tucked away on urban peripheries. The labour, capital, and technology invested in sanitation expansion and maintenance is, too, often invisible and therefore out of the public mind. The most attention many people give even to large projects like the Tideway Tunnel is little more than a cursory glance at a news article about the inconveniences of traffic divergences during construction or the potential environmental impacts.

It is a straightforward enough observation to say that cities are made up of *things*. Things compose citylife everywhere, and influence its conditions of possibility. When it comes to sanitation, the material realm is profoundly important. Things matter not just to how people experience and thrive in the city, but to whether the city is liveable at all. Understanding and addressing urban sanitation inequalities requires attending to the city's fabric. More than this, we need a politics of things that looks to improve and extend the materialities of the city in ways that help secure people's health, reduce their labour, and which can be relied upon to keep working.[3]

The prospect of the right to citylife rests on a world of things: toilets, pipes, drains, septic tanks, sludge, and sewers – sanitation's technosphere – each in their own way, and together, fundamental elements in the everyday life of the sanitary city. This infrastructure is fundamental to urban life, the substrate upon which pretty much everything else depends. As dense agglomerations of people and things occupying relatively small slithers of land, cities would simply not be possible without infrastructure. More than just the stage upon which urban life plays itself out, then, it is an active and dynamic part in the city's living conditions, social relations, and economic potential. Infrastructure is the hardwiring or bedrock of urban sanitation, and the right to citylife is unthinkable without it. But infrastructure is not distributed evenly or equally, is often ageing and in need of significant investment, and is frequently mismanaged.

Where infrastructure is inadequate and unequal, it is often – to build on the arguments in the previous chapter – 'peopled', made and remade in an ongoing way.[4] Communities become organised around infrastructure, whether to run stuttering water supplies, toilets, drainage, or septic tanks, or to come together to demand improved provisions from the state. As Ash Amin has put it, 'urban infrastructure turns out to be not only as active as any community or institution, but also the medium through which much of the latter is orchestrated'.[5] Infrastructure textures urban life and inhabitation, and it shapes both the possibilities and the constraints of urban living. At the same time, infrastructures also carry with them public or state imaginaries and aspirations, including ideals of progress, order, modernity, and the future.

The toilet

Where else to start other than with the humble toilet? Humble, yet also one of the most powerful symbols of modern civilisation. Struggles over how to build them and where they should be located, or even whether they should be prioritised at all, have been at the centre of urban modernity, colonialism, and development. The toilet has played a pivotal role not just in public health but in the production of cultures of privacy and notions of civic life, everyday habit and routine, gendered regimes of cleanliness, transformations and inequalities in public health, and the endurance of both cities and capitalist reproduction. If, as Henri Lefebvre put it, monuments are poems and buildings are prose, then toilets are street talk.[6]

It is also a universal technology, not in its form or reach but in its need, foundational for how we deal with our bodies. But if for many people the toilet is part of the hidden backstage of everyday life, in most of the urban world barely

Figure 3. Pit latrine, Delhi. Author's collection.

functioning toilets are a visible source of frustration, inadequacy, and labour.[7] They frequently break down or become blocked, and require regular investments of time and money. They can be life and death provisions.

German sociologist Norbert Elias argued that the progressive thickening of proximate connections between people – a 'social relational density' – generated all kinds of anxieties around waste and necessitated greater regulation of bodily practice by powerful groups.[8] This helped give rise to the corporeal practices and spaces that shape how toilets are seen and used. Infrastructures of sanitation, enabling as they did the circulation of water, waste, and better air while also enabling the movement of goods, traffic, and people, were critical to the social production of a self-governing hygienic, moral subject. But for all that the toilet is a hallmark in narratives of human progress, the history of the toilet is one littered with failure.

The population of sub-Saharan Africa, for example, has more than doubled in the past three decades, and most of that growth has been in cities. But while people hunt for jobs in informal economies, they are often hard pressed to find a decent toilet. Existing structures are typically ageing and poorly maintained, and there are anyway far too few of them. Many have fallen into disrepair, and despite growing need have not been replaced. In just two states in India, almost half of the 4.5 million latrines built during the 1990s are no longer in use.[9]

In poorer neighbourhoods, whatever toilets do exist are rarely part of an integrated city infrastructure system. From rudimentary latrines made of wood, corrugated metal, and jute to three-storey public blocks replete with decorated children's facilities, the 'what' and 'how' of the toilet is a litmus test of city sanitation.

Given that the state rarely provides the number of toilets needed, some of the poorest residents in the city are required to spend their own money building and maintaining them. The most common forms of sanitation are pit latrines (rudimentary, often makeshift toilets) with private septic tanks. These simple and often precarious toilets can cost between 128 and 759 percent of average household monthly income to construct. In very dense areas, or multi-storey buildings, where there is a lot of use, those provisions are woefully unreliable and vulnerable to breakdown and blockage, and local groundwater and soils often become contaminated from waste. In Dar es Salaam, 80 percent of sanitation provisions are pit latrines but less than a quarter of those are lined, meaning residents are often exposed to 'over-filled pits and illegal disposal near households'.[10]

The *number* of toilets is not the only, or sometimes even the most important, factor in sanitation improvements. Research on urban sanitation has continually identified maintenance of toilets and their surrounding infrastructure as fundamental, and here clarifying who is responsible and in what circumstances is equally important.[11] At the same time, toilets are not just material provisions but symbolic entities in the city.

For many poorer residents, a clean toilet is an indicator of progress, modern living, and cityness. The toilet is made up both of materials *and* social attitudes and beliefs. 'As soon as you flush the toilet, you're in the middle of ideology', Slavoj Žizek has written.[12] As a result, toilets are not just policy and budgetary preoccupations, they also become the focus of all sorts of political and social tensions all over the urban world. The toilet is at the centre of all kinds of identity politics, from those around trans rights activism to campaigns on disability, children's provisions, or travellers.

Toilets can function, too, as symbols of male privilege. In many cities, not only is there a profound imbalance of toilet provision for women and girls as compared to men and boys, the size, functionality, and location of public toilets are extremely circumscribed. This is particularly difficult for poorer women, who find it harder than their middle-class counterparts to access toilets in hotels or restaurants. Rather than build toilets, it is easier for states to point residents to private systems. Following the example of cities like New York, the South Delhi Municipal Corporation decided in 2017 to require all commercial establishments to make their toilets available to the general public, but – unlike New York, where larger restaurants must provide access for free – for a fee. This hardly works for many residents, especially women and girls. Mumbai, for instance, has both the highest number of working women of any city in India yet cannot manage to provide enough toilets for them.[13]

To understand the toilet, and to build an affirmative politics around it, we need to understand the social, political, and economic contexts that shape it as well as the material infrastructures that support it. A politics of things must begin with the recognition that making toilets work for the city demands an urban imagination that is at once infrastructural, social, and political. Efforts to find a 'technological fix' to save the day are misguided. One high-profile example here is the Gates Foundation's 'Reinvent the Toilet' competition. The foundation asked engineers to develop 'Toilet 2.0': a toilet suitable for hot climates with often little water and electricity, but cheap. A wide range of submissions were made, including waterless toilets that use solar panels or microwaves and which turn waste into fertiliser or charcoal. In practice, many of the winning designs were overly complex and largely inappropriate for many cities and poorer residents.[14]

There is now an active industry exploring all kinds of toilets, from eco-sanitation, VIP (ventilation improvement pits), and biogas centres to mobile toilets that can quickly be provided to emergency situations or temporary camps. There are experiments with biogas-generating toilets in Madagascar that are being used to create fertiliser and charge mobile phones. There are new toilet architectures, from public toilets in Hamburg made with one-way mirrored glass to the elaborate origami crane structures in Hiroshima Park.[15] There are container-based sanitation (CBS) systems that provide small individual toilets for the home; these often separate urine and collect faecal waste to be taken for treatment, and they are used in dense areas of Haiti, where they also generate compost.

These can be expensive systems that demand reliable and regular treatment providers, but they are sometimes managed by sanitary workers with inadequate equipment and protections. In some senses, these initiatives reconnect with early experiments in sanitation in the late eighteenth and early nineteenth centuries that sought to use waste productively at different locations in and around the city, rather than integrate it within vast systems of water-borne sewers. Even Bazalgette examined proposals, prior to the construction of London's sewers, that involved urine-harvesting and waste for agriculture.[16]

We need a large dose of caution with the technological fixation of some sanitation debates. When I argue for a politics of things, what matters most is the people the things are supposed to serve. Indeed, a politics of the sanitation technosphere must be about how things relate to people and place, and we need to keep one eye on that larger network and how each part of it might support the right to citylife. At the same time, it is important not to lose sight of the potential of technological innovation. It makes little sense to outright reject technological experiments in toilet form and design.

The question instead becomes one of connecting experiments to the wider ecology of conditions – economic, political, cultural, environmental, and above all, people's lived realities. After all, across the world a wide range of sanitation technologies is in use, from the squat toilet more common to Asia and Africa or the sitting toilet of Europe, to the high-tech toilets of Japan. There are flush toilets, composting toilets, toilets that freeze waste, toilets that incinerate it, and even plans to fit toilets with sensory devices that provide real-time updates on waste and health to your phone.

All kinds of forms have been tested, from British architect Graham Caine's 1972 *Street Farm House* – which connected waste to energy and food via solar collectors and a windmill, fishpond, greenhouse, sod roof, and waste-recycling system – to the twin-pit pour-flush toilets developed by Sulabh Sanitation in India, in which lower-caste residents access simple systems of alternating pits that, when full, generate fertiliser.[17] In a time of growing climate crisis, the ecological roles of the toilet matter enormously, from the amount and nature of water they use – clean drinking water as opposed to recycled water, for instance – to how their wastes are discarded and whether those wastes might be put to work to create energy or grow food. Toilets are increasingly seen as mini-power stations and agricultural sites. These different forms of toilet technology push at what some scholars have called our 'urban sanitation imaginary'.[18]

Experiments with the toilet can open new possibilities. Some eco-sanitation proponents passionately argue that the composting of human manure – 'humanure' – is 'a much better solution to the global sanitation crisis than installing water-flush loos'.[19] Following the 2010 earthquake in Haiti, temporary housing camps suffered severe sanitation challenges and there was a cholera outbreak that killed 8,000 people, while untreated sewage was being dumped into lagoons. Part of the relief effort included humanure composting. It is not difficult to see the attraction.

All this kind of toilet needs is a container and a handful of sawdust, grass, and leaves to control odour and deter flies; time and microbiology does the rest. After a year, you have compost from which to grow trees and crops. The toilets are cheap, work well in water-scarce environments, and have a strong track record, not just in disaster-emergency situations but in schools and community buildings. And yet given that they often require a good amount of space, dry materials, management of the compost, and technical training, claims that they are solutions to the global sanitation crisis are wildly overblown.

Why should poorer residents be expected to maintain eco-sanitation systems while richer neighbourhoods do not? In Buenos Aires, residents have described urine-diversion dry toilets with dehydration vaults as 'rural, underdeveloped, and backward'.[20] Should the fact that many residents across the world see sanitation not just as a provision but as an indicator of modern urbanity be subordinated to the well-meaning preferences of a liberal development class and urban elites who prescribe specific toilet forms? And will alternative systems be sustainable in the longer term if residents don't feel toilets reflect their sense of belonging as urban residents?[21] Relevant to these questions, too, is the fact there have unfortunately been some notable failures in eco-sanitation approaches.

Take the spectacular failure of a large dry toilet project in Ordos. The city is one of China's rapidly urbanising places, driven in this case by the coal, gas, and oil industries. The project was funded by the local state working with the Stockholm Environment Institute. It involved building a complex of 14 buildings and 830 apartments, all connected to an on-site compositing system, and promised to save water in an area of northern China where water can be in short supply. This was the first project on this scale in urban China, and it was beset with problems from the start.

The idea was to build systems that separated urine and excrement. The urine would be piped into underground storage tanks, the excrement covered in sawdust and transported by pipe into a separate tank, then emptied every couple of weeks. However, there were flaws in construction. Some urine pipes connected to ventilation pipes. There were breakdowns, blockages, and problems with bad smells. Some women complained that sawdust drifted and caused vaginal discomfort. There were cockroaches and maggots. Some residents were reluctant to carry buckets of their own waste to composting areas. One resident, Yan Jianping, said: 'I could hardly eat at home, and felt miserable on my way back after work,' while another described arriving home to be 'like stepping into a public toilet'.[22] Eventually, the entire system was replaced with conventional sanitation.

This is an extreme case of a system gone wrong, but there is nonetheless a broader question about technological experimentation and the sanitation crisis. To experiment with different toilet technologies may bring social and environmental benefits, but if the technologies don't work to the needs and aspirations of the people who use them, where have we got to? Even where alternative eco-systems do work, what may seem the best solution to external experts may be anathema to residents. At the same time, if eco-sanitation systems can sometimes offer a cheaper option, and one that helps cities meet environmental goals, then it's hardly surprising if municipalities see them as a good option. Even substantial budgets might not allow for everyone to get the toileting system they would most like to see.

As I will argue in Chapter 6, my position is, not surprisingly, that much more money needs to be spent on sanitation and that in the longer term it is a false economy *not* to invest substantially in it. But this is not to sidestep the compromised decisions city governments nonetheless often must make. These tensions are not going to go away, even if sanitation is placed where it ought to be, far more centrally on city and state political and economic agendas. Nonetheless, the plea I would make here, from a standpoint of sanitation as an integral part of the right to citylife, is that the decision on which toilets to build and where is made, first, with an understanding of the sanitation needs and aspirations of different residents in the immediate and longer term, and, second, not based on technological solutions alone.

Convenience or containment?

There are huge variations in public toilet provisions in cities across the world. You are never more than a five-minute walk from a public toilet in central Beijing. Paris has a greater density of public toilets per square kilometre than London or Berlin.[23] But in cities almost everywhere, public provision is collapsing. The United States has just eight toilets per 100,000 people, a similar ratio to Botswana.[24] The neglect of public toilets in cites has accompanied the larger process of privatisation and state retrenchment globally. Concerns over security and safety have also driven authorities to close public conveniences. These include worries over drug use near or in toilets to claims that terrorists might use toilets to conceal bombs, which led to the closure of many toilets on the underground systems of large cities like New York and San Francisco following the September 11 attacks.

Britain's first public toilets were introduced in 1852 and were often celebrated public institutions of Victorian grandeur and ornamentation, though it wasn't until the 1936 Public Health Act that local authorities gained formal power to provide them. That moment is long gone. Writing in the *Independent*, journalist Janice Street-Porter complained that the UK Conservative government's austerity programme led to local councils selling public property to raise revenue: 'Toilets have become tanning salons, wine bars, fast food outlets and cafes.'[25] For many urbanites in the UK and other parts of the world, the 'public' toilet has become a quick trip to Starbucks or McDonald's. At the same time, people working in lower-paid jobs, especially in the informal economy – as much as 80 percent of the workforce in some cities, ranging from construction and transport workers to market traders and street vendors – often lack decent toilets at their workplaces.[26]

While cafés, bars, and restaurants are required to provide toilets for customers in the UK, there is no statutory legal requirement for state provision of public toilets. Local authority spending on public toilets in British cities has severely declined in recent decades, and some regions have almost entirely stopped maintaining public toilets. The situation is getting rapidly worse. In the face of austerity cuts from central governments to local bodies, public toilets were among the first provisions to be cut. In London, more than half of all public toilets were closed after 1995. The central borough of Tower Hamlets has just one public toilet yet is the densest in the capital. Many British cities do not have dedicated public toilet policies, and because they have no legal duty to improve existing provision they typically do not have ring-fenced budgets for toilets.[27]

The London Assembly, a public body tasked with scrutinising the work of the mayor, has made the argument that public toilet provision isn't just a moral and health commitment, it's also an economic investment. People are more likely to spend time in High Streets if they know there are good facilities freely available, and tourists often place good public toilets high on their list for what makes a good visit to a place. There is plenty of evidence to support the need for more quality public toilets, including the London Assembly's *The Toilet Paper*, Age UK's *London Loos*, and data gathered by the Greater London Authority.[28] *London Loos* estimates that over 80 percent of Londoners think that public toilet provision in their area is bad and have considered provision before travelling to a particular place. Public toilets are considered poor in High Streets and parks, with cleanliness and opening times being among the biggest concerns. The numbers of people most affected in a city the size of London is remarkable. Over a million people over age sixty-five, over a million disabled, half a million with Crohn's and colitis, and many more breastfeeding, pregnant, or suffering from conditions that make getting to a toilet vital. The numbers are higher still in bigger cities like Mumbai, Lagos, or São Paulo.

Research by the Royal Society of Public Health shows that three in four people in the UK don't think there are enough public toilets where they live, and as much as 43 percent of the population have conditions that require frequent use of the toilet.[29] They show, too, that as many as 20 percent of the population experiences the 'loo leash', whereby inadequate toilets deter them from leaving their home as much as they'd want. Millions restrict fluid intake because of a lack of toilets, thereby causing or exacerbating poor health conditions. In addition to far greater attention and investment in toilets as essential to the British public realm, they have called for 'potty parity' in the form of legal stipulations that ensure fair provision for women and girls. This would mean, as seen in parts of North America, that there would be double the toilet provisions for women than men. All of these challenges and concerns can be exacerbated when the clocks hit 6 p.m., especially for nighttime workers, when most public toilets are closed and even the possible dash to a shop, café, or public building is off limits.

Not only are there not enough toilets, information on the ones that do exist is often out of date or missing. If signs exist on streets, they too often direct people to toilets that are closed. There has been a growth in websites and apps mapping free public toilets in cities. One of the better examples is the excellent Great British Toilet Map produced through the Royal College of Art's Public Toilet Research Unit. The website has data on whether toilets have adequate disabled access or whether they are gender neutral. As valuable as these maps are, they rely on local people updating them and they are sometimes out of date. People find that occasionally the toilets have fallen into disrepair, and not all of those in need – especially older groups or people with learning difficulties – are comfortable using websites or apps on smart phones. We need better and more regularly updated maps, both online and offline, across the urban public realm, especially at busier areas.

The impact of fewer public toilets is, obviously, reduced options for those who need them most, including elderly groups, those with disabilities, children, and pregnant women, all of whom are then forced to either use a private alternative or limit their trips out so that they don't stray too far from a known convenience. The failure to provide decent toilets could well be in violation of the UK's Equalities Act, given that many groups – disabled and elderly users, for instance, or those with certain illnesses – have very few sanitation options outside the home, especially those on lower incomes.

Over more than a century and a half, public toilets have gone from being key infrastructures of the public realm to then later being cast as nuisances – initially because of moral concerns about toilets being used for sex, mainly between men, and later as unsightly and unprofitable. Many have been converted to other purposes, some are derelict. There is one near Charing Cross, for instance, that is now a basement cocktail bar but which claims to have once been a toilet used by Oscar Wilde to meet men. In one case in London, a group of artists and activists sought to purchase a discarded public toilet only to find it was on land owned by the University of London. Their campaign to have it listed as an 'Asset of Community Value' failed, and the structure was later sold off to make way for a café chain. If, in a time of climate change, urbanites are to spend more time walking and cycling rather than driving, asked one of those involved, then why are public toilets not central to public, political, and planning debates and processes?[30]

If you look through state and municipal reports on sanitation, you see not just declining budgets but minutes replete with all manner of sanitation complaints. In one report by the House of Commons Communities and Local Government Committee, there are campaigners representing people suffering from incontinence, Crohn's disease, diabetes, elderly groups, pregnant women, and a range of disabilities, bemoaning the 'appalling' condition and the failings of 'poorly sighted' city councils. More than ten public toilets were closing in the UK every month, the report showed, and in bigger cities like London the transport networks lacked anything like systematic sanitation provisions for disabled users.

Even new flagship transport provisions in London lack toilets, such as many of the forty-one stations in the £19 billion Elizabeth line on the Underground network. Campaigners, and the occasional elected official, have argued that this is symbolic of a larger absence of public toilets on the Underground, which can carry 5 million people per day across more than 270 stations. Integrating toilets into Victorian transport systems can be an expensive and complicated task, and it is often cheaper and more practical to build toilets into large new developments, particularly in a big city like London where there are often sizeable urban development projects on the go. But the fact that one of the world's major metropolises has allowed sanitation in transit to become so thoroughly denuded is remarkable.

Still, toilets are not entirely off London's political agenda. The 2021 London Plan requires that new 'large-scale developments that are open to the public' should provide free publicly accessible toilets suitable for a range of users. This includes 'disabled people, families with young children and people of all gender identities', and free Changing Places toilets, which are larger toilets with the necessary space for wheelchair users and those with other needs. Smaller-scale developments are encouraged to pursue community toilet (CT) schemes, whereby local businesses are incentivised to advertise their toilet to the public when they are open.

CT schemes have had mixed success across cities in Britain. The scheme was abandoned in Newcastle, for example, and those London boroughs that have pursued it have had highly varied experiences. They depend on local businesses allowing everyone and anyone to use their toilets, but in practice some groups, especially those that business owners might look upon warily – the homeless and those who have been drinking or taking drugs, for instance – are often turned away. Toilet users sometimes feel they should buy something if they use the toilet, and business users occasionally request that they do. Nonetheless, the London Plan is at least making efforts here to grow access in the capital, particularly in a context of diminished resources from the central government to local authorities. The plan also notes the importance of providing twenty-four-hour toilets catering to the city's twenty-four-hour economy, including nighttime workers like bus drivers, and for the vital role of maintenance and cleaning. This is all welcome noise, even if the matching resources haven't materialised.

Across the urban world, recent decades have demonstrated a double process of the unravelling of public toilets in cities. On the one hand, existing public toilets have in many places been closed or so poorly maintained as to be largely unused. On the other hand, as cities have grown and urbanisation has continued, the public toilet has been largely neglected by city leadership. City leaders, it seems, have been more concerned with leapfrogging into the realm of the seductive digitalised and automatised 'smart city' than to bother too much with whether there are enough public toilets. There are, for sure, huge variations within and between cities in the distribution of public toilets, but what these two trends add up to is a systematic de-linking of the urban sanitation imaginary that connected 'public' and 'toilet'. In some cities, the link was scarcely there in the first place. As a result, there are a billion little ways, each day, in which people's well-being and health are at risk, or in which people calculate that it's best not to venture to certain places at all, thereby becoming closed off to parts of their city. The connections between public and toilet go to the heart of citylife.

At the same time, sanitation management has become more disciplinary. Writing about the impact of austerity budget cuts on public toilets in the UK, *Red Pepper* described how the police were more actively fining people for urinating in public, declaring it a public order offence in order to justify £80 fixed penalties.[31] Surveys of visitors to Manchester, the piece continued, placed a lack of public toilets in the top three complaints about the city centre, yet the council's response has been both piecemeal and gendered. For example, in one experiment, European-style plastic pissoirs were placed on weekends in Piccadilly Gardens in the city centre – dubbed 'piss daleks'. They only lasted a few months. There was no provision added for women, even though the council acknowledges there needs to be more toilets for women and girls.

Around the Toilet, an arts-based research project based at Sheffield Hallam University, has been collecting experiences of public toilets in the UK and considering the implications for provisions and design. Through a series of films and documents, the project details the everyday struggle of trying to find a disabled toilet, particularly one that has support rails or adequate space for wheelchair users. One wheelchair user describes how a trip to a zoo turned into a frantic hunt for a toilet that left her with 'my dignity forsaken' and wanting to 'sit and cry'.[32] Another talked about how she restricts what she drinks in a day. There are a range of invisible disabilities that are exacerbated by inadequate provisions, from incontinence and inflammatory bowel disease to 'shy bladder' syndrome.[33] Others talked about transphobic harassment because of the ways in which people read their gender, with security kicking people out of toilets, or finding that gender-neutral facilities have been vandalised. Parents quickly learn the geography of baby-changing facilities in cities, and one mother talked about feeling that 'I'm not meant to be here' in places lacking provisions.[34]

The question of good access to decent toilets is not just a question of convenience but of belonging and citizenship. Exclusion from toilets can equate to exclusion from public space.[35]

Toilets are both personal and political, about individual experience and social power and hierarchy. Historically, public space
in the city was designed for and largely inhabited by able-bodied
men, and any bodies deviating from the social norm were often
excluded and/or stigmatised. That inheritance has shaped what
in practice is the denial of citizenship rights. Citizenship is not
just an abstract working out of liberal values and regimes of
rights and responsibilities. It is lived, practised, and embodied.
It is constituted not just in law, regulation, and policy – vital
though all of those are – but in the experience people have as
they move through the city. One way to think of this experience
is through ideas like the 'loo leash and 'bladder leash', where
moving around and spending time in the city is dictated by the
scant geography of toilets or by how long people can 'hold it',
which is often simply not possible to do with conditions like
Crohn's disease.[36] In practice, it is a delimiting of citizenship and
equality that undermines the right to citylife.

And yet there has been a powerful silence on many of these
issues. Ableist assumptions are written into the city and urban
planning, leading to a kind of 'corporeal containment' in which
certain bodies – those that are disabled, queer, menstruating,
pregnant, ill, and so on – simply cannot participate in urban life
and city spaces equally, from cafés, bars, shops, markets, and
festivals to workplaces, bus stations, and open public spaces.
There is a long history at work here, one in which powerful
discourses of corporeal refinement render bodily difference out
of sight and out of mind.[37]

In the UK, one of the positive changes in public sanitation has
been the Changing Places scheme, which emerged from years of
lobbying by campaigners and councillors in different cities.
They highlighted the lack of adequate space and facilities in
extant public toilets for parents and other caregivers changing
babies, adults, and children, as well as for people in wheelchairs
and with other disabilities. In London, only a third of public
toilets are accessible to disabled users. The UK government's
Department of Health later brought campaigners together and

launched a fund to provide toilets across the country. Local authorities can now bid into the scheme – an additional £30 million fund was taking applications until September 2022. The scheme is welcome but there isn't enough money in it to come close to matching the scale of need, and the fund doesn't provide enough resources for maintaining and cleaning toilets when they are built, which means people might not be able to rely on them into the medium and longer term.

The question of public toilet provision, then, is both one of the micro-experiences and intimacies of everyday life in the city and one of the larger social, economic, and spatial inequalities that shape cities. San Francisco, for example, is one of the least affordable cities in the world for housing and has a tiny provision of public toilets when set against its population. In a city with growing homelessness, San Francisco has just a few dozen public toilets and there has been an increase in street defecation. As complaints about human waste increased by 400 percent, the city government's approach has too often been to clear homeless encampments rather to see the incidents as part of the failure of the state to provide the basics. The issue has become highly politicised in the city. As one former mayoral candidate noted, this 'fecal fiasco' unfolds even as San Francisco has an annual budget of US$9 billion.[38]

There are signs that this disciplinary sanitation trend is being increasingly questioned and there are cases of affirmative sanitation, like the Changing Places fund, that challenge it. The gender-neutral toilet, to take another example, is spreading across cities globally, and some cities – Philadelphia, for instance – have legislated it as a requirement in city-owned buildings.[39] At the same time, we have seen a backlash in some places. The gender-neutral toilet campaign is a reminder that the right to citylife does not stand still. It is an ever-expanding horizon, rather than a destination at which we finally arrive.

Solutions can sometimes carry their own problems. Standalone pay-for-use toilets, for example, have been an increasingly familiar substitute to the public toilet. They can be welcome provisions, especially in bustling city centre spaces. However, they are sometimes provided with a strong dose of the moralising that has long accompanied city sanitation debates. The City of Portland's sleek-looking solar-powered standalone public toilet has the advantage of meeting US disability standards for accessibility and is relatively easy to clean. The so-called 'Portland Loo' has been installed in several other US cities. It is often explicitly marketed as preventing graffiti, crime, drugs, and prostitution, stating that it prevents these kinds of issues in ways that more traditional public toilets cannot.[40]

The problem is not these interventions themselves, which are likely cheered in the places they are provided, but the failure to recognise the risks of connecting sanitation to disciplinary moralism. Doing so supports a discourse not of unconditional and universal public provisioning as part of a right to citylife but that of a fractured and conditional public, and at a time when the principle of the public toilet needs widespread support, promotion, and investment. This is important not just for sanitation itself, but for other priorities. Promoting cities that are inclusive, lively, and environmentally sustainable involves public toilets as a 'missing link', argues planner Clara Greed, encouraging people to spend more time using public transit and public spaces.[41]

Conditions of access to the most basic of provisions become more politically and publicly visible at times of crisis. Two examples from the COVID-19 pandemic illustrate this. During the pandemic, one of the biggest concerns for many people when they ventured out of their homes and into city spaces was whether the public toilet was open and safe to use. In the UK, the *Guardian* reported cases of women dehydrating themselves or confining themselves at home during their period.[42] They interviewed a pregnant woman who developed a urinary tract infection after being unable to find a toilet on a trip to Hyde Park in London. In some areas of cities, temporary solutions emerged that caused personal frustration and local consternation. One of the people featured in the *Guardian* piece in London, Marie, captured some of this: 'I've had to use the bushes and hidden corners, which is really embarrassing. Holding it in is also physically painful and not good for your urinary tract, but I've had to suffer for hours . . . In some parks, certain bushes end up as designated loos with a queue to use them.'

A second example: In November 2020, a group of residents living in vehicles on a municipal campground in Squamish, north of Vancouver, were removed. Sanitation was at the centre of the debate. The residents had been living in their vehicles at the site as part of the local district's attempt to support people who had hit financial difficulties due to COVID-19. The rate they were charged – $200 per month – was considerably lower than most other camps, but the council concluded it lacked the funds to 'winterise' the camp by ensuring water pipes to toilets did not freeze. Winter-proofing the camp would have cost an estimated $34,000, which one local councillor who opposed the closure described as 'more human and sustainable'.[43] Another councillor worried that people would end up back on the streets at the coldest time of the year. The municipal government decided to close the camp.

One vehicle resident, Rodney Moule, had written in a letter to the council: 'If there was somewhere affordable, I would be there. If the campsite closes, all of us will be forced back to parking on the streets again. We are all willing to pay for a spot to call home.'[44] Noémie Anselme, a co-director of the Vehicle Residents of Squamish advocacy group, wrote that despite the campground 'working very well', public hostility – particularly the unsupported claim that the residents were spreading COVID-19 – had not helped.[45] She worried about how the residents would be able to access water and sanitation as the second wave of COVID-19 spread.

Sanitation featured in two ways here. First, the situation involved meeting the needs of people in financially desperate conditions – and to whom the council appeared to give no assurances. Second, there was the age-old association of a poor, marginalised community as somehow insanitary, even

85

exacerbating a pandemic. The response was punitive rather than caring – 'cruel and shameful', in Anselme's words – and left residents fearful and upended. This is not an isolated case. Urban history is replete with cases of socially and spatially marginalising people forced into camps, or living in and travelling in vehicles, and sanitation has often figured centrally in these processes. In the UK for example, there has been a discursive slippage between stereotypes of 'gypsies' and claims about how travellers organise waste.[46]

The toilet, then, becomes a different kind of problem at different historical moments and sites, from moral panics about homosexuality to campaigns for disabled users or gender-neutral toilets, or during crises like the COVID-19 pandemic. The toilet is not one thing, nor are the issues attached to it. Its politics change over time and space. Where does that leave a politics of the toilet? First, we can say that there has been a broad historical trajectory in which the public toilet has shifted from a provision of convenience to a politics of addressing containment – the loo leash in all its forms, for example. Second, we can say that the public toilet is not just about built form, not just about the existing material thing – vital though that is – but about law, regulation, culture, power, and social difference.

This means that the politics of the toilet is locally situated and contingent, often morphing into different concerns and issues. This local specificity to particular places and issues, however, does not mean that we should abandon a universal politics of the toilet. Quite the opposite. The universal call for sanitation for all is more vital than ever. But the route to realising it is necessarily plural and varied, and it will expand and change over time. Just as sanitation is networked and the concerns attached to it are subject to change – including the very question of the what, where, why, and how of the toilet itself – so, too, must the politics of the right to citylife change and adapt across global space.

The social worlds of the toilet

Let's focus in for a moment on how the material configuration of the toilet can influence the social lives around it. Despite the crisis in public toilet numbers, there is a growing public and political awareness of the range of social needs toilets must respond to. They must accommodate for the elderly, children, gender and religious differences, identities that are non-binary, and those with disabilities. An array of smaller architectures can make a difference to a public toilet, from a bank of sinks that children can reach to adequate storage and provisions of tampons and menstrual pads, or changing platforms for carers. Some have imagined what a 'nonsexist bathroom' might look like and how it might support women and girls to live fuller lives in the city.[47] There is also a social conviviality in and around toilets – from bathrooms acting as sites of sociality and chatter in bars, nightclubs or sports clubs, or residents washing clothes or cooking food using water or gas pipes at toilet blocks, to how clean toilets enable kids to get to and stay in nursery, school, college, and university.

In some cases, the toilet is even a community centre. I have visited large public biogas toilets in Nairobi run by a group called the Umande Trust that include an upstairs library, office space, an internet café, a hall for community events, and water vending.[48] At one, a woman was cooking up a large pot on a biogas stove at the back of the toilet. While not all residents were comfortable with the idea of cooking food using fuel generated from their neighbours' bodily wastes, some welcomed a cheap local supply. The trust was also selling off containers of fuel to local business, including restaurants, at a cheaper price than other fuel supplies. There have been other interventions like this in Kenya, such as a public biogas toilet in a bus station in the town of Naivasha, two hours from Nairobi, which provides gas for cooking.[49] In some community interventions I have seen, it's almost as if the toilet block over time becomes less about toilets and more about community activities, from computing, dance classes, sports activities, and libraries to solar panels, rainwater harvesting, composting, and a host of local functions.

In these initiatives, community toilet blocks can become vehicles for local entrepreneurialism that creates its own opportunities and questions. In 2007, for example, a Mumbai toilet block was awarded the prestigious Deutsche Bank Urban Age (DBUA) Award. The toilet block is based in a well-established lower-income neighbourhood in west Mumbai. Describing why the award was given for this toilet block, Deutsche Bank wrote that the project 'is a striking example of the poor helping themselves, and gives the lie to the stereotypical depiction of slum dwellers as helpless or indolent victims'.⁵⁰ [50] The award is far more than just prestige – US$100,000 was given to the community-based organisation that runs the block, Triratana Prerana Mandal (TPM, 'triratana' means three jewels, and for the activists refers to education, sports, and culture). TPM has subsequently used the award to help fund the construction of a large community sports centre along the road from the toilet block. Suketu Mehta, author of a celebrated book on Mumbai, *Maximum City*, and one of the Urban Age judges, described the toilet project as 'an ingenious as well as indigenous solution that needed very little investment and could be replicated in slum colonies around the world'.[51]

The award was given not just because TPM built a well-maintained, clean block, but because it became the unlikely focal point for a range of social activities. When I last visited the site a few years ago, two hundred students from around the local area were enrolled in basic computer classes upstairs from the toilets, paying around ₹750 for a three-month class (around $US10 at the time). The block had attained solar hot water, set up a biogas plant, started rainwater harvesting and pulling ground water through boring – all through city and state environmental funding schemes. Here, the practice of the sustainable eco-city becomes embodied in a toilet block and is tied to generating capital through waste. 'Our aim is 0 percent garbage', one TPM activist told me. 'We are making

Figure 4. Toilet block, Mumbai. Author's collection.

money [from user charges] and reinvesting it', he went on, in everything from a gymnasium and computer or dance classes to a plant nursery behind the block, and of course the running of the toilets themselves.

There are other examples like TPM across the urban world. In these cases, the social world of the toilet is shaped by, and aligned with, a larger vision of how entrepreneurial civil society might tackle urban poverty. The local, regional, and central state and other actors, such as international agencies like the World Bank or the Gates Foundation, are cast as partners to proactive and efficient community organisations. On the one hand, these initiatives provide better toilets and generate new social worlds. On the other, they perform a familiar neoliberal shift of pouring added labour and responsibility onto already over-worked poor groups. They also often become isolated islands of provision, with clear demarcations of who can access and who can't, shaped around a politics of class, religion, caste, gender, and migrant status. Local neighbourhood leaders, often connected to political parties, can also use the existence of the toilet to promote their own influence, either by taking credit for the toilet or by identifying themselves with repairs or health improvements.[52]

Away from the world of award-wining toilets, finding the money for decent toilets can be a daunting task. If land is available, building large public toilets is often the most economically feasible step, even if only as an interim measure towards sanitation in the home. If in sub-Saharan Africa, an individual toilet can cost around US$300–450, a communal toilet block can be as little as $22 per household. Quite apart from the engineering challenge of installing toilets in individual homes in some of the densest streets and neighbourhoods, where there may also be several storeys of housing, some people do not want a toilet in a tiny home. Others are nervous, sometimes for good reason, that a toilet might lead landlords to increase rents. In housing that is deemed 'illegal' by the state, residents understandably worry about investing in a home that may not be there in the longer term.

Yet, larger toilet block structures are far from straightforward solutions. They demand maintenance, and if they lack supporting infrastructure – electricity, water, drainage, pipes and, where necessary, tanks – they can fall out of use, especially for women and girls, and so they can end up being little or no economic saving at all. In extreme cases, poorly maintained toilet blocks can become death traps, a strikingly different biopolitics of the toilet from the TPM case. There are horrific cases in Mumbai of children or adults falling through corroded floors, damaged through heavy use and cleaning chemicals, and into septic tanks.[53]

'I was submerged up to my shoulders in the slush . . . I could feel it pulling me down but somehow held on to a slab. Then some people pulled me up and I passed out.' Sirajjudan Turat's description of falling through a floor in a northeast Mumbai toilet block, while waiting in queue, is not an isolated case. In a three-month period of 2016 alone, there were seven deaths in the city from similar incidents. In 2018, a forty-year-old municipal block entirely collapsed, killing one person. Residents said the municipality hadn't maintained it in ten years. In 2020, a toilet block side wall collapsed and killed a woman. In 2019, a girl in Kenya died when the school latrine collapsed. In Limpopo province, South Africa, three-year-old Omari Monono died while visiting his aunt when he fell into the pit toilet near the house and drowned.[54]

When toilet blocks are vulnerable to collapse, and when most lack water, electricity, and in many cases functional doors, then the material shapes the social in profound ways. Privacy and safety become compromised, and the kinds of people who feel comfortable using them narrows. Add to that the sheer pressure of numbers using toilet blocks in areas that lack them, and the impacts on daily living and interaction are profound. India's Swachh Bharat Abhiyaan (Clean India Mission) has aimed at one toilet for every 25 women and 30 men. In some parts of urban India the numbers approach one in every 200 people, a torturous equation of urban density and woeful provisioning.

In addition, all kinds of regulations curtail access to community toilet blocks. For example, in Mumbai's Slum Sanitation Programme (SSP), which I mentioned in Chapter 2, an arbitrary and controversial 'cut-off' date of 1995 was identified that means only residents who can prove they lived in the area before that date benefit from the programme. This means that older residents who can provide documentary proof are eligible for a monthly pass of ₹500 (about US$6.50), while those whose tenure can only be evidenced after 1995 are technically excluded from accessing the provision. In practice, and here again we see how social worlds matter, some caretakers allow those residents to purchase monthly passes provided they have documentary proof of residence now.[55] Those who are renting, such as migrant labourers, usually men working in small manufacturing, do not have evidence to qualify for a pass and have to pay per visit, usually two rupees.

All of this is as much a part of the social world of toilets as the success stories, characterised not by entrepreneurial organisation but by exclusion, fear, trauma, and even death. The different extremes I have discussed here – from celebrated entrepreneurialism to deathly infrastructure – are not as distinct as they may seem. The neoliberal withdrawal of the state from basic provisioning is one that both promotes entrepreneurial forms whereby the poor 'pick themselves up by their bootstraps' and entails the abandonment of communities who seemingly can't or won't conform to the entrepreneurial script. Particular social worlds are valorised, others condemned. For all that the TPM model is an example of affirmative sanitation, and it surely is, it is situated in a larger logic that withholds and forsakes others in need.

Between these extremes, there are other scripts at play in cities that connect toilets and social worlds in different ways. This includes organisations of the urban poor – community groups and social movements – that do the slow, laborious, and unglamorous work of monitoring toilets in neighbourhoods and lobbying city and state authorities to address local problems. In Mumbai, I encountered one NGO that carefully ranked local toilet blocks on a scale of A to D, and which sought to negotiate with local landowners, municipal staff, and residents to work out solutions. The political and economic challenges are pervasive and ongoing. Some private toilet block operators, they said, treat the blocks as commercial enterprises rather than local services – toilets as 'cash points', as Mike Davis has put it.[56] Nonetheless, there are small victories: a water connection repaired, better lighting installed, doors replaced, septic tanks emptied, and so on. The small differences this kind of hidden advocacy makes to everyday living, work, education, and social life cannot be underestimated.

Different toilet interventions can generate quite distinct social conditions, from the home and school to the workplace and train station, which often change over time. In South Africa, the eThekwini municipality received the 2015 African Municipality of the Year Award for its work providing free water and water-less toilets to homes. The waterless toilets have proven more successful with younger residents who have largely grown up with them in the house, while older residents often prefer flush toilets. In one study, some residents complained that the waterless toilets, which are urine-diverting, were tricky to use, demanding care in diverting urine or faeces in the right direction (there is typically a urine collection basin at the front of the toilet bowl).[57] This can be particularly tricky for older women, children, or those with medical conditions.

The municipality has used shipping containers to build community ablution blocks (CABs), which combine toilets, showers, and laundry facilities. Eight hundred CABs have provided for half a million residents. Some CABs have had health clubs, kindergartens, and food gardens, all of which create their own social conditions, from enhancing community cohesion to prompting low-level disagreements over the disposal of laundry wastewater. There has also been theft and vandalism, and a growing problem with clogged sewage systems backing wastewater into the blocks and surrounding areas. The smell can be overwhelming and it is women who end up doing the work of clearing the sewage. 'Bring back pit latrines because we cannot live like this', one resident told *GroundUp*.[58] Compare the multiple social worlds around this kind of toilet provisioning to a quite different context in Blantyre, Malawi. Here, a school initiative supported by the NGO *Water for People* has used games and play to promote awareness among children about the benefits of toilets, including menstrual hygiene, and their connection to attendance rates.

The materiality of toilets is not just a technical question. It is not only about getting the most appropriate technologies in place, even though we have seen here how fundamentally important reliable materials are. It is, too, a necessarily social question. Materials are not simply passive backdrops to everyday life; they act and influence the full range of human experience and everyday life. If there isn't a careful attentiveness to what different social groups need and want, then even the most sophisticated toilet technologies can be catastrophic failures. On the other hand, getting the material configurations in place that do work for people, and ensuring they are adequately maintained in the long term, can save lives and expand social worlds.

The pipe

The origins of the pipe can be tracked back to Mesopotamia in cylindrical ceramic or clay *asurrû* (sewer) forms, usually maintained by residents. By the third millennium BCE, Mesopotamia had developed a system of urban drainage carrying sewage, sometimes into larger pipes running under adjacent streets and into seepage pits. Today sewage pipes are predominantly concrete or clay and have historically evolved through different materials – clay, copper, lead, bronze, iron, and plastic.[59] They have been a fundamental connective tissue and defining feature of civilisation, modernity, and everyday life, from water and modern plumbing to food irrigation and energy transfer. But the contemporary global geography of the urban pipe is markedly unequal, with powerful social and ecological consequences.

More than a third of the global urban population is estimated to lack access to a sewer connection. That number drops well below 20 percent in urban sub-Saharan Africa. In Kampala, just one in ten residents have toilets that are connected to sewers, in parts of Lagos and Mzuzu it is zero.[60] In Siddarth Nagar in Mumbai, over half of residents are forced to turn to open defecation. In contrast, more than 90 percent of households in Caracas and Santiago de Cali have toilets connected to sewers.

In poorer neighbourhoods, what are counted as 'sewers' sometimes barely function, if at all, because they lack the necessary daily water supplies. Typically, poorer residents who live closer to city centres are more likely to have access to a sewer connection than those on peripheries, reflecting the historic construction of underground pipes. But today poorer residents are increasingly likely to live in peripheries rather than near centres, as cities expand and real estate markets in pressured centres become ever more prohibitive. Urbanisation is continuing apace, but it is increasingly delinked from the sewer, and both the sewer and water pipe are deeply fragmented across urban space.

We see this, for example, in former colonial cities like Mumbai. Poorer areas have historically had some of the highest mortality rates in the city. In the 1890s, T. S. Weir, the municipal officer of health, worried that rapid residential expansion accompanied by a lack of sewer connections was leading to greater illness and death. In 1892, while the predominantly European south Fort area of Mumbai had a mortality rate of 8.6 per thousand, the figure rose to 46.2 in the relatively close 'native' locality of Kamatipura. That Calcutta already had a water and drainage system fed into a sense of urgency for planners who viewed Mumbai, then Bombay, as *urbs prima in Indis*.[61] The drains that existed posed serious health threats, likened to 'gigantic cesspools', and poured out sewage pollution along the sea front. Colonial officials complained that Bombay had only one-fifth of the average proportion of sewerage to population of England, and the sewers that did exist were located too close to the surface and not watertight, leading to contamination. The sewers that were built in response continue to serve the old colonial centre but have never been adequately extended to the rest of the city, which today is increasingly urbanising northwards.

Where they work well, sewers help solve several sanitation problems by safely moving high quantities of daily waste away. At the same time, they have shifted the question of dealing with waste from the home to the city. If there isn't enough of them or good treatment of the wastes they carry, sewers end up spewing their contents into surrounding areas and watercourses, particularly older combined sewers that run rainwater and sewage in the same pipe. This brings all kinds of ecological challenges, from contaminated water bodies and soils to wasted water and nutrients.[62] The history of the city is caught up in this shift from the household to the city via the sewer.

The urgency of removing waste from sight and proximity as a public health concern and sensorial affront has not been replaced with an equivalent concern for where that waste then goes and how it is treated and used. On the one hand, a public display of urinating or defecating in the street can generate public shock; on the other hand, untreated waste flowing into rivers and seas often goes unnoticed. In some cases, however, people do see and chose to act. Sydney's drains, for example, were built to the sea, a situation that came to a head in the late 1980s when protests took off against the Water Board's seeming indifference, and perhaps cover up, of high levels of coastal pollution, including faecal coliform and industrial waste.[63] The People Opposed to Ocean Outflows (POOO) and Stop the Ocean Pollution (STOP) groups organised rallies at Manley and Bondi beaches, attended by almost a quarter of a million people.[64]

Yet for most of the urban world, there never was a wholesale shift from waste at the scale of the household to waste at the scale of the city. The infrastructures of sanitation are, far more often than not, fragmented and textured into social and ecological inequalities woven into urban space. If the pipe is not spilling wastewater into the immediate environment around it, it is often located precariously close to the ground-level surface. The pipes that bring water to toilets or neighbourhoods are often broken and vulnerable to contaminants, and their material properties and placements are sometimes the subject of debate among residents, municipalities, and activists. We can follow the pipe on its path and see the material, metabolic, ecological, and social life of sanitation in the city as wastes make their way through neighbourhoods and watercourses.

In Mumbai, residents often pay 'plumbers' (brokers) to 'transfer' their water connections to different parts of the pipes when the water quality or quantity suffers. Tap owners, if there is enough water in their tap, may sell water to residents.[65] The longer the distance of the connection that residents possess, the higher the chance that the pipe will be tapped into by others or damaged, leading to residents following the course of their pipe to inspect it. The timings of water provision can vary, prices might change as pressure or circumstances alter – such as tenants moving in and out or vertical home additions added – while new connections appear as others dry out, and municipal staff may conduct raids to remove illegal connections. All of this requires that residents keep on top of what's going on, and here all manner of sometimes predictable, sometimes less so, urban relations play a role, from rumour, stealth, and speculation on everything from pipe locations, water pressures, and the timings and operations of valves to changing power relations between political parties, councillors, municipal staff, and landowners. Pipes, like toilets, are caught up in social worlds.

Even the *pressure* in the pipe is not just physical but political, and it is vulnerable to all kinds of changes in political, social, or environmental conditions. Nikhil Anand has shown the different ways in which 'pressure' in the water system is made and mobilised *technically*, via the work of engineers and the functioning of the water system, *politically*, via the influence of politicians, charismatic individuals and neighbourhood collectives, and *geophysically*, through the landscape of the city.[66]

While there is evidence that clean, functioning toilets are more important than clean water for people's health in poor urban neighbourhoods, clean and reliable piped water is clearly fundamental to urban sanitation. In the longer run, one doesn't

Figure 5. Water pipes, Mumbai. Source: Renu Desai
(reproduced with permission).

work effectively without the other.[67] But in most neighbourhoods on the economic margins of the urban world, water pipes,
like toilets, are rarely one kind of thing. Often, they are provided through a complex geography of spaghetti pipes, with
mixed levels of quality, quantity, ownership, and cost, alongside

deliveries from public or private tankers and bottled water. Typically, the poorest residents will pay more for water and exert more energy to get it than middle-class residents in the same city, and then for water that is of more dubious quality. Water is a significant urban economy and, given that many 'slums' are designated as 'illegal' by the state – typically the poorest and most stigmatised neighbourhoods – it is sometimes run through criminal intermediaries.

The pipe – whether it is water, sewer, or drainage – in the city is not the same sort of thing as the pipe in the village. In dense neighbourhoods where social and political pressures are high and water pressure low or changeable, and where wastes seep into porous materials, the pipe is no mere technical provision. And yet the work of technical provision is often vast, requiring engineers and residents to know the lie of the land in complex, tacit ways, given that siphoning water from here can mean a drop in pressure over there. Pipes come and go around elections, are changed in their material constitution, or become temporarily pivotal to the hopes of aspiring local politicos.

Decent sanitation in the city demands the pipe, but the city often has other ideas in mind for it. Data matters too here – and not just national averages, but finely tuned understanding of variation across urban space. Put simply, delivering pipes demands knowing which households and communities need them and where they are. As a starting point, then, the challenge is to *know* the pipe in the city. In poorer neighbourhoods, especially older and highly dense places, knowledge of local pipe conditions is often not held by any one organisation but instead is distributed across municipal officials, residents, and civil society groups of different kinds. Local governments need to develop the capacity to produce their own data and learn to work better with other groups gathering data, such as civil society organisations.

At the same time, rendering pipes 'visible' brings its own political challenges. Residents understandably do not always want pipes to be mapped and made visible, given that the history and procurement of those pipes may cast questions over their use of them. Data can bring its own politics, and states are not averse to using it to exclude or demolish 'illegal' provisions from particular groups. Yet it is difficult to see how better provisions might work without building a more accurate picture of what is there and seeking to improve and extend that. It is an uncertain political ground. How, then, to respond to the inequalities of the city pipe?

Big pipes, little pipes

When it comes to pipes, size matters. The Orangi Pilot Project (OPP) has been a hugely influential and well-publicised model of sanitation development at low cost, using a version of 'simplified sewerage'. Here, instead of large sewer pipes, a smaller system of collector pipes connecting homes and running next to streets is used, co-constructed and paid for by residents. Orangi Town is one of the poorer areas of Karachi, Pakistan's largest conurbation, a city where half of 17.5 million residents live in low-income neighbourhoods.[68] Almost all have piped water, but the supply is erratic and residents often have to buy water from tankers. When the OPP began its work in 1980, activists found that residents cited sanitation as one of their key concerns. Some residents were already fitting rudimentary sewer pipes around their houses, and the OPP began with the view that they could support them with technical assistance and low-cost pipes.

From there they developed an 'internal-external' concept for sanitation, with four levels: the house, a sewer in the lane, a neighbourhood collector sewer, and a trunk sewer and treatment plant. The fourth, given the cost and labour involved, was to be carried out by the state. Thousands of low-cost pipes were laid. By 2011, 90 percent of the sewer lines in Orangi had been constructed and financed by residents, improving public health and helping to foster other community spin-off activities – for example, around youth issues. Lanes were sewage-free, children could play in cleaner environments, the area was safer for women, and residents were healthier and able to get to work and school more often.[69]

OPP's approach splits the responsibility for sanitation provision between residents doing the 'internal' work within neighbourhoods and the state doing the 'external' delivery of capital-intensive trunk infrastructure. This approach to sanitation is one that is shared among many high-profile civil society voices globally. In Mumbai, for example, the Alliance civil society network – consisting of SPARC, Mahila Milan, and the National Slum Dwellers Federation – have described their view of the differential role of the state and communities in terms of 'big pipes' and 'little pipes'.[70] 'Only the city can handle these big pipe items, which involve politics and big budgets,' they have argued. 'Toilets and drainage lines, on the other hand, are genuine little pipe items and don't really require the city at all. They can be planned, installed and maintained locally, by communities.' For the Alliance, this is their 'deal' for cities: build the big pipes, and let communities and civil society organisations get on with the little pipes.

There is much to be said for this realpolitik, borne as it is from the hard experience of activists pressing for change over many years in cities in which it is notoriously difficult to move the dial. However, it is important, too, to identify the limits and drawbacks of this approach. Many of the efforts to replicate the OPP model in Pakistan have, unfortunately, been unsuccessful, mainly due to political parties becoming involved in projects and construction, although OPP has fed into national sanitation policies.[71]

Part of the issue is that residents who took part in OPP owned their homes and therefore did not need permission to take part in the work, and homes were typically large enough to allow space for installing toilets.[72] These factors are often not replicated across lower-income neighbourhoods in Asia. There are distinct advantages to models of simplified sewerage. The pipes tend to be laid closer to the surface, can be extended more straightforwardly, and are less expensive both as materials (typically plastic) and in construction and maintenance. However, they are also more vulnerable to blockage and damage than conventional sewers, are less able to cope with the very high levels of waste that dense neighbourhoods generate, and don't work as well in multi-storey housing contexts.

Many cities have committed to forms of simplified sewerage and there are examples of successful systems in other parts of the urban world. In Kenya, a coalition of Nairobi Metropolitan Services, Nairobi City Water and Sewerage Company, and NGOs has been introducing simplified sewers that connect to a new main sewer line.[73] In Tanzania, the Centre for Community Initiatives (CCI) NGO has successfully piloted simplified sewerage in lower-income neighbourhoods typically excluded from sanitation, connecting 170 toilets and feeding waste ponds. CCI director Tim Ndezi has described how the success of the project depended on collaboration between the utility, the municipality, ward officials, and the NGO.[74] This was especially important when the water utility began charging rates that were unaffordable to some residents following the construction, and CCI managed to negotiate costs down.

I was involved in a project evaluating some of this work with CCI and other colleagues, and it was clear that the project had led to very significant benefits. Residents reported reduced cases of illness and disease, including cholera. Women talked about how they felt more comfortable with their children using the new toilets, given that they sometimes suffered injury in the older, more rudimentary latrines. The environment around the neighbourhood was cleaner, because there was less waste spilling into streets from the old septic tanks when the rains came. And the system was overall cheaper to maintain. At the same time, there were ongoing challenges. The pipes, narrower than conventional sewers, were sometimes blocked, and even though the system was cheaper, some of the poorest residents, who often had only rarely paid for sanitation before, struggled to make the utility charges.[75]

Brazil has been at the forefront of simplified sewerage experiments. In the 1980s, the 'condominial approach' of iteratively connecting housing blocks through narrower and less expensive sewer pipes became established in peri-urban areas. In this system, the sewer network does not run through every street and home but instead provides a single connection to a block of housing, reducing the length of both sewers and water pipes. There are then branches that connect into streets and houses, and sometimes localised water supplies and sewage treatment systems. As with the OPP approach, local neighbourhoods are sometimes involved in the design, construction, and maintenance of their locally branched systems.

In Salvador, Brazil, 2,000 kilometres of predominantly smaller sewer pipes connecting 300,000 homes were laid between 1996 and 2004, alongside eighty-six pumping stations. Simplified sewers reach more than 1 million people in the city. In Brasilia, the approach has provided for 500,000 people in several areas at lower cost to the utility. Child diarrhoeal disease rates dropped in Brazil between 22 and 60 percent after sewerage was provided. At the same time, as with the Dar case, the demands placed on neighbourhoods to maintain condominial systems have sometimes led to functional problems in the systems, and lower-income residents have faced difficulty meeting user charges for connections and use.[76]

Notwithstanding the successes in Pakistan, Brazil, and elsewhere, the challenges of constructing and maintaining pipes have led some to argue that it is better to use approaches that avoid pipes altogether. Igmarrey Pacheco, architect and coordinator of Uruguayan NGO Centre for Appropriate Technologies, has argued that standalone eco-sanitation systems that separate urine and faeces in order to generate nutrients for agriculture, often running on collected rainwater, can work better. These systems have the distinct advantage of not requiring pipe networks and treatment plants and reduce or eliminate the level of contamination of the surrounding environment.[77] For Pacheco, the solution to the larger sanitation crisis lies in a combination of conventional systems and decentralised alternatives. This argument is part of a larger momentum against conventional sewers that has grown in recent years. As David Satterthwaite – who has been at the forefront of urban development debate for decades, including in relation to sanitation – has put it, sewers 'get a bad press nowadays'.[78]

It's not a difficult argument to make. If you are a committed policymaker in a city with relatively scarce funds and water supply and where urban densities are relatively low, sewers likely seem near impossible. Construction is slow. It takes years to see results. Sewer construction takes on average 1.4 months to reach 1,000 people. If the sixty fastest-growing cities in the world were to be sewered by 2030 – the timeframe of the Sustainable Development Goals (SDGs) – they would have to do so at ten to fifty times the current highest rate in the World Bank's Projects Operations Database.[79]

It can be expensive, too. Lagos will have to spend 14 to 37 percent of its budget per year to provide sewers to its growing population.[80] In the process, there are all kinds of large-scale disruptions that ensue in transport networks, which can lead to knock-on costs for those affected. And pipes require maintenance. It's also true that some sewers, particularly gravity-based sewers that combine waste and storm water and which are built with iron, can be carbon-intensive and prone to flooding – especially concerning as flooding is increasing in a time of intensifying climate change.[81] A decentralised system of localised structures, including eco-sanitation, brings the additional gains of being climate-friendly and generating resources for food and business.

So, why bother with pipes at all? I would put the argument this way. First, on the financial expense, what is often not factored into these calculations is the possible savings over the longer term of using conventional sewers. The savings are likely to be particularly high in dense areas, whether through reduced maintenance costs as compared with other systems (for instance, in situ septic tanks) and the sheer durability of sewers, or through improved health and the greater ability for people to get to work, school, or participate in urban life and economic activity. It is difficult, of course, to estimate those costs, but they will be vast. Some estimates have them as high as 7 percent of GDP.[82] And in some cases, the cost of providing sewers is actually much closer to that of other, often less reliable options. One survey of fifteen cities found that in some places household costs for sewer connections were on par with or less expensive than that of a private septic tank, though much depends on the topography of the existing built environment and natural terrain.[83]

Second, alternative systems typically do not have the longevity of sewers, and again particularly so in highly dense contexts where there is a lot of waste to deal with. Many cities have sewers that, while now ageing and in desperate need of attention, have successfully operated for well over a century. Alternative systems, on the whole, do not cope well with higher densities of use and waste. And third – and this too is a density-sensitive point – sewers can move very large volumes of waste in ways that no alternative system can and are better suited for multi-storey housing. This means that waste does not have to be managed and treated on-site and therefore is less likely to make its way back into the neighbourhood, groundwater, and food chain.[84] Sewers mean residents don't have to pay to have septic tanks emptied and waste transported away.

The United Nation's 2030 SDG deadline for sanitation for all plays a role here. I have read many pieces arguing that alternative systems are easier and faster to build than sewers and therefore make more sense against a tight deadline. Well, for a start, the chances of meeting the 2030 SDG target of sanitation for all are at this point vanishingly small. But the bigger point, surely, is that the target – welcome though it is as a way of focusing minds and money – is after all an artifice of development discourse. It would be better to miss the 2030 deadline if the reward was to build systems that might last longer and work better, rather than meet it with systems that may have to be replaced later.

At the moment, the neighbourhoods that lack access to sewers tend to be the poorest. I suspect that some of the proponents of alternative provisions such as eco-sanitation would be unlikely to opt for alternative standalone systems in their own homes and neighbourhoods. Alternative systems such as eco-sanitation can work well across cities with lower densities and adequate space, but in places with higher densities – and that includes large swathes of urban Africa, South America, and especially Asia – the case for sewers as a reliable underpinning of citylife is compelling.

If there are good reasons as to why sewers are economically, environmentally, or politically unfeasible in a given city at a particular time, then perhaps cities would be best placed considering a two-stage strategy. First, a model combining simplified sewerage – learning from cases in Pakistan and Brazil, for instance – and working with local NGOs and community organisations, with septic tanks, and eco-sanitation where appropriate and workable. Second, and alongside this, developing plans to extend larger sewer connections at a later date, starting by prioritising the densest and poorest areas where the first stage might be less appropriate. In order to maximise long-term impact, these sewers would ideally separate rainwater and sewage pipes, use recycled water in sewer networks, and be large enough to anticipate future urban growth.

Drains and tanks

Any benefits that toilets and pipes bring can be rapidly traduced if the waste remains in the neighbourhood. If waste is not safely removed, people can emerge from a clean toilet with a good piped water supply and have to hop and jump across seeping pools and streams of human waste. That waste can then get into food, water supplies, and even into homes if there are heavy rains. Ultimately, the health and ecological benefits of toilets would then be undone. Yet the truth is that the vast majority of the world's wastewater – as much as 80 percent of it! – is released back into the environment *untreated*. Globally, 36 million hectares of land, an area equivalent to Germany, is irrigated by urban wastewater that has not been treated, often disrupting entire ecosystems in and beyond cities.[85]

Drains and tanks are unglamorous and easily overlooked city technologies, but increasing urbanisation will make their importance all the greater. At the same time, they can be deeply politicised. In Gaza, Palestine, a collapsed sewage treatment tank submerged the Bedouin village of Umm al-Nasir, killing five people.[86] The documentary, *Gaza Is Floating*, shows homes and streets deep in raw sewage. There had long been concern that the tanks were over capacity, but repair was limited due to the Israeli blockade. Israel restricts the imports of 'dual-use' materials that it believes might be used for both civilian and military purposes, and this includes pumps and water treatment. The siege of and violence in Palestine have stalled sanitation projects, and workers carrying out repairs have been shot at by Israeli troops. The Israeli-occupied West Bank is a dumping ground for Israeli waste, and Israeli trucks empty waste onto Palestinian farmland.

Combined with ongoing water shortages, the consequences have been severe. More than a quarter of Gaza's reported diseases are caused by poor sanitation, exacerbated by one of the highest urban densities in the world.[87] Over 90 percent of sewage in Palestine flows untreated into local areas, farmland, waterways, and aquifers, combining with trash, pesticides, animal waste, medical materials, and construction debris.[88]

So'ad, a mother living in Al Saftawi, near Gaza City, describes how 'everyone here relies on cesspits which they empty in the area' and continued: 'There is now a large, deep sewage pool next to our home. This is dangerous for children, and the smell is terrible . . . In winter, sewage floods the street, entering our house. In summer we cannot sleep because of mosquito bites at night. My children suffer from skin diseases, colic, and diarrhoea.'[89] Tonnes of untreated waste are pumped into the Mediterranean every day, in turn seeping back into the city. Here, drains and tanks are as much about geopolitics and war as they are the body, senses, and environment.

As with toilets and pipes, they are both *things* and *expressions* of the politics, policies, decisions, inequalities, and cultures of a city and its global situation. There is no one model or quick fix where the technologies fall into place. The response must be place-based, which is to say it must deal with the political, social, economic, and environmental struggles and questions at work in different sites.

Access to sewers and the treatment of faecal sludge is generally higher in Latin America than in South Asia, and lowest in sub-Saharan Africa. Even well-sewered cities do not always treat waste well. In Cochabamba, Bolivia, 80 percent of waste goes into sewers but less than half ends up in a treatment plant, the remaining being discharged into watercourses.[90] Mexico City struggles to get rid of its waste partly because of its geographical context – surrounded by mountains and having drained most of its lakes and rivers – but when it does one of the places sewage ends up is nearby villages like Endhó, where pollution has destroyed considerable amounts of farming and watercourses and caused health problems. One activist describes the village as 'the toilet of Mexico City'.[91] Treatment plants themselves are sometimes overwhelmed, and untreated waste ends up in rivers, lakes, streams, farms, and coastal areas.

In late 2021, the UK Environment Agency began an investigation into water companies accused of illegally releasing raw sewage, with threats of criminal proceedings and fines of up to 10 percent of annual turnover if sewage works were found wanting. England's nine water companies pay their shareholders an average of £1.4 billion per year yet are rarely held responsible for pollution incidents and have been accused of not even properly monitoring sewage overflows. Campaigners have described the spillages as 'an act of violence against the environment', while government responses have been weak. The government's data on sewage spills relies on self-reporting from water companies that have been accused by groups like Windrush Against Sewage Pollution of 'sweating the assets' rather than upgrading them. The Environment Agency has now sought to step up

Figure 6. Drainage works, Mumbai. Source: Renu Desai (used with permission).

monitoring but is doing so on the back of a recent history of budget cuts.[92]

Across the urban world, wastewater treatment plants have been neglected, continually overloaded, or left defunct. They are typically not prioritised in city or state budgets, and many cities now lack the capacity in skills, expertise, and technology to build and maintain them effectively. Only around ten of Mexico's almost 200 wastewater treatment plants have been found to be operational, and just nine of Ghana's forty-four plants. Even those working are often in bad shape. More than half of India's have been described as operating poorly or very poorly. In the city of Blantyre, Malawi, huge volumes of faecal sludge lie buried beneath the city, neither collected nor treated, constituting an impending 'sludge bomb'.[93]

Clearly, sewers do not always lead to better managed waste. Lagos has built new sewer connections but only around half of all human waste is safely treated, roughly the same proportion as Mumbai despite the city having almost a third of its inhabitants connected to sewers.[94] If local authorities are proactive and engaged, then it may be the case that on-site septic tanks can work as well or better than sewers, especially in contexts where sewers do not receive regular daily water flows. Like the treatment plant, however, the tank typically falls off the radar of political debate and economic prioritisation. These are the city's unthinkable spaces, adrift from the urban imagination and the political machinations of policy and debate, beneath and beyond the toilet and the immediate drama of the sanitation crisis.

In dense neighbourhoods, the tank can fill up with remarkable speed, backing up toilets and emitting its contents into public space. Little wonder, then, that public health experts often argue that meeting sanitation needs demands a shift away from septic tanks. Septic tanks, rather than sewers, are especially pronounced in poorer neighbourhoods. They serve three quarters of homes in Dhaka and approaching half of all residents of Colombo and Maputo. Most tanks discharge directly into the drainage system and lack soak pits (which allow for waste to drain into porous chambers).[95] In areas with narrow lanes, it can be difficult for vacuum trucks to access tanks to empty them.

There is a plethora of small-scale entrepreneurs and distinctively named technologies – from gulpers, nibblers, and gobblers

to rammers and MAPETs (manual pit-emptying technology) –
that have emerged to get around this, as well as exploitative
and often horrifying practices of manual cleaning without
equipment and protection.[96] Gulpers, for example, are portable
vacuum pumps invented by British engineer Steve Sugden in
2003. They have played a significant role in Kampala's waste
treatment. Here, the gulper was highly effective in lieu of sewer
construction, but it was also limited by the fact that the fees
for use are too high for many households, meaning wealthier
neighbourhoods have benefited most.[97]

Septic tanks, then, often go wrong, but there are some attempts
to experiment with their form. There are innovations that offer
possibilities for temporary solutions in crisis circumstances,
including experiments with 'septic bags'. One example is the mem-
brane septic tank kit developed by a sanitation NGO, the
Bremen Overseas Research and Development Association,
which has been used in the Surdash refugee camp in Iraq. The
septic bag is a prefabricated foldable structure that can be
rapidly deployed, moved, and reused. These kinds of systems are
promising but are yet to be tested systematically at scale for
effectiveness and affordability.[98] Another option that is similar
to the septic tank but which can treat waste faster is the anaer-
obic baffled reactor (ABR). ABRs use a series of baffles
containing microbes that control flows within the tank and
enhance the digestion of organic matter, and they are often promoted to treat wastewater. However, they have also been found
to contain high levels of pathogens, the effluent needs to be
treated, they require a water supply, and they can take a long
time to get started.[99] The consequences of tanks and drains not
being up to scratch for the population they serve can be severe.

While in wealthier cities like New York the staffing and
machinery exists to deal with unwelcome moments when the
bodily wastes of the underworld return to the city, in Dar es
Salaam excrement sometimes lingers in the urban environment,
allowing bacteria such as cholera to find its way perniciously
into the lifeworlds of the city. As a coastal city with poor

drainage, Dar es Salaam has been relatively badly hit by cholera outbreaks, particularly during heavy rainfall and floods, and with climate change the regularity and severity of flooding is likely to worsen. In the 2015 and 2016 outbreaks, 5,000 cases were recorded. Given that Dar es Salaam's poorer neighbourhoods are growing at twice the rate of the city more generally, the sanitation challenge is likely to become much more severe before it gets better.[100] Local governments are often better at emergency responses than ensuring the necessary investments and preparations are in place for the longer term.

Despite their importance to the city, especially in poorer neighbourhoods where their coverage is most patchy, data on the extent of drains and tanks is weak. In the absence of state-sponsored comprehensive drainage, waste often runs into poorly constructed and maintained open sewers – some of which are wrongly counted as functioning sewers by the state – or through self-provisioned drains directly into the closest storm water drain or watercourse.[101] Residents with means are often forced to pay local companies to do the work, or themselves put together informal regimes to manage them. If these regimes are vital for public health, they are vulnerable to conflict among neighbours and often unable to cope with sudden surges during intense rainfall, which can push the contents of drains around neighbourhoods. Improving drainage is good for flood-risk reduction as well as healthier cities, and it can support local ecosystems.

Unsurprisingly, illness is often higher among people living closest to open drains, yet the drain is also a space where children play in neighbourhoods lacking public space or playgrounds.[102] There is a long history of celebrating public spaces in city thinking, and rightly so, but for growing numbers of the urban poor local public space is as much about negotiating potential health hazards as it is sociality, play, mobility, or economic activity. In Accra, a drainage project in Jamestown and Ussher Town used local materials to sanitise the living environment. Alleys in the neighbourhoods that were flooded during the rains, creating pools of stagnant waste that attracted mosquitoes, were paved with cement blocks which were manufactured locally and laid by employing residents. The result was not only a cleaner, healthier environment, but transformed public spaces. These areas have subsequently had street lighting and are now safer for social and economic life, especially for women and girls.[103]

Little surprise, then, that if the drain typically receives scant political attention, it can loom large in the daily concerns of residents.[104] It may seem an unlikely rallying cry, but committed plans for faecal sludge management (FSM) are vital to the modern city and its futures. Faecal sludge refers to undigested or partially digested slurry or solids resulting from storage of waste in non-sewered conditions, and it is typically untreated. There have been notable successes in FSM in some South East Asian cities, including in Indonesia, the Philippines, and Malaysia. There have also been improvements elsewhere, including in Kampala, Uganda, where between 2003 and 2015 the amount of human waste being treated increased by thirty times.[105]

Where there has been significant success, it has been driven by a combination of policy, legislation, planning, and budgetary provisions operating citywide. For example, San Fernando in the Philippines safely manages 99.6 percent of its faecal waste with the support of a reliable vacuum truck service, and its success is likely due to the fact that city authorities manage the whole process and fund it through a designated tax. Successful cases also often have the involvement of good quality civil society and private actors that formally and informally remove and treat faecal sludge. Part of the challenge is that FSM is often 'invisible' to policymakers, and many cities – from Delhi in India to Managua in Nicaragua – have virtually no official FSM delivery framework or services at all.[106]

More typical are the modest improvements we see in cities like Dakar, over 70 percent of which lacks sewer connections, particularly in poorer areas. Here, FSM has led to minor improvements in places using pour-flush latrines and septic tanks or pits. Contractors known as *baay pelle* do most of the city's desludging work, in which waste is removed, usually manually and unsafely, from tanks and pits. There is an association of mechanical operators that remove sludge either to treatment plants or, to avoid the treatment fee, dump sludge illegally. The amount of household human waste collected and treated is not likely to be more than a quarter of the city's total, but there are signs that the proportion is at least increasing.[107] The challenge here lies in expanding existing services, incentivising legal treatment over illegal discarding, and integrating practices more robustly into an FSM framework that is properly funded and actively monitored.

Too often, sanitation debates and interventions focus on just one aspect of the material chain of provisions, usually the toilet. It's not surprising that this would be so, given that much of the global headlines and charity appeals fixate on access to a decent toilet, and doing so can be a useful way to gather attention to the sanitation cause. FSM is often ignored, and so the impacts on land, water, agriculture, food supply, and public space will continue, especially in and around denser areas, where larger quantities of waste are generated.[108] Peter Hawkins, a senior sanitation expert at the World Bank, has described FSM as 'the elephant in the room' in urban sanitation.[109] The Bank has developed FSM tools to guide cities in decision-making, including diagramming faecal waste flows, assessing the quality of service delivery along sanitation chains, identifying the political-economic factors that block action, planning a more enabling environment, and identifying options for technical intervention.

These tools tend to work best when they are part of national policy, legislation, citywide planning, and funding, with clear roles for relevant institutions, regulations, and finance.[110] They emphasise a coordinated and incremental approach, neighbourhood by neighbourhood. In Malaysia, for example, the central government provided substantial subsidies to improve waste collection services and treatment plant operation, keeping household fees relatively low. But these cases are unfortunately

few and far between. Most Asian cities have poor waste collection, mainly due to an inadequate number of vacuum trucks,
and treatment practices and technologies are typically not much
better.[111]

Waste beyond infrastructure

From the toilet to the pipe and drain, the tank and the treatment
plant, the things of sanitation need to be planned and mar-
shalled together. In the background to all of this is the question
of what people have to do when the infrastructures of sanitation
are unavailable. Those moments when different elements break
down and become unusable, or when toilets become so busy at
particular parts of the day, or in such a poor state of maintenance or cleanliness, as to force people into alternatives.

'Open defecation', another strange catch-all phrase of sanitation discourse, is the descriptor that is typically used here. It
hides all kinds of practices. Without reliable toilets, people are
forced to use an array of urban marginal spaces, from railway
tracks and garbage grounds to riverbanks or peri-urban fields.
Even people who have at least some access to toilets sometimes
practise open defecation, especially children. There is evidence
that residents with good connections to local leaders – 'fixers',
often well connected to political parties – are more likely to
have access to toilets.[112] Big, dense cities where there is insufficient sanitation investment can place huge demands on limited
provisions and have some of the highest rates of open defecation, including 15 percent in Mumbai and 10 percent in Karachi.
In one estimate, residents in sub-Saharan Africa can spend as
much as sixty hours per year trying to find a safe and private
place outdoors.[113]

In Agra, India, residents have described the sheer amount of
labour and inconvenience of open defecation.[114] The tiring and
difficult work of having to find somewhere relatively private
when it's not nearby and families are preparing for work and
school can take huge amounts of time, especially for women

with small children. If you are ill and need a toilet, the problem is obviously magnified. Open defecation can be a social act – when, for instance, groups of women and girls go to find space together.[115] Not for nothing has the polite term 'convenience' been historically attached to the toilet. Open defecation is not just a term for the act of passing waste outdoors, but a set of everyday relations that surround that act: timing, family pressures, work, school, health, fitness, sociality, privacy, and so on. It is an unsafe, sometimes humiliating, often burdensome practice.

In research in Rafiq Nagar, Mumbai, Renu Desai, Steven Graham, and I found that residents were dependent on six public toilet blocks – three public and three private – providing one toilet seat for every 263 persons.[116] While the official acceptable standard in Mumbai is to provide just one toilet seat for every 50 persons – a number that emerged as part of the city's SSP, a number that accepts sanitation poverty as inevitable – toilet surveys found that each toilet seat was used by many more – between 80 and 115 persons in most cases. Inadequate toilet numbers meant that open defecation in Rafiq Nagar was unavoidable.

In addition to the larger city politics that stigmatise and exclude these areas of the city from decent services and infrastructure, the micropolitics of toilet access, territoriality, and control are important factors shaping the emergence of open defecation. Caretakers might restrict access to residents, or to particular religious, gender, or caste identities. Some residents might only have access to private pay-per-use blocks, and these might be a distance away. If people are ill or have conditions that require frequent use of toilets, they often cannot afford to pay for repeat visits. Even when residents can access blocks, the inadequate number of toilets typically leads to large queues where tensions might arise. All of this can lead to abdominal pain, psychological stress, and in some cases chronic constipation and other longer-term problems. Women try to cope by controlling their bodies and its excretions.

The local garbage ground, the largest in the city, provided a topography for creating gendered separations for open defecation. Men often used open spaces at the lower edges of the ground, especially along the water channel along the ground's western edge, while women walked up onto the garbage ground, finding spaces behind garbage heaps or in the ditches created by garbage to shield themselves from sometimes prying eyes. People described cases of women and girls being harassed and raped, which is partly why women often go to open areas with other women. Using the garbage ground poses other hazards too, such as being bitten by aggressive stray dogs, falling into deep ditches, and sinking into the garbage, especially during the monsoons.

The better news is that the number of people forced into open defecation globally has been steadily decreasing by a rate estimated at 20 million per year, from 1,229 million at the turn of the century to 892 million by 2015.[117] Still a staggering number, but at the least one moving steadily in the right direction. Ethiopia, for example, has been one of the big successes, with a 57 percent drop in open defecation, owing to a 1995 decision by the government to incorporate public health in its Constitution and to develop its centrally supported National Hygiene and Sanitation Strategy in 2005, followed quickly the next year with the National Hygiene and On-Site Sanitation Protocol.

Cambodia, too, more than halved its level of open defecation following a sustained programme of infrastructural investment and extension across sanitation networks. Here, the extent of what the UN defines as 'improved' facilities increased from 19 percent in 2000 to 88 percent in 2015, although people living in urban peripheries, on lower incomes, or with disabilities were often left out of the picture. In both Ethiopia and Cambodia, improvements in sanitation have accompanied large reductions in poverty more generally, although inequality has been increasing.[118] The bad news is that the aim of eliminating open defecation altogether by 2030, as per Sustainable Development Goal target 6.2, is very unlikely to be met. In fact, in some of the poorest and most affected regions, such as sub-Saharan Africa, the overall number of people resorting to open defecation is *increasing.*[119]

In the past few decades, many urbanists have become wary of universals. I share that wariness. Totalising positions often don't work for cities. There is just so much variation within and between them. But if there is one universal we can all surely agree on, it is sanitation for all. The kick here, though, is that materialising that universal means being highly localised, discerning what works according to the specific configurations, economies, politics, ecologies, and social worlds of cities as we find them.

A widening range of material options and possibilities exists, but the central question that remains is: what kind of urban imagination is needed to think through the politics of the toilet, pipe, drain, tank, and sewer *together*? This is an imagination that needs to connect things to policy, law and regulation, budgeting, social attitudes, and the different kinds of people, bodies, and life. This is the promise of understanding sanitation as a network, even if that network might be pursued and built as a materially decentralised one. Whatever it looks like, a networked plan for the materialities of sanitation is a prerequisite for the right to citylife.

This means thinking big – being prepared, for example, to embark on the necessary capital spending and urban disruption that a large project of sewer construction would entail. While they are not always the most feasible solution, sewers work, especially at densities, and they have longevity. The commitment to longevity is perhaps what is missing above all else. Even the best built and maintained toilets can struggle if the tanks can't cope with the capacity, and the costs in public health and lost work and education are colossal. Research has shown that improving one aspect of the sanitation network but removing others can lead to little substantial change. The prevalence of rotavirus, for example, which causes diarrhoea and is highly contagious, in the surface waters of many cities may not reduce significantly if only particular parts of the network are supported.[120]

As I argued in Chapter 1, the current global discourse around what constitutes 'improved' sanitation provisions is clearly not enough to meet 'sanitation for all' in a meaningful sense. Too many substandard systems can be counted as improved. Attempting to define a threshold of material provision is notoriously fraught and can militate against the need for flexibility. The highest JMP categorisation of service levels ('safely managed') – decent toilet facilities with waste safely disposed of in situ or transported and treated off-site – represents a valuable aim. But what, beyond this, can we say as a minimum? In closing, I would spotlight three guiding principles for the material provision of sanitation.

The first demand is that sanitation must be *predictable*. Whatever system is used, residents must be able to depend on it. There must be a long-term plan to build reliable, quality systems that can endure heavy use, with the funds to match it. This means the system must have maintenance and longevity.

Second, provisions must have *capacity*. This requires three elements. First, there needs to be a good ratio of toilets to people, and far more than the one seat for every fifty people that was built into projects like the Mumbai SPP. Public toilets should be at least able to provide for busy periods by keeping queues to a minimum. Second, if toilets cannot be connected to sewers, simplified or otherwise, then there needs at least to be tanks big enough that are – safely and affordably – emptied regularly enough, and not by residents, to cope with levels of use. And third, toilet provisions in a given site must have a degree of in-built flexibility for the social heterogeneities of the city that I have discussed in this chapter, while accepting that it is not likely that systems will be able to provide for everyone all the time. The combination of majority preferences and available budgets might mean compromises on the degree of flexibility in material provisions, and as ever the devil is in the detail of the compromise and how it's attained.

Finally, as the third demand, sanitation must be *connected*. By connected, I do not mean that the sanitation chain needs to be *literally* materially connected in the form, for example, of water to toilets to sewers to treatment plants – though in most cases such an approach will likely be the best one in the longer term – but there has to be a clear and transparent city plan for removing and treating waste. This means bringing tools like faecal sludge management plans, unglamourous though they may sound, to the centre of urban policy and planning. It is self-defeating to get one part of the material provisioning right – toilets, say – while having waste churn out into the local environment.

4

Life

Nicole Eisenman's 2008 painting *Coping* shows a fantastic cast of characters walking through a town, possibly in Germany or Switzerland, with mountains in the background. It is a surreal scene: there is a man smoking a pipe, another in a suit, a naked woman, a man pushing a bike, a mummy, and a cat with a parrot on its head. The faces are calm, appearing thoughtful, sad, or resigned. In the distance people sit and talk. Even more bizarre than the cast of characters is that they appear to be wading through a river of shit, waves of brown lapping at their waists.

The noxious river might be a metaphor for the shit humans collectively have to wade through, fostered on them by the political, economic, or cultural subjugations and calamities of history. For writer Olivia Laing, the painting is a powerful image of the urban crowd and our shared vulnerability: 'Aren't we in it together, up to our necks, trapped in the outflow pipe of history?'[1] But whatever the metaphorical or symbolic qualities of Eisenman's river of waste, the truth is – as Laing knows well and has shown across her remarkable catalogue of work – that we are not all 'in it together'. Some of us are very much more exposed than others.

Another way of looking at Eisenman's painting is to see how it uses life, in all its variety. Life registers in the movement of wading through, in working bodies in the street, and in the promise of untouched and serene green fields and mountains in the bright distance. Life, here, is expansive, cast widely as an ecology of struggle, difference, and possibility. What life has in common in this depiction is not so much those quintessential infrastructures of urban public life, the street and the square, but the waste that fills those spaces. Waste runs through and grips urban life, and urban life in turn generates waste. We might see *Coping* as a dramatisation of the historical relations between life, waste, and the city.

The city demands and forges an expansive conception of 'life'. Human bodies, microbes, insects, animals, metabolisms, resources, soils – waste in the city is an ecology that connects all these forms of life. I will focus on the nature and radical differentiation that accompany the relations between life, the city, and waste. After all, if we really were 'all in it together', conditions would have by now been transformed. Those in power would not have stood for the daily inundation of excess waste.

The life of sanitation is manifold and diverse, shaped according to the histories, inequalities, and conditions of different places. It is haunted by illness, disease, and death. How does the urban sanitation crisis appear when we focus on the being, presence, and movement of different life forms and their ecologies? This question matters, because if we fail to see that sanitation is an ecology of life we risk isolating or ignoring fundamental dimensions of the crisis. Whatever else sanitation is, it is an ecological question. It takes shape at the intersection between different forms of life, from bacteria and viruses to rivers and forests. What is the 'life' of the right to city*life*?

While the right to citylife points our attention to humans, including how they live and move around the city, there is a tendency to lose sight of the fleshy, metabolising, microbial and animal ecologies that co-constitute human life. It's an odd omission from the mainstream of policy and debate on urban sanitation, as well as much of the run of research on it, given both that sanitation is above all else a bodily act and that its neglect is so physically and ecologically damaging. The right to citylife demands a kind of zooming in to the microbial and out to the national and global.

This shifting perspective is a version of what Ash Amin has called 'telescopic urbanism', roving between and in and out of different levels and perspectives.[2] Zoom in close enough, and a teeming microbial world comes into view. A world often busy and dynamic, sometimes held in place and persisting, moving in and out of human and animal waste, gathering and dispersing, seeping and absorbing, infecting and contaminating. Zoom out and there is a world of animals, or human bodies, of soils and watercourses, garbage grounds and blocked drains, and of wastes flooding through homes through monsoon downpours or becoming airborne through bodily respiratory systems or burning wastes. Move the lens again and we can see the impact of transformations in global climate, shaping and reframing the experience and future of urban sanitation by becoming emmeshed in other drivers and processes in and beyond the city.

The new urban ecology

Climate change is steadily reshaping urban life. It is no longer possible, materially or imaginatively, to separate out the climate crisis from life in all its forms. Climate change is newly configuring people, infrastructure, and ecological conditions. Understanding and addressing it demands a 'system of systems' approach that integrates people, economy, the built environment, and ecology, and it pays close attention to local conditions and configurations. Cities and urbanisation are the primary cause of the climate crisis and the sites where solutions will need to unfold.[3] But if it all comes together in the city, the impact of climate on life in cities is uneven and unequal. It is not just that climate change impresses upon citylife – for example, through heating or flooding – in ways that affect sanitation conditions, but that it is actively changing it. Greater rainfall, flash floods, landslides, heat islands, drought, lower dam levels, reduced water supplies, failing drainage, damaged infrastructure, the production of new defences, new viruses and bacteria as well as

Figure 7. Flooding in Manila. Sustainable Sanitation (licensed under CC BY 2.0).

resurgent old ones, and so on. The deep entanglements of climate and city are reforming life.

This new urban ecology shapes the nature and prospects of the urban present and future. Increases in global temperature are linked to higher rates of diarrhoeal disease caused by bacterial infections. The WHO has estimated that climate change will cause almost 50,000 more deaths from diarrhoea in 2030.[4] Extreme weather events can increase the risks of water supply contamination, and flooding can spread infection across an urban area and find its way through water supplies, including via wastes from seeping septic tanks. Outbreaks of leptospirosis, cholera, hepatitis A and E, and pathogenic *E. coli* have all been linked to floods, and some pathogens – legionella and pseudomonas, for example – appear to thrive in warmer conditions.[5]

In one report featuring 530 cities, the top five climate hazards were flash/surface flooding, heat waves, rainstorms, extreme hot days, and droughts, all of which directly impact sanitation.[6]

Often, cities experience these hazards at the same time. Economically richer countries have greater resources to anticipate and react. In large swathes of urban Africa and Asia, increasingly intense cycles of drought and flood are damaging economies, ecologies, and social worlds. What some analysts call 'the poverty penalty' is shorthand for the dual impact of these hazards: not only are poorer groups and places more exposed, they have access to fewer resources to respond and adapt. In Dar es Salaam, a water shortage was declared in late 2021 following record high temperatures and little rainfall, leaving the River Ruvu – the city's main source of water – at extremely low levels, with many residents relying on boreholes, wells, or private vendors, who sharply increased their prices.[7] This was on top of the fact that the poorest often pay more for water and sanitation in the first place.

Across the urban world, poorer homes are particularly vulnerable to heat increases because they are often already up to 10°C warmer than surrounding temperatures, given their close proximities of activities like cooking and work. These are homes that are already linked to higher rates of mortality in elderly and young people.[8] Development agencies like to talk about the poor being resilient and adaptive in the face of crises. In truth they are increasingly just coping and surviving. In those cities that are trying to respond, from Dhaka to Nairobi, municipalities are working with water and sewage companies to build lower-cost systems such as simplified sewerage.

Not only does less rain mean less drinking water, higher temperatures can increase evaporation losses from reservoirs, damage agriculture and food supplies, and intensify the concentration of pathogens and chemicals in local watercourses.[9] But cities like Dar es Salaam can suffer from both too little water and too much, and climate change is intensifying the extremes. A clutch of cities are particularly vulnerable to flooding – Mumbai, Guangzhou, Jakarta, Shanghai, Miami, Ho Chi Minh City, Kolkata, New York, Osaka-Kobe, Alexandria, and New Orleans among them. The Intergovernmental Panel on Climate

Change (IPCC) predicts that sea level could increase by as much as 1.1 metres by the end of this century, affecting 190 million people. Another estimate predicts that by 2050 there will be 340 million people on land likely to be flooded.[10] The threat to certain cites – Jakarta or Miami, for instance – is existential, and there are plans to move Jakarta inland en masse. In Miami-Dade County, Florida, rising the sea level will flood two-thirds of residential septic tanks by 2040.

Heavier rainfall can increase waste discharge from sewers into watercourses, while urbanisation reduces permeable green space and can mean that residents, often the poorest, end up living in floodplains. Low-lying coastal cities are especially vulnerable to a confluence of intensifying monsoons and rising sea levels, alongside intensive urbanisation and destruction of natural flood protections such as mangroves. In Mumbai, 26 July 2005 is a prominent date in the city's memory. An estimated 944 millimetres of rain fell in a five-hour period in the city, creating floods that covered a third of the city's surface and which reached almost five metres in depth in low-lying areas.

This was the heaviest rainfall since records began in 1846, yet there was no weather warning. Electricity supplies were cut, mobile phone networks faltered, public transport ground to a halt, and the city's suburban rail system – key to the economy and social fabric – was out of service for eighteen hours. More than a thousand people were estimated to have been killed in the destruction, predominantly in poorer neighbourhoods – drowned, electrocuted, or buried in landslides. The drainage system was overwhelmed, and in places floodwaters did not recede for days, leading to localised outbreaks of malaria, dengue, and leptospirosis. In one neighbourhood in Govandi, north Mumbai, a toilet block, as the highest structure in the area, provided refuge for local people as floodwaters washed away or destroyed fragile housing and infrastructure.

At the time, the media sought explanations for the extent of the flooding but only rarely mentioned the important Brihanmumbai Storm Water Drainage (Brimstowad) report. That report had been produced in response to flooding from the 1985 monsoon floods. It had outlined the need for major infra-structural improvements to the storm water drainage network. The improvements were stalled through a combination of a lack of state investment, delayed projects, and the state's inability to satisfy World Bank loan conditions. In the ensuing public debate, blame for the flooding was assigned to a variety of causes: 'slums' blocking drains and developers obstructing drains with construction debris; inadequate state investment in drainage; rampant, uncontrolled development, resulting in the loss of mangroves, river space, and the natural drainage of green spaces; a freak episode of rainfall; rising sea level and climate change; poor state planning for disaster management and abil-ity to respond to crisis; and the flouting of construction regulations.

While the levels of rainfall were indeed unprecedented, the state exercised simple political expediency by blaming 'nature' for the event. In truth, the loss of life and damage to housing, property, and infrastructure was a result of decades of lack of investment in drainage, violating building regulations, uncon-trolled construction – often by developers in collaboration with state officials – and a lack of disaster planning and coordination. However, given that 'nature' is an unwieldy target, it was the poor who shouldered much of the blame for the floods as the alleged cause of clogged storm drainage infrastructure. The Chitale Commission, a state investigation into the floods focused on the part of Mumbai around the airport and the Mithi River, pub-lished its findings a year after the floods, and within days the state announced a new three-year deadline for 'slum' clearance around the international airport.

The crisis, and the responses to it, was not simply 'natural' but politically constructed. As with the sanitation crisis more generally, it is often easier for those in positions of political responsibility to blame the poor rather than deal with the under-lying processes. Some powerful voices in Mumbai sought to target the most marginal rather than a hugely damaging urban development model in which the state is not only complicit but an architect. As Neil Smith argued in the wake of the devastation Hurricane Katrina wrought on New Orleans in 2006, 'there's no such thing as a natural disaster.'[11] Who escaped and who was victimised, Smith argued, was predicated not on 'nature' but on race, class, and the historic, systemic inequalities of urban capitalism.

When floods happen, women and girls often suffer most as people limit their trips to toilets outside of the home and sometimes reduce the amount of water they consume.[12] As urban floods in Mumbai and other cities have vividly demonstrated, sewers that operate using gravity are particularly vulnerable to flooding, especially so when they are combined sewers that carry both sewage and storm water to struggling treatment facilities.[13] The pressures arise not just from intense rainfall but from rising seas and melting ice. In Bangladesh, rising sea level has increased water salinity in some areas. From Nepal to the Andes, groundwater or water from glacier melt and snowmelt, a lot of which hydrates urban areas, is coming under greater pressure. More water is being withdrawn from groundwater sources than is refilling aquifers and by 2040, 2 billion people will be experiencing the consequences of a groundwater crisis.

Set against this backdrop, there is the very real possibility that wealthier residents will continue to locate to more favourable, cooler, less risky sites in the city, serviced by privatised and customised water and sanitation systems, while poorer residents will be forced into increasingly hazardous urban environments. Addressing these climate impacts will necessarily entwine sanitation, environment, and inequality. Much of what is needed to improve urban living in poorer urban neighbourhoods overlaps with what is necessary for climate change: better housing, sanitation, piped water, solid waste management systems, storm drainage systems, reliable electricity, and so on.[14]

A lot of what's been done in response by cities focuses on both identifying risks – flood and heat mapping, for example – and supporting infrastructure through better storm water capture, tree planting, and so on. The German government, for example, has provided €12 million to the large Bangladeshi NGO, BRAC, as a 'Climate Bridge Fund' to finance infrastructure and livelihood support in poor neighbourhoods, while in Kenya climate change runs through the 'Kenya Vision 2030' development plan, including providing resources for infrastructure and services to rapidly urbanising areas.[15]

While large, capital-intensive infrastructure spending is comparatively rare at the moment, a host of interventions have proven useful. Sand dams have been shown to help reduce flooding. In flood-prone areas, elevated sanitation and water systems, improved drainage systems, and sea walls can be effective, and in-situ sensors and monitoring and communication systems are important. Greater investment will be needed to protect drinking water sources, but in populous urban areas governments and utilities will also need to diversify and recycle water sources where they can. For instance, there is evidence from Egypt, India, and Pakistan that the use of treated wastewater in small-scale agriculture can reduce pressure on freshwater sources and increase supplies for drinking. While the new urban ecology demands a system of systems approach to an unprecedented coming together of climate crisis, urbanisation, and inequality, solutions do not need to be singular.[16]

Of course, sanitation interventions can bring their own environmental costs. The construction of sewers, for instance, can be carbon as well as capital intensive, especially when materials such as iron are used over polyethylene, yet that too can be reduced by decarbonisation in feeder networks, such as electricity, and through techniques like narrower pipe diameters where possible.[17] In balancing environmental and economic costs, global finance funds ought, as UN-Habitat has argued, to prioritise sanitation interventions in low-income neighbourhoods. Important here is ensuring there are clear mechanisms to allow local authorities and civil society groups to access climate finance sources directly to develop locally relevant solutions and capacities.[18]

Nature-based solutions (NBS) are a growing part of climate responses that impact sanitation. This includes the construction of wetlands, wastewater treatment ponds, soil infiltration systems, or green roofs and vertical gardens. These interventions use microbial and plant life to support human life and ecological conditions by generating clean water, reducing waste through bacteria, encouraging nutrients, absorbing high rainfall, and potentially supporting livelihoods.

The Science for Nature and People Partnership (SNAPP), which aims to promote nature-based development solutions, has been experimenting with ways of naturally treating wastewater but notes that planners often have little experience with such initiatives. They have mapped global 'hotspots' where sewage is damaging ecosystems, often closely linked to cities, and argue for municipal-scale solutions such as the Omni Processor, which uses physical, biological, or chemical treatment processes to treat waste, remove pathogens, and stop the spread of disease.[19]

Philadelphia has embarked on the most comprehensive green infrastructure campaign in the United States, tax-funded at $2.5 billion over two decades. The project entails thousands of rain gardens and tree trenches across the city, on streets, parks, schools, residential and vacant land, designed to collect runoff. The alternative – a tunnel that would store excess sewage, which is what Chicago, San Francisco, and Washington, DC, have pursued – would mean tripling the cost. The aim is to remove 9 billion gallons of sewage overflows from waterways by draining storm water at the source.[20]

In the 2020 Human Development Report, the United Nations Development Programme argued that the challenges of growing demand, deepening inequality, and the climate crisis point to the need for greater green infrastructure, from NBS such as landscape restoration and urban greening to improving urban watersheds (drainage and catchment basins), making water storage and distribution more efficient, installing permeable pavements and roof gardens, repairing riverbanks, interconnecting watercourses, supporting ecologically enhanced urban agriculture, and improving waste treatment by better filtering pollutants, biodegrading, and recycling.[21] There are cases where wetlands have been successfully constructed to treat wastes in water-scarce environments, including both human waste and industrial waste like gas and oil in the United Arab Emirates.

To date, most of the thinking and experimentation with NBS has been on constructing ponds, lagoons, and wetlands, with less use of options such as soil infiltration, green walls (composed of plants chosen to help recovery of greywater), or willow-based systems (where willow trees are used to treat waste owing to their capacity to remove nitrogen and heavy metals).[22] Part of the challenge is that in dense cities with limited space, nature-based interventions can require a lot of space. As welcome as these different possibilities are, the scale of the climate crisis demands radical political and economic reprioritisation that goes beyond technical fixes.

'In the twenty-first century,' Kate Aronoff and colleagues write in *A Planet to Win: Why We Need a Green New Deal*, 'all politics are climate politics. The politics of climate change and the transformation of the built environment are the same damn thing.'[23] They argue that those residents most exposed to pollution should be first to receive provisions like improved housing, clean electric buses, street trees, and so forth. Addressing urban sanitation inequality can simultaneously be a climate politics, at once improving ecological conditions locally and downstream, decarbonising infrastructure investments, and enabling new social and economic possibilities.

The body

Over the last few decades, there has been a growing focus in both the social sciences and wider public debates on the different ways in which the body becomes political, yet human waste has typically remained marginal.[24] In Chapter 2, I focused on the impact of the crisis on people. Here, I want to build on that by briefly reflecting on what the sanitation crisis means for a politics of the body, focusing on four aspects: *metabolising, vulnerability, spatiality*, and *restoring*. First, metabolising.

The metabolic processes of the body – eating, drinking, secreting, menstruating, defecating, urinating, sweating, medicating, sleeping, moving – are profoundly shaped by processes external to it. Contaminated water weakens bodies through diarrhoea and illness, bodily wastes seep into water and food supplies and enter back into bodies, dysfunctional or broken toilets can lead to injury, and people miss work and school to care for themselves or family members. The climate, too, is metabolised in the body, whether through climate-induced flooding and heating that can spread infection or in the kinds of investments and infrastructures needed to protect bodies from hazards. Metabolism is not only an anatomical, biochemical, or functionalist self-regulatory system but also a set of distributed processes that connect bodies to material things, local and regional environments, changing economies, political priorities, cultural power, and global processes.[25]

Bodies produce waste. Waste is then, in theory, deposited in toilets, and moved away by infrastructures. The body and the material world are, thus, part of the same process: the metabolising of human waste. This metabolising – not just of waste *in* bodies but of the production and movement of waste in and beyond the city – is one of the ways in which the body is rendered a deeply politicised site.

Inadequate sanitation precludes the potential of the body to live, act, and flourish, yet bodies are very often curiously absent from mainstream sanitation debates. Bodies are not equally vulnerable, and this is the second aspect of the politics of the body that is vitally important here. Women and children's bodies are especially at risk. The issue is not simply that there aren't enough toilets, but that the toilets that do exist can be downright dangerous.

We have seen how people can fall through shoddy structures into septic tanks or pits, but there are also more routine cases of people being injured by broken tiles, protruding pipes, or rudimentary doors, especially those with disabilities or health conditions like arthritis, or among children and the elderly. In some places, the risks of being bitten by rats and venomous spiders or snakes are real enough, in addition to mosquitoes. And that's if there's a toilet you can get to at all, whether in the home, neighbourhood, or across the city.

In addition to the risk of harassment and rape, the consequences of supressing bodily flows and secretions are discomfort, pain, and dehydration, a host of urinary tract and bowel infections, complications with menstruation, and serious impacts on pregnancy and breastfeeding. Children are particularly vulnerable. Some estimates suggest that diarrhoea kills more children than any other illness except pneumonia.[26] It is one of the main causes of child mortality for the under-fives. In some of urban India's poorest neighbourhoods, the infant mortality rate is 100 per 1,000 births – one in every ten babies dies before turning one due to diarrhoea and other preventable infections – more than triple the average the World Health Organization has found for sub-Saharan Africa.[27]

Usually the result of food or water contaminated with faecal matter from sewage and animals, diarrhoea is fundamentally woven into the experience of the city for much of the world's urban poor. It dehydrates and malnourishes, stunts growth and keeps kids out of school and adults from work. It is exacerbated by malnutrition. Urban disruptions and emergencies, from floods to war and breakdowns in infrastructure, can make conditions far worse. We know that bodies grow better when there are decent toilets. One study in Mali found significant impacts on the height and weight of children, especially younger children.[28] Soap and clean water can make a big difference, as can breastfeeding over bottled milk.

In 2016, the *Lancet* published a 'revolutionary' study on diarrhoeal disease among children in Africa and South Asia.[29] The study, produced by the University of Maryland's Global Enteric Multicenter Study (GEMS), focused on more than 10,000 children in Bangladesh, India, Pakistan, the Gambia,

Kenya, Mali, and Mozambique. It found that diarrhoea is generally caused by seven key pathogens and that interventions should be prioritised to tackle these.[30] We know that some of these pathogens can move with astonishing speed between people in conditions of poor sanitation and high urban density. Diarrhoea is easily treated, but for the poorest the costs are often expensive and parents are often forced into impossible choices between hydration, eating, and medicine. Yet the cumulative costs of treating diarrhoea and its consequences could well be more than investing in decent water and sanitation infrastructure.[31]

Third, to understand the politics of the body in sanitation, it helps to focus on the *spatiality* of bodies and their excretions. In many marginalised, low-income neighbourhoods, human waste is not controlled, moved out of sight and treated, but *there* in urban space, gathering in open drains, spilling into narrow streets and areas where children play, finding its way through insects or unwashed hands into food and water, oozing through rivers and streams in the city. The presence and smell of urine can become synonymous with certain kinds of urban spaces. Transport hubs, public toilets, car parks, waste grounds, alleys, bridges, and so on. The important difference between urine and excrement, of course, is that urine is usually sterile and less of a hazard (although urine from animals that gets into water supplies and local rivers can spread illness and disease, such as leptospirosis). The smell and sight of human wastes of different kinds are linked to an urban waste sensorium that can serve to stigmatise different places.

Henri Lefebvre, in *The Production of Space*, noted that it is smell, more than the visual realm, that most powerfully lends the 'sensual rapture' to urban space, from 'villainous smells' to 'fragrances of all kinds'. Lefebvre went on to argue that 'everywhere in the modern world smells are being eliminated' through an 'immense deodorizing campaign', everything visceral usurped by a world of spectacle.[32] Lefebvre may be overstating the case here, but he was not wrong to identify the inflection of the sensorial and social in city sanitising campaigns. In these campaigns, in the rush to produce chic and attractive neoliberal urban spaces, the urban poor are excluded while at the same time being narrowly incorporated in accordance with dominant social and economic forces.

Not imaginatively difficult, for example, for the powers that be to portray places and people with a waste problem as places and people that *are* waste. And yet bodies that are so often excluded from decent sanitation provisions also at the same time do much of the labour of cleaning the increasingly sanitised city spaces primarily geared to middle and upper classes, investors, and tourists.

Waste has historically operated as a marker of social distinction and projection onto bodies. Histories of the United States have shown how immigrants were taught particular ideas of cleanliness as part of their route to citizenship, while British imperialism connected mundane provisions like soap to ideas of social purification and white dominance, and apartheid legacies in South Africa continue to populate racist imaginaries of cleaning practices. These and other histories continue to become entangled with the urban present, in projectisations of women's bodies as 'excessive, disgusting and wasteful' or 'disabled bodies as monstrous', or of Black male bodies as 'polluting, aggressive, perverse and filthy' and threatening to white women.[33]

Finally, the right to citylife must be a politics of *restoring the body*. This is not just about protection. It is, for sure, a politics of recognition of the body and of different kinds of bodies, indeed of different metabolisations, from the circulation of pathogens to breastfeeding and menstruation. But it is more than this. It is nothing less than being able to live life to a greater potential, to grow the opportunities to be creative and inventive, to participate in different kinds of activities beyond work and the labour of social reproduction, to be a greater part of the social, economic, and political life of the city. The right to citylife leads to the potential not just of safety and basic health, fundamental though they are, but of differentiation: the historic promise of the city and urban living.

There is an important feminist tradition that helps us to think about the politics of the body here. In both public debate and intellectual contexts, the body is often either reduced to passive object, its capacities already mapped and decided upon, or ignored altogether. A feminist politics of the body involves moving beyond the inherited dualisms of mind–body, public–private, knowledge–feeling that limit our ability to understand the nature, capacities, and potentials of bodies. Bodies are generative, and what they generate in their different relations to other things, activities, and bodies can be surprising and unpredictable. It is helpful to focus not just on what bodies are, but what they can *do*, including how that is shaped and delimited by social and economic divisions around class, sex, race, disability, and so on.[34]

The restoration of the body in the right to citylife leads, to use Annemarie Mol's phrase, to 'the body multiple'. On the one hand, there is an imperative to place 'the body' at the centre of sanitation interventions and to recognise the toll and daily hardships that mark bodies. On the other hand, the body is a radically differentiated and changing entity caught up in all kinds of activities from one day to the next. How, then, do we tack between the singularity of the body and the multiplicity of the body-in-the-city?

Mol's focus is not on sanitation but on how medicines treat disease, but her thinking is helpful in this context. She focuses on atherosclerosis of the leg arteries and how it is treated in a university hospital in a Dutch town. Different medical approaches measure, count, and know the body in different ways, so that a single object in fact appears multiple. In the treatment of disease, cells, bodily fluids, unexpected responses (such as a patient allergy), pre-existing heart problems, changing doses of drugs, and the decisions of individual doctors, can all play large or small roles depending on how situations unfold.[35] There is, then, always the possibility of difference and alternative configurations.

A politics of restoring the body operates in this tension between what 'the body' needs and the sheer multiplicity of bodies and their needs in practice. Bodies that are breastfeeding, menstruating, ageing, disabled in different ways, ill, and differently sized must occupy the imagination of urban sanitation interventions and their material configurations. Otherwise 'sanitation for all' will continually run aground of the body multiple, reproducing all kinds of exclusions and inequalities.

The four aspects of the politics of the body I have identified here – metabolising, vulnerability, spatiality, and restoring – situate the body in a wider urban context with which the rights to citylife must contend. That context is made through the powers and inequalities of capitalist urbanisation, cultural and political subjectification, and bodily and ecological processes. Understanding the body in the urban sanitation crisis demands a zooming into the scale of the micro and then out to the scale of economic disinvestment and political marginalisation.

Microbial urbanisation

The term 'excrement' comes from the Latin *excernere*, to 'sift' and 'separate'. This etymological root is interesting. On the one hand, there has been a colossal historical effort to separate excrement from bodies, places, and cities. On the other hand, language itself is used to sift and sort through ways of talking about excrement that, in a curious sense, often add up to *not* talking about waste or at least to talking around it. While some terms keep some hold of the messy realities of human waste, including sludge and sewage, others – faeces, stools, scat, bio-solids, humanure, and so on – can serve to obfuscate them.

The word 'shit', with its proto-Indo-European root of separating things from each other, has a remarkable versatility and is used in all sorts of ways. Nonetheless, that familiarity of use is more cultural than biological or chemical in register, belying a more general discomfort with talking about excrement. What is often lost here, argues David Waltner-Toews in *The Origin of Feces*, is the sheer matter of excrement, the question of what it actually is, materially. If we could zoom in, we would see that excrement in an adult human contains 10^{36} bacteria per cubic millimetre from 500 to 1,000 species, bacteria that variously aid digestion or deal with pathogens, or which can make people seriously ill if exposed to it, or which is simply 'hanging around' from distant biological pasts.[37]

Bacterial cells in the body outnumber human cells by ten to one. As a collection of chemicals – nitrogen, phosphorous, potassium, calcium, magnesium, and copper, among others – excrement can be nutrient-rich. However, human excrement is a risky fertiliser because it is particularly high in nitrogen, and so it is typically separated out from urine in eco-sanitation processes. Urine is directly siphoned off as fertiliser and excrement goes to composting or bio-digesters. The problem of human excrement is both what's in it and how much there is of it – if there was around 88 billion kilograms of it on Earth in 1900, by 2013 the estimate was closer to 400 billion kilograms.[38] More people, more shit to deal with.

Since World War II, more than 300 diseases have been identified. The expectation is that many more will emerge, particularly as a result of peripheral growth on the edge of cities, combined with intensive agricultural practice, the increasing global demand for commodities, and climate change.[39] As Creighton Connolly, Roger Keil, and Harris Ali have argued, capitalist urbanisation is continually 'producing new ecological niches for disease spread'.[40] Most emerging and re-emerging diseases are zoonoses that originate in wildlife.[41] Viruses are the most frequent pathogen group, and they have driven recent epidemic and pandemic zoonoses, including Ebola, SARS and COVID-19. These pathogens can be life-threatening or life-changing, such as *E. coli* 0157 and haemolytic uraemic syndrome, which can damage blood cells and cause kidney failure, or *Campylobacter* and Guillain-Barré syndrome, in which the body's immune system attacks nerves.[42] Yet water and sanitation experts have been slow to work with disciplines specialising in pathogen preparedness, emergence, and transmission.

What, then, if we turned the lens not onto people or materials, technologies or politics, economics or cultural practice, but on *pathogens*? Urban sanitation specialists tend to debate technologies and costs rather than focusing on the specific processes and sites at which pathogens are released within a city. Pathogens, oddly, have rather fallen from view in the research and debates on urban sanitation.[43] This is odd because diarrhoea kills more people, mainly children, every year than malaria, measles, and AIDS combined, and it is typically caused by faecal contamination of food and water. In places where water and sanitation are inadequate, diarrhoea is obviously more prevalent. Stubbornly persistent intestinal parasites like Giardia will infect around a third of people living in such places at some point in their lives.[44]

Describing the intimate links between sanitation, water, and diseases, one overview rightly identifies the fundamental need for reliable, continuous piped water supplies to homes, health care settings, schools, workplaces, markets, and transport hubs, so that the wider urban environment can maintain hygiene and close off possible pathogen emergence and transmission routes.[45] Yet we know too that piped water is just one part of the geography through which pathogens can move, and our view has to be wider still. Doing so reveals sometimes unlikely routes. While *E. coli*, for example, normally lives in the intestinal tracts of animals, in 2011 a powerful antibiotic-resistant strain of it turned up in fenugreek seeds in Egypt. It was later traced to a farm in Germany.[46] Understanding how pathogens emerge and move is a vital and increasingly important task.

Indeed, over the past few decades, epidemics and pandemics of faecal-associated infectious diseases have become worryingly routine in industrial agrifood networks. The combination of cities spreading into new habitats, massive agricultural economies, climate change, ecological destruction, and mass global trade has led to new pathways for infection, to which vulnerable and previously unexposed people are most susceptible.[47] Agents like salmonella, *E. coli*, Campylobacter, and coronaviruses are now more likely to move from animals to humans, often through manure. Urbanisation is a key driver here. As Roger Keil argues, emergent novel diseases such as COVID-19 are linked to 'the immense expansion of urban life around the globe . . . the tentacles of urban society reach to far flung mining camps, logging operations, agricultural regions and the like that make urban life possible elsewhere'.[48]

The epidemiology of disease is at once geographically intensive and extensive in cities. On the one hand, agglomerations of people, insects, rodents, waste, and food create, alongside inadequate health provisions, 'hot spots' for the rapid spread of infection. Particular spaces can generate pernicious pathogens. One study, for example, found that washing sinks in health care settings can contain organisms that resist powerful cleaning agents and antibiotics.[49] On the other hand, the mobility of people and goods across cities, regions, and national borders can promptly turn localised outbreaks into regional or global concerns. While there is evidence that urbanisation has reduced malaria in some places, diseases like cholera, tuberculosis, schistosomiasis, trachoma, and soil-transmitted helminthiasis are all more prevalent in poorer neighbourhoods, while infections typically seen as rural are themselves urbanising. One example is lymphatic filariasis, caused by worms and transmitted through mosquitoes, which can damage the lymph system and for which there is no vaccine or cure.[50]

Microbial urbanisation is shaped by processes both in and beyond the city – from food webs, watercourses, seas, farms, and the migration of people, animals, and birds to urban soil, water and atmospheres, peripheral urbanisation, global supply chains, and climate change.[51] The atmosphere, for instance, is both 'a source and a sink for the urban microbiome and acts as a pathway through which microbes move between urban areas and their surroundings, even between very distant regions'.[52] Water pollution, to take another important concern, is often the result of untreated and partially treated wastewater flowing into local water bodies, and it is common in cities.[53]

In Taiwan, rapid urbanisation since the 1970s has led to many waterside areas being built upon, leaving sites such as the Tainan green with toxic contaminants and dead fish.[54] Not only does waste end up in local rivers, streams, canals, and dikes, it can also make its way into farming, drinking supplies, and food. In Uruguay, sewage pipes in cities transmit bacteria to beaches.[55] Veronica Antelo and colleagues have been organising sewage pipe samples into a Bacterial Biobank of the Urban Environment, which allows them to examine how bacteria interact and respond to antibiotics. Urbanisation can alter soils, plants, green spaces, and atmospheres in ways that have uncertain consequences for microbial extent, diversity, and geography.[56]

The connections between urban density and poverty can also be important for infection. As Ebola spread rapidly across the three worst-affected countries in Africa in 2014 – Sierra Leone, Guinea, and Liberia, where more than 10,000 people died – and through, for a period, Mali and Senegal, good sanitation, water, hygiene, and health care was identified as vitally important. In poor, dense neighbourhoods, as well as in busy road networks and workplaces, increased contact combined with inadequate sanitation kept rates of infection high. In some areas across West Africa, public handwashing stations were provided. However, health facilities often lacked clean water and sanitation facilities; in some places, even just water and soap may have reduced the rate of infection.[57] Indeed, poor health care facilities have become occasional epicentres of infection with Ebola, as they have with cholera. There is a growing body of work examining the intersections between density, public health, planning, and microbes.[58]

While Ebola has acted as a spur for investment in sanitation in dense and often impoverished urban spaces in Africa, albeit in a patchwork way, in Brazil the Zika outbreak also drove sanitation further up the political ladder.[59] Zika can cause birth defects and Guillain-Barré syndrome, and it is usually spread by mosquitoes where there is limited drainage, unclean water, and untreated human waste. The virus's link to neurological illnesses in unborn babies resulted in a level of public concern that diseases like dengue – another disease that can thrive amid poor sanitation and urban density – doesn't quite generate. Dengue 'moves people less, despite the high mortality rate', writes Edison Carols of the Trata Brazil Institute, whereas Zika 'has a baby's face'.[60]

There's no doubting the challenges that dense spaces present. A city of 1 million people will discharge 1,500 cubic metres of human waste per day. Dhaka, for example, has some of the planet's highest densities, with areas of more than 1 million people per square kilometre. Only 25 percent of Dhaka is connected to sewers, and most people depend on pit latrines, septic tanks, and makeshift drainage. In Karachi, densities can be as high as 3,500 people per hectare and eight people to a small apartment, with extended families of twelve to fifteen people sharing one toilet. In Mumbai's poorer neighbourhoods, the ratio of toilet seats to people varies from 58:1 to 273:1.[61]

But if for some sanitation is a 'demon of density', that has nothing to do with there being 'too many people' and everything to do with the politics and inadequacies of historical patterns of provisioning.[62] Paromita Vohra's film *Q2P* vividly portrays Mumbai's snaking queues of people at toilets in poorer neighbourhoods as a social compression of relations of gender, caste, ethnicity, and class. The queue is a measure of the city: of bodies in dense space, of social relations that dictate who gets to be where when, of the lack of toilets and water pipes, of the lack of money invested by the state, and of the residents the state does not see or care for.

To be sure, density can be a resource for people living on the margins. The concentration of people in place can be the foundation from which community organisations develop and become strong, from loose affiliations of neighbours maintaining drains or caring for children to more formal nongovernmental groups that raise funds for sanitation improvements or lobby the state for better provisions. Density can provide what Jane Jacobs memorably called 'eyes on the street', through which the sheer presence of people can help promote safety.

But it is also the case that densities of people, waste, and vectors like flies and mosquitoes can work together to generate or intensify illness and disease in neighbourhoods suffering from sanitation disinvestment. At the same time, there is growing concern and debate about how some pathogens are developing antibiotic resistance, including multi-drug resistant TB, which can be exacerbated in dense urban spaces with inadequate sanitation. What emerges is not just at an equation of poverty + density + inadequate sanitation = microbial threat, but a more nuanced appreciation of how density operates in the rhythms, possibilities, and hazards of urban life. Not because that equation is itself wrong, but because being attentive to how cities generate the conditions to cope with and change everyday life is itself a vital part of the understanding how the right to citylife is expressed and potentially realised (more on this in the next chapter). 'Not only are urban settings and edges sites for intense contagion,' writes Steve Hinchliffe, they are also 'places of cultural diversity, spatial difference, potential solidarity and assistance'.[63]

Just as illness and disease linked to inadequate sanitation travel through insects, so too can vectors move through the ground at our feet. Soil and ground materials can matter enormously for the life of sanitation. Soil-transmitted helminth (STH) infections – intestinal worms – do particularly well in warm and wet sites with poor sanitation, and they affect pre-school children disproportionately.[64]

The Centers for Disease Control (CDC) in the United States identifies STH as a 'neglected disease' because it can inflict 'tremendous disability'. Yet it can be controlled, treated, and even eliminated from places. Hookworm, for example, is a form of STH that emerges when eggs get into food supplies through open defecation. People become infected when they ingest the eggs. Symptoms include diarrhoea, stomach pain, blood loss, physical and cognitive damage, and rectal prolapse. Yet in addition to better availability of medicines, decent toilets and waste treatment would all but remove the risk.

In the absence of reliable and well-maintained septic tanks, pits, and sewers, waste can leach into surrounding areas, including watercourses, soils, and streets. While it is a long-gone chapter in the history of disease in many cities, there are still outbreaks of cholera in some cities that derive from these bursts of wastes into public environments. Cholera brings with it a host of horrific symptoms and can kill within twelve hours.[65] It is increasingly rare as sanitation capacities, waste treatment, and water provision improve and as vaccination capacities in major hotspots, such as the Democratic Republic of Congo, Haiti, and Somalia, increase. In 2018, for example, there was a 60 percent global decrease in cases.[66]

But there are also signs that cholera is making a worrying return, particularly in places where infrastructure has become damaged through war, disaster, and severe economic crisis. When sanitation systems falter, cholera can thrive in unclean water and spread with alarming speed. In Lebanon, economic crisis has rendered various key infrastructures dysfunctional, including electricity, treatment plants, water, and sanitation. The last known cholera outbreak was thirty years ago, but in recent years there have been hundreds of suspected cases.

Hussein Ali, a resident of the town of Bebnine, in north Lebanon, told journalist Anna Foster how he had lost his brother to cholera and that some of his family was infected.[67] 'We don't know where we got infected from . . . Is it the air or the water? We are living in a state of panic, we are afraid of everything now.' A river of brown water runs through the centre of the town, piped into some homes and spilling into nearby cropland. Residents worry about whether the crops they grow are safe but there is little alternative food. Cholera can be treated fairly easily, but rapid care is important and health services are struggling to cope more than ever. While the government has said it will cover the costs of cholera for its citizens, there are a million refugees in Lebanon, many from Syria, who cannot have costs covered but who are among the most vulnerable.

The legacies of war and conflict in Afghanistan and Syria have similarly led to thousands of new cholera cases. Twenty-nine countries reported cholera outbreaks in 2022. In the summer of that year, cholera cases climbed in Syria to nearly 25,000 infections; refugee camps, often crowded and lacking basic infrastructure, had the highest levels of infection. Water and sewage infrastructure in Syria has not recovered since the war began in 2011. The World Health Organization believes the outbreak was worsened by people consuming water from the Euphrates River, which is overrun with raw sewage. Some groups are attempting to purify the water using chlorine tanks or boiling water. The WHO describes the global rise in cholera as 'unprecedented', noting that at the same time there is a global shortage in vaccine supply.[68]

Tackling the world of microbial urbanism demands a focus on the geographies of emergence and infection. Some scholars have argued for a 'source–pathway–receptor' approach. This entails pinpointing pathogens and their sources and how they travel to 'receptors' (a category that includes, rather clunkily, 'people').[69] Tools like faecal sludge management plans (FSM) are helpful, although these tend to stop short of really focusing in on pathogens. And there is a plethora of other mapping tools – from material flow analysis that quantifies waste inputs, flows, treatment, and outputs to risk-mapping approaches that identify physical, social, or economic hazards – which share similar limitations. The source–pathway–receptor approach involves experts calculating pathogen concentrations at different points in the waste flow, identifying the health risks at those points, and targeting improvements accordingly.

What's especially useful is that it identifies the nature and extent of pathogens at different scales, from the household to local area, community, and city, but in a way that assesses the likely impact of pathogens at different sites. The relative presence of different pathogens – bacteria, protozoa, viruses, helminths, and so on – across localities makes a difference to public health and the local environment, as does the extent to which the pathogens may or may not become diluted or change form in different conditions.[70] It is an approach that sets priorities by being attentive to spatial differences and vulnerabilities. So, for example, pathogens flowing away from the city in a watercourse are of course a challenge now and potentially later, but pathogens flowing into a local drain in an area where children play is likely to be the more urgent problem.

Being attentive to these spatial distinctions in and around the city can reveal important new challenges. For instance, the WHO guidelines state that if pit latrines are located in areas where groundwater is used for drinking, then they should be 1.5 metres above the water table and fifteen metres down-gradient from the water supply in order to reduce contamination.[71] But that is often extremely difficult to ensure in high-density areas with limited space. The source–pathway–receptor approach can provide a geographically nuanced understanding of the microbial life of waste as well as a tailored plan of action in response. It may be, for example, that the local drain is where infections from viruses are most likely, while the downstream environment is where certain bacteria are more common.[72] In contexts of finite resources, it is an appealing approach and a useful step in creating an accurate picture of the urban microbiologies of waste.

The right to citylife demands strategies that work with the liveliness and geographies of life beyond the human realm. In 2012, the World Bank's Global Water Security and Sanitation Partnership developed a new tool for assessing what happens to human waste in the city, which they called a Shit Flow Diagram (SFD). Following initial funding from the Gates Foundation, more than a hundred SFD reports were compiled for cities across the world. The purpose of the diagram is to provide a snapshot illustration of how excreta 'flows' through a city from defecation to end use.[73] Waste is tracked through containment, emptying, transport, treatment, and end use or disposal, then grouped into 'off-site' and 'on-site' sanitation. The SFD for Dar es Salaam, for example, shows that 90 percent of waste is treated on-site – that is, it does not go into a sewer – only around a third of which is emptied from tanks, with just 5 percent of that being treated. The diagram underlines the need for greater collaboration across the water and sanitation sector in the city, with clearer aims and coordination that runs from the national state to local contexts.[74]

The SFD is a useful device for focusing minds on the life of sanitation as a network of relations. Other approaches, such as the Sanipath assessment tool, provide a more detailed focus on where people and environments may become exposed to human waste.[75] The tool was developed by the Center for Global Safe WASH at Emory University in the United States; it tracks 'exposure pathways' through quantitative microbial risk assessment. These assessments are supplemented with local interviews, transect walks, and an open-source data repository. In Accra, Ghana, the tool identified the consumption of raw produce as a dominant exposure pathway.[76] Another study of microbial contamination of piped water in Kumasi, Ghana, found *E. coli* in a quarter of samples, indicating the presence of faecal matter caused by uncovered and cracked pipes.[77]

If SFDs and the Sanipath exposure tool are concerned with tracking human waste, metagenomic surveys look more closely into the microbial world and what that might mean for sanitation responses and interventions. Metagenomic surveys sample highly trafficked urban sites in order to identify microorganisms, and they can reveal how microbial populations change across urban space and over time. The MetaSUB project – Metagenomics and Metadesign of Subways and Urban Biomes – a global research consortium examining the relations between density and the microbial in cities, coordinated at Weill Cornell Medical College in New York, has produced city profiles of the 'urban biomes' carried by mass-transit systems.

The project began in New York, when the Mason Lab surveyed the New York subway to identify 'bio-threats' and found that almost half of all DNA sequences did not match any known organism, and that 28 percent of live bacteria had resistance to at least one common antibiotic drug.[78] They also found that events can make a significant difference to microbial populations. Hurricane Sandy, for example, left marine bacteria on the subway walls as a 'molecular echo'. From there, the consortium has sought to build a DNA map of microbiomes in mass-transit systems, taking samples from turnstiles, emergency exits, ticket kiosks, benches, handrails, garbage cans, elevators, and other surfaces, from Lima and Hong Kong to New Delhi, Cairo, and Paris.

There is evidence, too, that microbial diversity can vary across a day – for instance, at peak travel hours – and that there are some surprising microbial densities around us in our cities. In another project in New York, for instance, researchers took almost 600 soil samples in Central Park and sequenced 16S and 18S rRNA to identify the bacterial, archaeal, and eukaryotic composition. They were surprised to find that the soil's microbial diversity compared with places of very high biodiversity that you would find in the tropics. The nature of microbial communities can in turn significantly impact plant life – and therefore animal and human life.[79]

Initiatives like MetaSUB seek to examine the points of intensive contact between humans and the microbial world, and to understand how bacteria thrives, evolves, and interacts over urban space and time. 'Urban genomes' may be used to develop new avenues for novel drugs and antibiotics or to recommend urban materials that might enhance good bacteria so that it can compete with bad bacteria, or to develop educational programmes and outreach, or to train a new generation of students to work across disciplinary perspectives. In the process, we are learning not just about cities but about microbes, too, mapping a new bacteriological frontier as life increasingly urbanises.

A new field is being produced that intersects planning, design, architecture, transit, public health, ecology, biology, and geography. We are only beginning to uncover the microbial diversities of city subways, shaped by conjunctures of density, temperature, and humidity, as well as commuter geographies and architectural features.[80] The new emphasis on mapping changing urban biomes developed through initiatives like MetaSUB provide the possibility of rapid detection and response to pathogens, improved water safety, and tracking the highly dynamic metagenomic complexity of cities. This may allow, for instance, predictions of how large and small events or forms of construction and development might shift microbial ecologies, from new housing developments to infrastructure extension, or climatic changes that impact insects, mould, humidity, and materials in myriad ways. It might also allow early identification of the people and places most vulnerable to new infections and potential outbreaks.

The risk with approaches like source–receptor–pathway, SFD, and metagenomic surveys is that for all their attentiveness to the geographies of waste and infection, they can mean losing sight of the political, cultural, and economic factors that shape sanitation. These too need to be included in our roving sanitation telescope. The links between density, cities, sanitation, and disease outbreaks demonstrate the connections between the microbial and the economic, political, cultural, and ecological. The toxic combination of poor sanitation, a lack of clean water, uncollected solid and industrial wastes, inadequate drainage for wastewater, and malnutrition can generate high rates of respiratory disorders, skin and gastro-intestinal infections, frequent fevers, tuberculosis and hypertension, as well as occasional outbreaks of typhoid, hepatitis, and cholera.[81] The distribution of vulnerability is not just a technical question of mapping waste, vital though that is, but of economic disinvestment, political neglect, and inequalities such as those of gender, race, and class.

Microbes – bacteria, viruses, archaea, fungi, and single-celled eukaryotes that include amoebas, slime mould, and paramecia – exhibit vast diversity and adaptability, often working together or in competition with one another. There is much we need to learn about how they interact with cities and urbanisation.[82] They are not always the enemy. There is a growing awareness of the vital role of microbial diversity in the human gut, and here there is a nascent research area that brings the body, the microbial, the infrastructural, and the environmental into alignment in order to understand the urban microbiome.

The gut microbiome and the urban microbiome are not separate, and the ways in which they interconnect can be wildly varied across urban space. If you are living in a neighbourhood with a sewage and wider sanitation problem, where there is poverty that impacts nutrition and diet, then your gut biome is likely to be quite different to those middle-class residents across town who can maximise the ingestion of good bacteria in sanitised environments. There are even efforts underway to develop apps that connect to sensors in toilets that bring 'real time' data on the composition of excrement, providing read-outs of mineral and vitamin health while potentially ringing alarm bells about disease and illness.

More broadly, microbes are central to managing waste in the city and are increasingly being put to work in a new economy of virtuous urban sanitation ecologies. A new experimental moment is at play as activists, businesses, and municipalities begin to look upon growing piles of human waste as an opportunity rather than a problem. Development NGOs and local entrepreneurs are making a case for the social and economic potential of turning waste into energy, fertiliser, compost, and food, and private companies increasingly talk about how to build 'circular sanitation economies' that connect farms, food production, waste, treatment, and water capture.[83]

In places where rural and peri-urban farmers sometimes fertilise land using untreated septic tank waste, the addition of 'effective microorganisms' might assist waste treatment as well as enhancing decomposition and soil fertility, something the WHO has explored with some success.[84] Eco-sanitation initiatives seek to transform excrement into fertilisers for high-yielding fruit trees but struggle to cope with dense conditions and are sometimes shunned by residents, while sometimes very large bio-centres siphon off gas from chambers underneath 'community' toilet blocks.

One example is the growth in commercial enterprises such as biogas sanitation centres in different cities, with mixed consequences for local economies, socialities, and politics. In Nairobi, for example, biogas centres have spread rapidly in recent years, with more than fifty serving 20,000 persons daily. Biocentres link generative microbial processes to livelihood and business opportunities that can upend how waste is perceived. In Rwanda, the Kigali Institute of Science, Technology and Management has developed large-scale biogas plants in all kinds of sites, from schools to prisons. The impact of this is not just to produce energy – and bio-effluent used as a fertiliser – but to reduce demand for fuel generated from deforestation in rural Rwanda.[85]

At the same time, there can be conflict around how these resources are used, what is and what is not an appropriate way to use energy derived from excrement, and who is or is not included in the opportunities it generates. There are complications to how biogas centres enter the urban environment. For example, in March 2017, the largest garbage ground infrastructure in Ethiopia collapsed, killing more than a hundred residents at the Koshe landfill, Addis Ababa. Some blamed the construction of a new biogas plant built to meet social and environmental goals of improved energy through waste. The government argued that it had sought to close the site but met with local resistance. The collapse generated debate about how the city should dispose of waste while meeting the needs of local communities and building sustainable metabolic systems.

The microbial world, then, co-constitutes all kinds of conditions, coalitions, conflicts, and changes in the city. We can zoom into the microbe, isolate and study the pathogen, and that task is vital. But it also risks missing the larger picture, which is to do with the relations among microbes and what they form in and beyond the city, the complex geographies through which they travel, the new – and old – threats they bring, the vulnerabilities they expose, and the opportunities they present. When we zoom out and pursue the routes through which they travel, we see that microbes become part of all kinds of relations in the urban sanitation crisis, from climate change and war to economic crisis, infrastructure policy, and cultural politics that impact refugees and other marginal groups They become part of the networked nature of sanitation, inexorably constitutive of the potential for the right to citylife.

The life of sanitation is at once pathogenic and political-economic, playing on existing urban poverty and sanitation inadequacy, taking advantage of urban travel and density, or becoming the source of new social economies and risks. If this is a wide-ranging and growing debate, the event that, more than most in the past hundred years, cemented the relationship between pathogens, sanitation and the city, and propelled public and political debates in and beyond cities globally, is the COVID-19 pandemic.

'Picture the city in daily life'

Local and global disease outbreaks are becoming increasingly common. Before COVID-19, we had already seen them in rapidly urbanising China and Africa, including SARS and Ebola. These diseases moved from urbanising hinterlands to cities, including Hong Kong, Toronto, Freetown, and Monrovia. Across the world, the urban periphery is undergoing an increasingly intense transformation, and with it enhanced zoonotic risks can quickly become regional and global problems. The land mass of cities globally has increased at a faster rate than their populations. Research using population data and satellite maps has shown that sprawl is outpacing densification across the world.[86] Yet the immediate focus as the COVID-19 pandemic emerged was not on peripheral urbanisation and the conduits of global trade and travel, but on high densities at the core of large cities.

Concerns over density and sanitation emerged early in the pandemic. The high death toll in New York, the initial epicentre of the outbreak in the United States, led then-governor Andrew

Cuomo to espouse his own version of telescopic urbanism: 'I touch this table – the virus could live here for two days. You come tomorrow, I'm gone, you touch that spot . . . In New York City, all that density, a lot of people are touching a lot of spots, right? Park bench, grocery counters. Just picture the city in daily life.'[87] In other cities that were initially badly impacted by COVID-19, including Milan and Madrid, density was often identified as the progenitor of transmission. There was a form of 'sanitation syndrome' or 'hygienisation' connected to density in these discourses, a geographical imagination of the city as so many sites of contamination resulting from too many people crowding into the same places.[88] Urbanist Joel Kotkin argued that high-density living was central to the crisis from the start, 'from the pandemic's genesis in crowed, unsanitary urban China to the much higher rates of hospitalization and death in large cities'.[89]

It is not surprising that this view emerged, given that the virus did grip a large urban agglomeration – Wuhan – and in its initial stages quickly became connected to big, dense cities and urban regions, including New York, Milan, Madrid, and London. The flipside of these sanitation syndromes was the idea that low-density spaces are safer from contamination.[90] It was also reflected in a much more serious, sinister politics, such as efforts to 'de-densify' townships and informal settlements in South Africa and India, including shocking stories of opportunistic urban eviction and demolition by the state.[91] In South Africa, the government used 'heat maps' to identify twenty-nine areas for 'de-densification', lower-income neighbourhoods that were to, in the disturbingly sanitised words of one minister, 'relocate and decant'.[92]

However, even in the early stage of the pandemic, there were counter-examples to the 'blame density' position and its attendant sanitation syndromes. Most obviously, there were those cities with high densities in which authorities had relative success in managing the virus, including South East Asian giants Singapore, Hong Kong, Taipei, and Seoul. Moreover, it appeared that their relative success was in fact partly to do with their high densities, including in pursuing contact tracing, the extent of public health infrastructure, investment in sanitation across the public realm and transit systems, the uptake of face masks, and the fact that many people live with the memory of the 2003 SARS outbreak and quickly changed their practices. In Hong Kong, the 2019–20 protests against the Chinese state extradition bill helped ensure that a ready civic infrastructure was in place to facilitate community responses and provisioning. Evidence emerged that higher density areas often have better quality health care and greater amounts of both formal and informal mutual support networks.[93]

Rather than density, it was particular spatial conditions that were seen to be especially impacted by COVID-19. Roger Keil, for example, noted that it was 'care homes, prisons, camps, reserves, some work environments such as meatpacking plants and among migrant farm workers' that were sometimes the worst hit by infection, hospitalisation, and death.[94] While Singapore was praised for its handling of COVID-19, there were spikes in recorded infections among the city's migrant worker population, including in crowded dormitories housing up to twenty male workers from China and South Asia in a single room.[95] If density played a role in increasing COVID-19 infection levels, then, it was a particular expression of it: overcrowded, often poorly ventilated domestic and labour conditions, with insufficient investment in sanitation provisions.

Residents in poor, dense neighbourhoods were still likely to have higher 'exposure density' to the virus – a term historically linked to radiology – than those in other areas.[96] In Karachi, for example, the urban poor often occupy tiny plots of packed land a fraction of the size of wealthier neighbourhoods and share infrastructures like poorly maintained toilets.[97] Social distancing is nigh on impossible in such conditions, and indeed transmission rates were much lower in middle-class areas. People have much higher rates of contact with one another in the home and across the neighbourhood, and they are far less able to work at home, leading – as with flu outbreaks – to higher and quicker epidemic peaks in poor, dense areas with inadequate sanitation.[98]

In one estimate during the pandemic, only 2 percent of health care facilities in low- and middle-income countries, or at least those with data, had adequate amounts of water, sanitation, hygiene, waste management services, and personal protective equipment, and those resources were often especially scant in dense, deprived neighbourhoods.[99] Yet, water, sanitation, and hygiene were not being prioritised in COVID-19 funding when compared to support for research, equipment, industry, business, detection, and other priorities.[100] At the same time, poorer residents often lack access to quality, affordable health care. Arundhati Roy's prediction at the start of the outbreak was all too often realised in practice: 'India's public hospitals and clinics – which are unable to cope with the almost 1m children who die of diarrhoea, malnutrition and other health issues every year, with the hundreds of thousands of tuberculosis patients (a quarter of the world's cases), with a vast anaemic and malnourished population vulnerable to any number of minor illnesses that prove fatal for them – will not be able to cope.'

While politicians like Cuomo and much of the media worried about density in general, others warned early on that it was residents living in overcrowded homes in dense neighbourhoods with poor sanitation, and who had to keep working outside the home, who were most at risk. UN-Habitat set out an agenda early in the pandemic to support community-driven work and local governments by providing data and mapping areas of priority and emerging hotspots. This included, for instance, collecting data on water and sanitation in order to identify areas in need of additional support in Kenya or installing public handwashing stations in key locations in Myanmar. Residents in Nigeria, Ethiopia, and Congo accounted for a third of those in sub-Saharan Africa lacking soap and water at home, while a third of all school-age children across the region lacked basic handwashing facilities at school.[101]

Some local governments and utilities rapidly scaled up affordable water and sanitation, for example in Kibera in Kenya, Kigali in Rwanda, and Freetown in Sierra Leone, mainly through handwashing stations.[102] A thick tissue of community support grew up across the urban world, with nongovernmental organisations, charities, churches, temples, mosques, and mutual aid groups distributing food and medicines to those in extreme need, especially those who had lost their jobs or were sick, while short-term government grants were often rolled out. Density kicked in as a resource for meeting basic needs even as people so often sought to escape it.

COVID-19 ought to have been a wake-up call to the extent of the global sanitation crisis. It shone a huge spotlight on the uneven geography of risk and on the intimate links between poverty, overcrowding, and sanitation. It threw the relationship between sanitation and the urban experience into sharp relief. It also showed what is possible when an emergency hits. It triggered a vast economic response consisting of trillions of dollars, the invention of new vaccines, radical changes in governance and lifestyle, and in some places a public health transformation. The deep and extensive urban sanitation crisis that has been escalating across the world, particularly in poorer cities, demands at the very least a similar response and ought to be viewed as the emergency it is. In the past, crises have led to radical changes in sanitation and cities. But not even the pandemic, it seems, is quite enough to place the rallying call of sanitation for all at the centre of the urban agenda. Instead, millions of urbanites were pushed into extreme poverty, infrastructure projects were put on hold, sanitation systems were not as maintained as before, and city and national budgets were squeezed by the economic hit.

At the same time, however, the crisis did provoke a new conversation in some policy, civil society, and academic quarters about city sanitation, densities, and their futures, including on how to ensure greater attention, investment, and care towards areas where the inhabitants have been badly affected by the virus even as they provided essential labour for the rest of the city. In places that urbanist Jay Pitter referred to as 'forgotten densities', where dense populations are found alongside high rates of health, class, race, gender, and socioeconomic inequality, it is clear enough that a new approach is needed.[103]

This approach demands addressing the vast inequalities in housing, services, infrastructure, and labour conditions through which pathogens can move – in other words, sanitation as part of a much wider network underpinning the right to citylife. The pandemic was a stark reminder of the need for a new focus on infrastructure provisioning, maintenance and repair, and especially on water and sanitation, particularly in neighbourhoods where they fall short of everyday needs. It is not so much a question of addressing a virus, or even of preparing for the next one, but addressing the urban inequalities, including sanitation poverty, that disease and illness align with and entrench.

Animal geographies

While there is debate, it is likely that the origins of COVID-19 lie in human contact with bat droppings in peri-urban Wuhan. It would be wrong to position animals as an enemy when in fact what is so often needed is a much better coexistence with them in our cities, but it would be wrong too to underestimate the scale and threat from animal faeces. Yet, this is precisely what has been done in sanitation research, policy, and practice.[104] Animals – goats, cows, chickens, pigs, dogs, cats, rodents, birds, and more – are important parts of the ecology of sanitation.

They defecate into water, drains, open ground, and soil. They rummage through heaps of solid waste scavenging for food. They pass on parasites. They provide milk and food. Meat hangs in kiosks and provides sustenance not just for people, but for flies and microbes. Discarded animal parts rot in garbage grounds, where birds and insects clear the debris even as they spread infection. Then there are the rats, history's most vilified vectors. 'We are scared of getting bitten by the rats while using the toilet,' said Aarti Shinde, a resident in Jai Santoshi Mata Nagar, Mumbai, of the local toilet block: 'The rats that climb up from the toilet are big and children get scared.'[105]

Poultry, cattle, sheep, and pigs generate 85 percent of the world's animal faecal waste, much of which ends up in cities.[106]

Figure 8. Chicken and toilet. Source: Renu Desai (reproduced with permission).

Contamination of food and water sources is common, particularly in poorer urban contexts. Pigs, for example, can be 'mixing vessels' for influenza, combining both bird and human flu. A study of free-range pig rearing in Guwahati, a city in northeast India, found that pig sheds were often poorly maintained and that the combination of inadequate hygiene, poverty, and density posed particular risks for zoonotic infection.

For some in public health and epidemiology, dense low-income neighbourhoods with inadequate sanitation are 'petri dishes' for new threats to human health.[107] This kind of language, however, walks a risky political line. It can easily fall into pre-existing stereotypes that stigmatise and sometimes are used to justify the demolition of poorer neighbourhoods (the 'de-densification' drives during the COVID-19 pandemic were not unique, one-off events).

The history of urbanisation has depended on close links between humans and animals, from fertiliser, food, and leather products to horse-drawn carts, pets in the home or streets, chickens in gardens, pigeons on rooftops, and more. In *Animal Cities*, Peter Atkins explores the 'de-animalisation' of cities from the nineteenth century on, when animals were removed typically in the name of sanitation.[108] Concerns with health or with 'offensive odours' led to animals being progressively separated into designated areas or removed from cities altogether. Atkins calls this 'the great separation'.

There is a long history of urban damage to animals, from the concretisation or contamination of lakes, rivers, and soils to deforestation and intensive small- and large-scale agribusiness that overwhelms ecologies, harms wildlife, and increases opportunities for zoonotic transmission. These practices are intimately woven into the fabric of capitalist urbanisation, industrialised agriculture, and global consumption practices.

The paradigmatic figure of industrialised agriculture is the broiler chicken, grown to twice its size in half the time it took fifty years ago, managed by poultry workers subsisting on exploitative wages, demanding the industrialisation and homogenisation of grain and oilseed, and intensifying the risk of avian influenza.[109] For some commentators, the broiler chicken is effectively 'a genetically engineered monocultural technology', produced in the main by just three companies and kept in horrendously cramped conditions. Outbreaks of avian flu among chickens on poultry farms have been increasing and the chance of mutations that carry over to humans is high both in contact with workers and in the transfer of birds across borders. Improving the conditions the birds are kept in could help reduce the risks, but the extraordinary appetite of the poultry market – 69 billion chickens were slaughtered in 2018 alone – demands otherwise. The global politics of urban sanitation is also a global politics of food and ecology.[110]

Animals can suffer from infection, illness, and death in cities due to sewage and garbage. Stray dogs, for example, can contract rabies feeding from open garbage grounds, markets, or near homes. In Cameroon, research has shown that the growth of cities has been accompanied by an increase in stray dogs, and children are more likely to be bitten than adults. Across the world, urban shelters for dogs are often insanitary and disease is not uncommon. In one in Chennai, India, an investigation in 2021 found that almost sixty dogs died in just over a year due to poor conditions and that others were suffering from helminthiasis (worm infection), respiratory disease, and wounds.[111]

Cities have historically generated new habitats for animals, from rodents and lizards to threatened bird species, from langur monkeys in India or chacma baboons in South Africa, to black bears or coyotes in the United States or kittiwakes in the UK. Cities can both reduce biodiversity and damage populations of birds and other species as well as act as sites for animal protection – for instance, through new wildlife parks and corridors.[112] In many cities the great separation never occurred to anywhere near the extent it did in Western cities, both for cultural and economic reasons. Nonetheless, coexistence between humans and animals in cities is often a fraught and complex affair, and here waste is one among many problem areas.

India has an estimated 5 million stray cows roaming the country. Cows are sacred in Hinduism and are often fiercely protected in law and culture. This can generate difficult encounters in congested cities. When cows stop giving milk, it is often easier for owners to set them free than to pay to care for them, while cow shelters are often overcrowded. Cows have been hit by cars, consumed dangerous amounts of plastic, and left excrement and urine across streets and public places. The response has ranged from frustrations over waste to sharp increases in fines for allowing cows to block roads and campaigning groups insisting cows be left alone. In spring 2022, the High Court in Gujarat, refusing to allot further land for cattle, captured this range of responses by insisting that people had to learn to better live alongside cows: 'It's called coexistence,' the judge concluded.[113]

Another example is bird life. In her research on kittiwakes in Newcastle, in northeast England, Helen Wilson shows the range of encounters and responses different groups have to the seabird in the city, from concerns over excrement and noise to affection and protection. This reflects the larger 'inherent ambivalence' that shapes how birds and animals figure in urban imaginations, politics, and experience.[114] For all that coexistence is a multiple and ambivalent terrain, it is also where the links between non-humans, sanitation, poverty, and disease come sharply into view.

Nearly two-thirds of human pathogens are zoonotic in origin, and urbanisation, climate change, and inequality are increasing the risks of successful leaps from animals to humans. Most of these pathogens lack the high infection potential of the coronavirus that led to the COVID-19 pandemic, but that does not mean they are without serious consequence. In addition to the risk of industrialised food production, especially through poultry, there is exposure to animal faeces in cities through household livestock, small-scale farming, markets, slaughterhouses, and free-roaming animals. All of this is linked to a range of health consequences, from diarrhoea, soil-transmitted helminth infection, and trachoma to environmental enteric dysfunction, stunted growth in children, and long-term consequences for pregnant women and those who are immunocompromised.[115]

The transmission of zoonotic pathogens to humans occurs through both direct and indirect means. Direct transmission occurs in *contact* with body fluids and tissues from sick animals – rabies and brucellosis, for example – *inhalation* of aerosolised pathogens from infected animals – including influenza viruses and *Mycobacterium bovis* – and *ingestion* of contaminated animal products – for example, salmonella and *E. coli*. Indirect transmission emerges when people encounter a site or object contaminated with pathogens, including soil, water, or animal excrement. Some pathogens can survive for weeks and even months, including those passed from rodent waste like leptospirosis, arenaviruses, and hantaviruses.[116] A third of deaths among children under five are due to diarrhoea caused by pathogens that can be found in animal faeces.

Sanitation interventions can falter if they focus on human waste to the neglect of animal waste. Part of the solution here is to reduce human cohabitation and contact with animals, as well as controls on animal movement, the creation of safer child spaces, better veterinary care and hygiene promotion, and in some cases even provisions as simple as animal faeces scoops. In the pre-emergence stage of new pathogens, ensuring clean and protected drinking water for livestock can prevent contamination by wildlife or pest hosts and reduce inter-species transmission.[117]

Hygiene education plays a role. One study in Thailand found that even where personal protective equipment was provided, less than 1 percent of households with backyard chickens used gloves as a measure against avian influenza, although people were more likely to wear boots. Research in Chile found large disparities in the participation of lower-income urban neighbourhoods in safe animal waste disposal practices, even in neighbourhoods adjacent to one another, and argued for greater tailoring of educational materials and public health outreach to specific places.[118]

There are also ways of using new technologies to identify risks as they are emerging. For example, the Monkeybar project uses drones to detect malaria carried by macaques in South East Asia. The drones provide data on land changes, including deforestation or changes to agriculture, which can be used to better predict the movement of animals, insects, and people.[119]

The risk with some of these measures, necessary though they are, is that they often focus responsibility on poor residents. Or, worse, they can serve those who would attribute blame to residents for the emergence and spread of new disease, even when infection may in fact have arisen from illegal poaching, hunting, and wildlife trade, from the larger production of urban inequality, or the intensive global production of animal meat. Better real-time data, for example, is good, but it does not operate in a neutral political sphere and in some contexts could be used not to generate progressive interventions but to advance damaging pre-existing political agendas. It is crucial to invest in primary prevention activities such as disease surveillance, preventive veterinary care at the level of animal populations, waste disposal, rodent extermination, and secondary practices such as education and personal protective equipment when handing animals.[120]

It is important, too, not to lose sight of the fact that farming is often economically vital for livelihoods in cities. It provides essential food in often under-nourished areas, and there are sometimes cultural concerns at stake, from traditional practices of animal husbandry that are tied to pre-existing patterns of rural and tribal living to the religious reverence attached to cows, elephants, and monkeys in Indian cities. Urban farming can also be an ecological good, bringing diversity, ecosystem services, and lower-carbon agricultural practices, as well as functioning as a kind of 'outdoor classroom' for urbanites on food and environment.[121]

In navigating these tensions between threat and contamination, on the one hand, and investment and support, on the other, sanitation as the right to citylife can play a role. If the right to citylife is being safe in and thriving in the city, then the challenge is how to support places, livelihoods, and human–animal relations and practices and to confront a politics of stigmatisation and removal. This means building alliances and dialogue between, for example, local states, civil society groups, and peri-urban farmers, as well as forming collaborative forums that look to use data in genuinely progressive ways. The result ought then to be agreed frameworks for investing in local housing, infrastructure, services, hygiene education, and protective practices as required, with residents involved in the planning and implementation.

Inevitably, there are cases where the hazards mean that certain practices do have to stop, but if that is necessary then it needs to be clear to all involved as to why and it must be done with a genuine commitment to long-term support for affected groups. Easier said than done. The role animals play in the urban sanitation crisis has to be understood not just as a question of agricultural practice, but in the context of contemporary urbanisation and capitalist ecologies, as well as all the ambivalences that come with urban coexistence. Alongside the provision of appropriate equipment, regulations, and planning, then, there is a deeper and more intractable politics of production and consumption at stake.

Paying greater attention to the 'life' of 'citylife' in the urban sanitation crisis is a thorny politics and a constantly changing one. But it is a politics that is likely to become more intense and frequent rather than less so. 'City' and 'life' shape each other far too indelibly to make any separation especially meaningful. The stuff of life – climate ecologies, bodies, animals, and microbes – are 'written into' one another, and the consequence is that neither citylife nor the right to it are fixed. We are dealing, then, with a highly dynamic and expanding confluence of life, requiring ever greater vigilance and care.

5

Protest

Human waste is political. Whenever any of us use a toilet, we are bringing together an immense historical apparatus of infrastructure, knowledge, policy, regulation, and investment. This apparatus has shaped moral codes separating the private and the public and typically has all kinds of in-built assumptions about the sorts of bodies that will make use of it, usually privileging the able-bodied adult male. Who gets what, where, and how in the city is a reflection of historic and contemporary cultures, economies, and inequalities.

So, when human waste is used in protest, it is not that it then *becomes* political. Instead, what is happening in those moments is a *re*politicisation, a becoming-political in a different way. These moments are powerful expressions and demands for the right to citylife. They are usually aimed at transforming sanitation conditions in a site or across a city. These protests are typically a desperate politics of last resort, when residents or activists arrive at the view that no other political channel is available to securing better sanitation conditions. In some cases, they might use human waste to express a political demand distinct from sanitation itself, and the fact that human waste is the vehicle of politicisation means that the protest takes on a particular resonance with the cultural politics and histories of waste and bodies.

The making public of private bodily materials in political acts gets to the core of what is thought to be legitimate protest. It brings the political question of disobedience and the cultural question of what represents proper conduct into sharp and often explosive relation. For protestors, such acts are calculations that weigh increased public attention against the risk of being vilified through creating public disgust.

This is more than a politics of acceptability; when people express anger or discontent through human waste they are often traduced as 'uncivilised'. Political and legal figures frequently condemn residents and activists who vent anger through bodily waste as 'animalistic'.[1] As a demand for the right to citylife, the use of human waste in protest is a high-risk politics, typically generating a shocking spectacle and strong affective and discursive response. It can shift a debate about sanitation conditions or the political settlement in a city, but the direction of that shift might not necessarily be what protestors intend.

This is a tradition of sanitation politics that exists both in relation to and beyond the global apparatus and debates of liberal sanitation discourse. While these protests may sometimes speak the language of liberal inclusion, they more often take the form of a guttural, frustrated cry that rejects the development-talk of local states and international agencies as either spin or woefully insufficient, demanding instead a more radical horizon of change – even if the content of that horizon is not always mapped out. These are forms of protest historically stigmatised by elites in power as the irrational outbursts of the 'rabble' and the 'mob'.[2]

Very often, the response by those in power is to try to connect the act of protest – using human waste as a political weapon – with the protestors themselves: in using waste, conservative voices have long argued, they reveal themselves to *be* waste. But what these protests point to is the conscious choice of the dispossessed, the systematically exploited, and the despairing crowd to articulate the fundamental right to human dignity and potential. They operate in an alternative global tradition and marginalised archive of the right to citylife.

Smearing the enemy

In Jharkhand, India, activists have been involved in a series of ongoing protests against the central government's land reform bill. Amendments to the 2013 Land Acquisition Act have been referred to as a 'death warrant' by activists because they threaten to dispossess tribal groups of huge tracts of land to make way for industry. Moreover, amendments were introduced that exempted the government from conducting social impact assessments, which would take account of those most likely to be affected by developments, a measure normally reserved for emergency situations.[3]

Rallies and meets have taken place in response, but, in what one of the activists called 'an act of desperation', they turned to what some media and activists referred to as a 'public shit protest' or a 'poop protest'. In Latehar, a town in the centre of the state, a group of around sixty men sat in a row in public and defecated on copies of the bill, with the aim of creating 'a shock'. In a country where human waste has been historically connected to caste labour, stigmatisation, and 'untouchability', this kind of protest – not entirely unfamiliar – has political potency.

'We have got immense support for the poop protest from the Adivasi [tribal] regions and many have invited us to collectively do poop protest in their areas,' said one activist. 'With the poop protest in Latehar, we have begun a fight and we have promised ourselves not to leave it unfinished.'[4] He went on to reflect on the historical use of what he called 'shit as arsenal': 'Throughout history, whenever oppressed masses have dropped their shit as arsenal, rulers have been shaken because it often marks the beginning of a social uprising.'[5] These kinds of short-lived shock protests are part of a longer repertoire of what Sudipta Kaviraj has called 'small rebelliousness' around waste, where improvised defilement becomes a political outlet using the power of smell and disgust.[6]

There is a global history here, taking on distinct cultural and political inflections in different cities. Some examples illustrate the diversity of this. In France in 2014, a protestor smeared excrement on bank machines to protest capitalism. In Zimbabwe in 2013, a twenty-six-year-old was arrested in a bar and charged with insulting President Mugabe and defacing election materials, both criminal offences, after he allegedly used a campaign poster as toilet paper. But – and pointing to the ambivalent status of shock protests that use human waste – the main court in the country later demanded that the government prosecutors explain why the action was in violation of the Constitution's free speech provisions. Following a protest in Stuttgart in February 2014, excrement became part of the contention between Christian protestors and gay rights groups. Some Christians in Stuttgart protesting against teaching about homosexuality in the school curriculum claimed that people charged at them, threw excrement, and wiped themselves with pages torn from the Bible, which they subsequently threw at them. It was claimed by some that this story was invented by Christian activist groups.[7]

In Texas in 2013, state authorities claimed that jars containing urine, excrement, and feminine hygiene products were confiscated from anti-abortion protestors demonstrating outside the Senate. Activists denied this and claimed that what was actually going on was a deliberate strategy to smear protestors by associating them with bodily wastes. In Bristol in 2021, police alleged that activists protesting against the UK government's controversial Police, Crime, Sentencing, and Courts Bill – which hands draconian powers to the police, allowing them greater scope to prevent protests that might become noisy and disruptive – defecated on their shoes. The city's mayor described the protests as 'worse than pathetic'.[8]

The attempt to associate protests with waste in order to delegitimise them and alienate support has a long history. For example, during the 2012 G8 meeting in Chicago, police wore masks to protect themselves from protestors throwing excrement and urine. Michael Shields, Fraternal Order of Police president, complained at the time that 'rioters' who attend

NATO and G8 meetings 'have been known to throw bags of urine and bags of faeces at police', arguing that Chicago police need an adapted shield that can protect officers from waste.[9] Activists insisted that the accusation was a deliberate effort to delegitimise the protestors and their agenda. In the same year, there had been accusations, often from conservative commentators, that protestors at the May Day protests in Seattle were planning on throwing faeces.

The encounter of human waste and protest generates intense ambivalence, can become weaponised in different ways, and is vulnerable to an often unpredictable politics of blame that shifts attention from grievances to the alleged character of protagonists. It is not just places, bills, and buildings that becomes physically and symbolically smeared, or even the claims and counter-claims of political actors, but the participants themselves.

In the lead-up to the 2008 political party national conventions in the US, both the Democrat and Republican parties accused each other of planning to weaponise human waste. All kinds of rumours flew, including that the police were going to use a weapon that caused protestors to involuntarily defecate and that protestors were going to spray urine or excrement on the police. Ahead of the Democratic National Convention in Denver, local newspaper *Westword* initiated, with tongue in cheek, what they called the 'NoCRAP' campaign – Normal Citizens Rising Against Poo – and called for a 'moratorium on the public throwing, spraying, smearing, hosing or inducing of excrement for the week', and set up a 'Doo-Doo Accord'.[10] But there was a serious politics lurking in the background to the puns and jokes around human waste.

In 2011, as the Occupy protests railed against the financial system, there were efforts by city governments across the world to remove occupiers on the grounds of sanitation. The Occupy protests seized urban public space, turning those spaces into debating chambers, ongoing rallies, libraries, and, for a while at least, places to live and socialise. In New York, occupiers at Liberty Plaza had their belongings – everything from clothes

Figure 9. Day 31 Occupy Wall Street, 16 October 2011.
Source David Shankbone, CC PDM 1.0.

and books to food supplies, medications, and laptops – cleared by police and taken to the sanitation station. Max Liboiron, who was involved in the occupation, described how the next day, when protestors returned to Liberty Plaza, any object they placed on the ground was seized and taken to a garbage truck: 'One security officer explained it to a friend: "Anything that touches the ground is garbage." He looked at her feet suggestively.'[11] Protestors at the site had been increasingly portrayed by the mayor's office and hostile sections of the media as 'dirty, filthy and unsanitary', claims that were made against Occupy protests elsewhere, including Los Angeles and Paris.[12] This occurred despite efforts by Occupy Wall Street and other Occupy protests to set up their own Sanitation Working Groups.

No amount of 'clean up' by the protestors would have made much difference, however. For many political authorities, the very presence of the protestors was an affront. It didn't matter that protestors at Liberty Plaza had organised their own toilets through an alliance with the United Federation of Teachers or that they had their own laundry group, or that principles of cleanliness were often explicitly written into the rules of Occupy camps. Political opponents of Occupy explicitly connected the politics of the protestors to dirt and lack of hygiene so as to question the very legitimacy of their concerns and presence in the city.

As prominent Republican politician Newt Gingrich put it at the time: 'They [Occupy] take over a public park they didn't pay for, to go nearby to use bathrooms they didn't pay for, to beg for food from places they don't want to pay for, to obstruct those who are going to work to pay the taxes to sustain the bathrooms and to sustain the park, so they can self-righteously explain they are the paragons of virtue to which we owe everything . . . you need to reassert something by saying to them, "Go get a job right after you take a bath." ' Gingrich was not subtle in his replaying of the old discursive slippage from 'unclean places' to 'unclean people' cast as social, political, and economic waste. The fact that the protestors were so often demanding the 'cleaning up' of Wall Street capitalism or the ending of flows of 'dirty money' made the claims for sanitation from the powers that be all the more incongruous. 'We can see,' wrote one Occupy activist, 'that ideas about filth, waste and transgressions make up an ongoing political debate about the ideal society by both Occupiers and [their] opposition.'[13]

There is a wide and dizzying history of politics here. We might think of the Israel Defense Forces spraying 'skunk', a concoction that smells like sewage, against Palestinian demonstrators (an act known in Arabic as 'kharara' or 'the shitter'). Or, in 2017, protestors in Venezuela led by right-wing opposition parties used what they called 'Poopootov cocktails', consisting of water and human waste, against the National Guard and police.[14] Then there were pro-democracy protestors in Hong Kong having excrement and dead rodents thrown at them by disgruntled neighbours. There was the Queer Student Union at California Polytechnic University staging what they called a 'shit in' to protest the university's lack of toilets for transgender students. Or – very different again – an incident outside the French Parliament when a lorry load of manure was emptied as part of a right-wing protest calling for the president to resign over his agricultural policy, in what the police called 'un attentat à la crotte' or 'poop attack'. There is a historical litany of shit in social and political debate, from descriptions of 'slums' as 'filthy' or racial and class-based slurs about particular neighbourhoods to Trump referring to 'shithole' nations and the more general phenomena of 'shitposting' on social media.[15]

Using human waste to smear the enemy is a form of protest that can combine bodily intimacy and intensely private acts with disgust at life choices or at political positions, organisations, and ideologies. In August 2014, Egyptian feminist activist Aliaa Magda Elmahdy protested against the Islamic State (IS) by releasing, via Facebook, a picture of herself menstruating on the IS flag. Alongside her was a woman dressed in a black hijab defecating on the flag. Elmahdy has political asylum in Sweden and works in conjunction with Ukrainian feminist group Femen. The picture was aimed at IS and its supporters, although most media in the Middle East deemed the picture too offensive to publish.

This is obviously a very particular expression of disgust at a political ideology, but there is a wider global politics of menstrual activism that seeks to unsettle the inherited ideas of what is and isn't 'sanitary' and how that becomes linked to ideas of shame and humiliation. There are, for instance, 'stain protests', such as athlete Kiran Gandhi's free-bleeding during the 2015 London Marathon or Rupi Kaur's Instagram stain protest. If these acts tend to highlight the connections between periods and questions of cost, taxation, leave from work, and period poverty, they also point to a larger politics of bodies and shame that takes shape in and beyond cities.[16]

Menstrual blood is seen as deeply offensive in some cultures, or as marking a threshold moment at which women must be married, and in some contexts – Malawi, for example – cultural stigma attached to it can result in girls leaving school.[17] As Mary Douglas argued in *Purity and Danger*, the body and its excretions – 'spittle, blood, milk, urine, faeces or tears' – are shaped by social norms.[18] What's important about Douglas's argument is that menstrual blood, for example, becomes a particular kind of political 'problem' not so much in general, but specifically when it is *out of place*, which can then entail all kinds responses: solidarity, support, disgust, the reassertion of social power, and so on.

Chella Quint, a UK-based artist who has been a menstrual activist for over thirty years, is sharply critical of the corporate and public discourse around 'feminine hygiene' and 'sanitary protection' – 'what makes us unsanitary for having periods?' – and campaigns for changes in advertising and school messaging on menstrual discourse to encourage a more positive relation to blood. She uses discussion, dance and art to tackle taboos, arguing that the 'reframing of menstruation as not shameful and certainly not dirty can be achieved through joy, humour and, of course, evidence-based social change and policy change'.[19]

The idea of 'reframing' is to enable women and girls to see bodily secretions as part of everyday life rather than 'dirt' and shame. If many of the examples briefly mentioned above use bodily waste either to express their disgust and anger at a set of conditions and actors – land reform, global inequalities and climate damage, the Occupy protests, the political violence of IS, and so on – or to find ways of depicting political opponents as dirt or as dirty, the politics Quint advocates offer a different approach. Here, the politics of sanitation becomes a question of critiquing and changing the symbolic projection of human wastes as negative, a kind of 'de-smearing' of menstrual cultural orders. The politics of smearing does not have a straightforward relationship to the right to citylife, given how ambivalent, charged, and vulnerable it is. The struggle for activists is to shape the discourse of waste that surrounds the protest. As an intimate but pervasive relation of the body and the social, waste is both biopolitical and biomoral.

This is why the emphasis on reframing matters. Who gets to frame the politics of the protest in the city? Who is being smeared? What cultural and economic histories are being conjured up when one groups smears another? What might it take for activists, typically having less power and less capacity to broadcast than the state, to turn the dial so that their struggle – and indeed they themselves – are not depicted as dirt, waste, and unsanitary? Often, the act of using human waste is born from sheer frustration that a people and their cause is being ignored or not making needed progress. It is a desperate throw of the dice, a social and political gamble, and activists are typically aware of just how risky it can be to use human waste in protest for how they and their cause are portrayed. In the contexts I turn to now, the range of political options for protestors are still more circumscribed. Here, as we will see, bodily wastes become intimately linked to a politics of refusal and (dis)respect.

Bodily dissent and dirty protest

In March 2015, it was reported that inmates at Guantanamo Bay prison began assaulting prison guards with bodily fluids, a practice the US military calls 'splashing'. 'They concoct a cocktail,' said General John Kelly of the US Marines. 'Usually it's faeces, urine, sperm, vomit.' When guards come into the cell, they are splashed.[20] Kelly described the practice as opportunistic and 'vile', contrasting it with what he saw as the military's 'dignified' approach to detainees, that 'sees to their every need'. A Guantanamo camp commander claimed that splashing was a near daily practice.[21] Cell doors were fitted with 'splash boxes' to stop or at least limit the exposure guards experienced.

While agencies like CNN that have had some access to Guantanamo claim that the splashing is based on objections by

Muslim inmates to being guarded by women, there is little information about the context for splashing.[22] The repeated allegations that conditions in Guantanamo – which the Obama administration announced in 2009 would be closed down, Trump insisted would remain functioning, and Biden is aiming to shut down – were inhumane, and that most prisoners were held without charge, sit alongside numerous allegations of force-feeding and sexual torture.[23] These body politics were difficult to monitor, partly because lawyers weren't allowed to speak to their clients and media reporting was so tightly controlled.

The so-called 'dirty protest', which itself sometimes takes the form of smearing, generates vociferous responses. The dirty protest operates at the level of the senses and crashes through the moral line in the sand that separates 'decent' behaviour and 'legitimate' protest from what some would diagnose as 'animalistic' acts. It might be an act of non-compliance, a desperate attempt for some measure of justice, an effort to have a struggle or situation be acknowledged, an expression of disgust with those in power, a statement of refusal, a spectacular critique, and more.

In the context of the prison, the dirty protest brings with it the shadowy uncertainty of what goes on behind closed doors in some of the world's most disciplined and controlled spaces. At the same time, it is the powerful – the generals and governors – who have the greatest capacity to control the discourse around dirty protests, while protestors often have no or at least highly restricted capacity to 'reframe' events. The dirty protest in the urban prison is, in these ways, the politicisation of human waste *in extremis*.

Despite often being among the most insanitary spaces in cities, prisons are often forgotten or ignored in global sanitation debates. Across the world, prisons house some of the poorest urban residents in the worst sanitation conditions. Prisons tend to be overcrowded, with poor environmental health, and as with some other marginal sites in the city, such as homeless shelters, they often have higher proportions of people with physical and mental health conditions that can be exacerbated by inadequate sanitation.[24]

Inmates are typically poor, and often disproportionately Black or from ethnic minorities. In the US, African Americans are incarcerated at a rate five times that of whites, while in the UK a quarter of prisoners are from ethnic minority groups despite constituting 14 percent of the population.[25] In India, Muslims, Dalits and tribal groups make up hugely disproportionate numbers of the prison population.[26] Malawi's biggest prison – Mauli – contains large numbers of Ethiopian migrants who were locked up following a government crackdown on migration. The combination of overcrowding, malnutrition, and poor sanitation in Mauli has intensified outbreaks of scabies, skin infections, tuberculosis, hepatitis, and malaria.

The prison may seem like a strange place from which to consider the right to citylife, given that it is designed specifically to prevent it. It also profoundly shifts the legal, social, and spatial relations between private acts and the public. But the prison matters for how we understand urban sanitation, and while it is a place apart it is also nonetheless physically, legally, and discursively part of the larger city and society. It matters, first, because imprisonment itself reflects the wider inequalities that shape cities, second because it is such a powerful arena for reflecting on protests that deploy human waste, given how disciplinary power and control typically operates in prison, and third because sanitation conditions are sometimes among the worst in a city.

For the International Committee of the Red Cross, the disposal of human waste, as a key source of illness and disease, has been one of the most intractable problems of prisons globally. Toilets often take the form of pit latrines that are unclean, poorly maintained, and regularly blocked. Overcrowded, insanitary prisons, and rudimentary toilets – including buckets, basins and chamber pots, and insufficient menstrual products – have been found to cause higher rates of intestinal parasites, water shortages, and greater susceptibility to disease outbreaks, as we saw during the COVID-19 pandemic, in cases from Ethiopia to Panama. There are cases of women and children trading sex for access to water, food, and blankets. In the US, critics point to a lack of adequate regulation on maintaining hygiene in prisons, from not enough soap in New York to sewage backups in Texas.

They often lack privacy. In London, inspections of Pentonville Prison in recent years have described it as 'overcrowded and inhumane', including blocked toilets, leaking sewage, and little privacy, with inmates sharing small cells with badly screened toilets. [27] At the same time, research in prisons in Myanmar has shown how prisoner pecking orders can mean that some are forced to sleep nearer latrines, pointing to the important olfactory micro-geographies of waste. Tomas Martin describes how political prisoners explained to him of 'learning to accept the smell of shit': 'Two, three or four cellmates had to manage bodily positions and practices of excretion in an extremely cramped space and against the grain of their securitized environment' (indeed, these 'shit buckets' were sometimes used to hide the smell of contraband from authorities).[28] Prison suspends personal freedom; it cannot be right that it so often suspends sanitation, dignity, and health, too.

When inmates turn to protest, it is often their own bodies – and wastes – that seem to be their only weapon. One of the most high-profile dirty protests in prisons was carried out by inmates at the Maze Prison and Armagh Women's Prison in Northern Ireland in the 1970s and 1980s, where the relations between the body, politics, and rights formed a geopolitical battleground. It began not with waste but with food. In July 1972, a hunger strike by Irish Republican Army (IRA) prisoners in Maze Prison, then called Long Kesh, led to Special Category Status being introduced by the UK government across prisons in Northern Ireland.

This placed prisoners on a par with prisoners of war and thereby provided certain rights, such as not having to do certain forms of work, being placed with others in the same category, extra visits and food parcels, and not wearing prison uniforms. Four years later, however, this status was nullified when the Gardiner Committee argued that it weakened prison discipline and undermined staff. This led to growing unrest, including the death of several prison staff. The initial response involved the 'blanket protest', in which prisoners refused to wear prison uniforms and instead made clothes from blankets, if they didn't simply go naked.

This bodily act was followed by another, as prison authorities refused to let the inmates leave their cells for exercise and some prisoners declined to leave their cells to use toilets or to shower or even use the water basins that were installed in cells. Instead of leaving their cells to empty chamber pots, some prisoners began smearing excrement on the walls of their cell. Officers would spray disinfectant though windows or forcibly remove prisoners to be cleaned. By late 1979, an estimated nine in ten new prisoners were joining the protest. In February 1980, more than thirty women at Armagh Women's Prison, located in the centre of Armagh town, joined the dirty protests, an act that was to prove all the more shocking beyond the prison walls because it involved women. The gender politics created a scandal: it was one thing having men behave in this way, quite another seeing women so profoundly flout bodily and behavioural norms.

The protests at Armagh had emerged in the context of violence from prison authorities following a 'no-work' protest. Women were confined to their cells and some began to push urine through the spy holes in their doors and to throw excrement and menstrual blood from windows. Regimes of waste management also emerged in the cells. One woman in the prison wrote: 'Our walls are covered in excrement. There was nothing else to do with it. You can't pile it up in the corner – that would be unbearable. This way it's not half as bad. It dries and the smell isn't so bad after an hour or so. The urine is the worst smell. You'll probably find that hard to believe. But the stench of it just seems to cling in the air'.[29] While guards were often hostile and disgusted, especially at menstrual blood, many in the public and among feminist groups, and within the powerful Catholic Church, rallied around the women and criticised the prison.

The events have lived long in cultural and political memory and have come to resonate with other moments that entangle bodily waste, prisons, and geopolitical conflict. The hunger strikes of 1980 and 1981 at Maze Prison are an example. These led to the deaths of seven inmates, including high-profile figure Bobby Sands, who was elected member of Parliament during the strikes. These body protests led to changes in prisons in the 1980s that met many of the demands and left a long legacy in Irish politics.

If prisons are kept overcrowded and under-provided, it shouldn't surprise anyone that there will be unrest, nor that one of the few vehicles for expressing concerns and politics for prisoners is their own body. The prison is an extreme staging for the intimate relations between bodies, waste, control, and power, but these sites are nonetheless a measure of how the urban sanitation crisis and its politics unfolds. Dirty protests are struggles for rights, albeit in the context of citylife suspended, and they are a test of a universal commitment to adequate sanitation. That struggle is being fought all the time in all kinds of spaces. I now turn to another context and example, from South Africa, of using human waste as a political weapon.

'This is not our shit'

It was a hot summer afternoon in Cape Town, and my colleague Jonathan Silver and I were standing in the car park of a shopping centre in the upmarket suburb of Constantia. For the first time in my life as a researcher, I was holding a clipboard, and I had a set of survey questions. Given what we were researching – the politicisation of sanitation in Cape Town – we had initially baulked at the idea of a survey. What, in the context of deep-seated historical struggles and politics around race, infrastructure, and services, could a survey possibly achieve? While Jonathan was experienced in researching urban infrastructure and services in Cape Town, I was new to Cape Town.[30] Perhaps the survey, superficial though it may be, might add a layer to the research interviews we were doing. We did a few of these surveys in different parts of the city, but the survey at Constantia was, for me at least, the most striking.

We asked respondents what they thought of the recent spate of protests in which activists threw excrement – dubbed 'poo protests' in the media – at public buildings to vent their anger at worsening sanitation conditions. For people who have been the victims of bellicose racist slurs in Cape Town and beyond, the comments we heard – delivered often with unbridled confidence and certainty – must be rooted in long and ongoing histories of violence and trauma that are deeply felt and lived. It would not be right for me to replay in detail the range of offensive statements here. Most respondents did not think protest was justified at all, and the few who did certainly did not think throwing excrement was justifiable – as one respondent put it, 'People should protest in a dignified way.' One middle-aged white man who sympathised with the idea of protesting sanitation inequalities quickly added that 'the poo protests were revolting' and dismissed the actions as pre-election politicking.

Perhaps most disturbing was that for many respondents, the acts reflected the character of the protestors, and indeed residents, themselves. Many blamed migrants from the Eastern Cape, who were often portrayed through historical racist tropes linking race, waste, and moral behaviour. There was a lot of talk about people not 'appreciating what they get', or of 'always complaining'. One white woman, for example, ranted about how her parents were farmers and had built their own toilets: 'They didn't ask anyone for help . . . do it yourself!' A small number were more ambivalent. One white woman reflected simply that 'people are desperate'. But the most vocal supporter was a young student, a Black man from the township of Khayelit-sha who had a job at the shopping mall. For him, the protests 'exposed the treatment of Black people'. Throwing waste was an act of those deprived of a voice – 'the government doesn't listen . . . [we can't just] write letters.' These encounters were brief and took place during just one afternoon in the course of a research trip, but the ugly politics of division and prejudice set along lines of race and class were laid glaringly bare.

The relations between race, disgust, oppression, and protest have a long history in South Africa.[31] As David Atwell has argued, however, waste can be politicised in sometimes surprising ways, 'flinging the disgust back to its point of origin'.[32] In October 2011, Ayanda Kota, chair of the South African Unemployed People's Movement (UPM), emptied buckets of waste in the entrance of Grahamstown City Hall, in Makana. He was protesting the bucket toilet system in the Grahamstown township, whereby buckets of waste from outside toilets are collected and cleaned once a week.

The Grahamstown protest was a part of UPM's larger struggle, linked at the time to the Occupy Grahamstown movement, for basic provisions and security in townships and informal settlements (water, sanitation, electricity, protection from rape, and other fundamental concerns). Fiercely critical of the ruling African National Congress (ANC), the movement questioned the entire post-apartheid project. Kota, a revolutionary activist who, it is claimed, was brutally attacked by police in custody (in front of his distraught six-year-old son) led the protest.[33] A video of the protest shows Kota addressing a small group of activists and a few bemused passersby in the centre of Makana, yelling: 'This is not our shit.' Before emptying the buckets, Kota shouts: 'It is enough . . . this we will dump here, it does not belong to us.' To applause and cheers, followed by photographers, Kota enters city hall and pours the buckets out over the floor.

In his short speech, Kota says remarkably little about sanitation itself. Instead, he connects human waste to the wider condition of poverty and inequality and to the failure of post-apartheid democracy. He links the failure of the state to collect waste to its failure to represent and defend ordinary South Africans, including in relation to rising food prices. The ANC is the focus of much of his critique. In Kota's account, the party is no longer interested in the poor, has abandoned the struggle for justice, and has become corrupt, more concerned with its own financial gain and political power: 'We are denouncing the party of the elite . . . for the death of democracy in this country,' he states.

This is not just a question of poor sanitation but about sanitation alongside substandard housing, safety for women and girls, health and dignity, and unemployment – about, in short, the politics of race, class, and political economy that underwrite the post-apartheid condition. South Africa, he argues, cannot consider itself 'free' from apartheid. 'When there is freedom,' Kota has written, 'people are free from hunger, poverty, disease, homelessness and the inability to meet basic needs. Justice, peace, dignity and access to the country's wealth are central to freedom . . . We must struggle and we must fight for our rights.'[34]

As Mandy De Waal has written of the UPM's work in Grahamstown, sanitation struggle here is a generalised urban struggle, because life entails toiling with a series of disinvestments across urban life support systems: 'Township people struggle daily with crumbling houses, corruption, water taps that don't work, the degrading bucket system, increased food prices, hunger, unemployment and the unending disappointment of political promises that fail to amount to anything.'[35]

Activists like Kota rail against the humiliation of Black lives treated *as* shit, and living *with* shit, turning that politics outward to the reproduction of urban socio-spatial inequality and the right to citylife.[36] Here is human waste dramatically and spectacularly 'out of place' – breathing new life into Mary Douglas's well-worn description of dirt – but at the same time, from Kota's perspective, being returned in a sense to where it ought to be. It is the responsibility of the state to ensure people do not have to individually and collectively live with their own waste, and so here it is presented materially and symbolically to the state. In insisting that 'this is not our shit', Kota and his fellow activists are launching a wider critique of the contemporary condition and the failure of the state to provide a basic service. It is the neglect of the state which is cast here as 'shit', a condition that demands an out-of-the-ordinary response ('it is enough . . .').

Maynard Swanson argued over forty years ago that sanitation in Cape Town exists not just as a specific service delivery problem, but as a sociopolitical syndrome.[37] The question of addressing excess human waste in Cape Town has always been inseparable from the question of race. The sanitation syndrome links race and class to spurious notions of contamination and disease, and it manifests as socio-spatial segregation. The historical conflation of racial prejudice and an erroneous construction of the Black body as a contaminant in relation to the plague led to often violent geographical displacement and separation. This is not unique to South Africa, of course. In Brazil, for example, others have described similar processes of 'hygienisation', whereby spaces are 'decontaminated' through displacement of the poor, or in which the favela is linked by powerful actors to the idea of 'contagion'.[38]

Many Black residents in Cape Town were forcibly removed under the Public Health Act to Uitvlugt (later Ndabeni), a sewage farm on the Cape Flats. Sanitation in Cape Town is a process of racialised segregation that can be traced back to forms of early settler colonialism across the continent and beyond, and it is linked to the larger inequalities in housing, infrastructure, services, and opportunity. While there is some evidence of racial upward mobility in Cape Town, the gains for Black professionals have been offset by growing unemployment among poor Black residents.[39]

Using human waste as a political weapon in the city is not a discursive political claim but a tactic of spectacle that plays on the senses and connects the urban sensorium to the cultural politics of disgust and contamination as well as the histories of race, poverty, and urban space. It inverts the notion that waste belongs with poor urban peripheries and out of sight by casting it where it has absolutely no business being: the spaces of the elite and often hyper-sanitised city.[40] One example here is the Ses'khona ('We're here') People's Rights Movement. This was the movement that had so sharply offended the survey respondents I described earlier. Ses'khona involved activists and residents of poor and marginalised neighbourhoods emptying buckets of uncollected waste at targeted sites of the city, including the airport, a main arterial road, the provincial legislature, and the mayor's car.

The movement started in 2011 with residents in low-income neighbourhoods who were angry when the municipality, in the lead up to the municipal elections, provided communities in the poorer parts of the city with open-air toilets – toilets with no walls. While the City of Cape Town (CCT) claimed to have

Figure 10. Toilets, Cape Town. Author's collection.

conducted consultations with residents on how to spend the budget for sanitation, such an affront to dignity infuriated many residents and gave rise to what was termed the 'toilet wars'.[41] The open toilets – which were facetiously referred to as the 'loo with the view' – were 'improved' by the CCT using walls of corrugated iron, which ANC Youth League activists tore down amid claims of insults on the dignity of the predominantly Black poor, demanding concrete forms instead.[42]

Protests and campaigns led to the 2011 decision by the new mayor, Patricia de Lille, to fund maintenance services through national funds from the Expanded Public Works Programme for sanitation in 'informal settlements', with an initial investment of R138 million (£6.5 million) per year. This took the form of a janitorial service aimed at maintaining neglected infrastructure. However, like the open-air toilets, this too was an underfunded provision. Janitors working in the Barcelona informal settlement were given restricted hours and therefore less pay than the previous contract. In protest they went on strike against the portable flush-toilet private provider, Sanicare, and some dumped bags of faeces and garbage on the highway in protest. After a month or so without the 'buckets' from toilets being collected, the conditions in Barcelona were terrible.[43] In desperation, activists decided to deal with the excess of human waste by transforming it from a symbol of post-apartheid failure into a political weapon.

Initially, the buckets of uncollected waste were emptied over the N2 road, a main road leading to the airport.[44] Subsequent protests targeted the state legislature in the central city and the hyper-sanitised space of Cape Town International Airport, with activists calling the media in advance. After the airport action, nine protesters were found guilty and given three years' imprisonment, suspended for five years, for contravening the Civil Aviation Act, which was used by the authorities to criminalise what was in fact an act of civil disobedience. Passing the sentence, and with little sense of irony, Magistrate Nonkosi Sabi said that Ses'khona was 'not only embarrassing to the country as a whole, but [had] infringed on the rights and human dignity of others' exposed to faeces at the airport.[45]

These protests operated through multiple registers: first, at the level of the urban sensorium – so that the politicians could appreciate, as one activist put it, 'how it smells' to have uncollected human waste in your neighbourhood. Second, and through the media, to raise awareness about the sanitation struggle. And third, to prompt the CCT into dialogue with the activists. For some observers, the presence of political parties in the dispute was a persistent risk. Kota, reflecting on the Cape Town protests as they were emerging around the city, expressed his concern that the actions would collapse into party politicking between the two major forces in the city, the ANC and the Democratic Alliance. Kota urged the protestors to remain focused on politicising the 'suffering' people experience and on bringing that to 'elite spaces'.

Later, in September 2020, residents in the neighbourhood of Dunoon prevented Sanitech, a CCT sanitation contractor, from providing services, and in protest at the municipality they emptied buckets of faeces on the N7 road. *GroundUp*, a critical journalism outlet in South Africa, described the protest in August of that year: 'With bare hands, residents removed septic tanks from communal chemical toilets, loaded them on shopping trolleys and emptied then at the exit of N7 at Dunoon.'[46] Residents complained that the contractor had not cleaned their toilets in three weeks and should instead be replaced by the previous toilet operator, Mshengu.

Twenty septic tanks were emptied, with the threat of more protests to come. Once again, this form of protest proved controversial, even among sympathetic groups in the city. The South African National Civic Organisation's (SANCO) Sinethemba Matomela said: 'As a SANCO leader we condemn things like that, especially if it's going to affect other people. We can't stop people when they are angry. The City needs to come and engage with leaders properly.'[47] Sanitech complained that their staff were being threatened and were unable to do their work, while the CCT Waste and Sanitation Department insisted the company be given the chance to provide its chemical toilets and for its work to be monitored.[48]

Given that toilets and sanitation more generally are intimately tied to basic rights and questions of dignity bound up with the Constitution of South Africa, sanitation goes to the heart of the country's post-apartheid urban crisis. From the start, these protests were about the larger struggle for the right to citylife.[49] As Veronica Baxter and Mbongeni Mtshali have put it, the protests were a 'confrontation of Black life in the townships as ontologically *shit*', where marginalised people are forced to live and die as 'the wasted remains that "the city" quietly expels and hides away'.[50] In response, the protestors seem to say, with Mary Douglas, that the margins of the body and the margins of society become dramatised together – symbolically and materially – through a profoundly political sensorial shock tactic.

A time of transformation?

There have been other instances of what journalist Mark Hay has called 'diarrheic dissidence' in urban South Africa. In the spring of 2014, a group of students at the University of Cape Town (UCT) protested against the Cecil Rhodes statue on campus by throwing excrement at it. 'As Black students we are disgusted by the fact that this statue still stands here today as it is a symbol of white supremacy,' said Chumani Maxwele, one of the students involved. 'How can we be living in a time of transformation when this statue still stands and our hall is named after [Leander Starr] Jameson, who was a brutal lieutenant under Rhodes.'[51]

Maxwele argued that excrement here represents not just a critique of how colonial segregation logics linked Black bodies with the contamination and threat of waste, but also of the shame of Black people having to historically live with waste: 'By throwing [excrement] on the statue we are throwing our shame to whites' affluence. As Black students here we have to change our ways just to fit in . . . It is time for all of that to change.' Maxwele described how activists wanted to express their collective disgust at the 'fraudulent relationships' that make up the urban landscape – the juxtaposition of buildings and streets named after figures like Mandela and Biko with colonial figures like Rhodes. One activist said the act was a critique of the idea of the 'rainbow nation'.[52]

Rhodes is a material representation of imperial historical geographies in a city that remains deeply racially divided. The encounter with excrement was a confrontation of history, power, race, and space; it folded the urban order of imperialism into the present moment of urban inequality and segregation in three ways: First, the protests co-located the colonial production of urban space – segregation and later apartheid – with contemporary politics. They insisted that history is not past, but active in the life and stakes of the present. Second, the protests actively addressed the making of urban space, in that they framed the presence of Rhodes as a material-symbol and antagonistic site of Black power. And third, they invested in the transformation of urban space as vital to producing an urbanism not of shame and power over, but of possibility and empowerment.

This architecture of protest – from critique to investment – represents one possible route for a politics of sanitation in the right to citylife. But there is another connection to space, time and politics in this protest, and that is its staging as spectacle. The image of a renowned colonial figure covered in excrement has the potential to force a public debate in ways that more conventional protest – say, a demonstration about colonial symbols on campus – is unlikely to achieve. The act involving a small group quickly travelled through social and mainstream media and became part of a larger debate about the transformation of the university and its role in the larger direction of South Africa.[53] UCT security were well aware of the potential power of the images that might result and were filmed handling a photographer from the *Daily Voice* as he repeatedly tried to take photographs of the excrement-covered statue. The images nonetheless travelled nationally and globally, forcing a debate about colonial legacies in the urban landscape and their social, economic, and political consequences.

Excrement was a political vehicle here for the students, who also sought to generate debate about alleged institutional racism at UCT, a university that at the time had never had a South African–born Black female professor. The protests turned into the temporary occupation of university buildings. On a sign outside the building, the occupiers placed a poster over the building's nameplate which read 'Azania House' – a reference used as rejection of the colonial name 'South Africa'.[54] In April 2015, the Rhodes statue was removed from campus to the cheers of students, with a plan to eventually house it in a museum.

The protests' influence rippled through South Africa. Students at Rhodes University were mobilised by the acts and demanded that the name of the university be changed. At the University of KwaZulu-Natal (UKZN), two students were taken into custody at the Alexandra Road police station in the middle of the night for carrying a large bag full of excrement onto the university's premises. No charges were brought but, in another example of the ambivalence towards protests that use human waste, the Student Representative Council at UKZN condemned the idea of a poo protest. In March 2015, at the UKZN's Howard College campus, a statue of King George V was covered not with excrement but with white paint. A sign was hung reading: 'End White Privilege'. And there were influences beyond South Africa: in the UK, for instance, a campaign by students at Oxford University targeted the campus's Rhodes statue, though not with human waste.

The various protests discussed across this chapter collectively pose a powerful question of the city and urban conditions. Much as we can learn from and find inspiration in the work of activists, there is also the risk that activism, much like policy, can lose sight of the sanitation crisis as a *networked* crisis. There is sometimes a fixation on toilets at the cost of other parts of the sanitation technosphere, including waste management and treatment. Nonetheless, across the different examples in this chapter – from the Occupy movement or the politics of bodily waste in prisons to the connections between waste, protest, and race – is a larger message.

More important than the sheer power and range of waste as a political weapon, more remarkable than the struggle to wield this most unpredictable of tools, is what these moments express. They are languages of suffering that use not words but the body and spectacle, a cry for the most basic forms of recognition, a desperate hope for a better city and urban condition. They reject the liberal platitudes of those in power, the hollow claims that things will get better that appear empty when stacked against the extent of urban suffering, exclusion, and neglect. They are the shocking markers of life impeded and denied, evocations of the great drama of the right to citylife as a fight for citylife, simultaneously despairing and raging, shaped by the long arm of history and focused on the profound urgency of now.

They are both about waste and often about much more than that – better sanitation, yes, but with an understanding, born from hard experience and frustrated struggle, that sanitation is always already about very much more than toilets and services.

6

Allocation

The small town of Centreville is one of the poorest in America. Here, residents have been living with raw sewage for decades, accustomed to the thick stench in the air. When it rains, the sewage spills out of the network and across the city, into homes, gardens, play areas, and open spaces. The pipes, pumps, and drainage are old and damaged, and manhole covers 'spout sewer water like geysers' at pressured times. The water doesn't taste right. Illinois American Water, which supplies much of the town's water, insists it is safe, but people often buy bottled water. The smell means that it is sometimes difficult to sit outside. Some worry about the effect of the air on their lungs. There are stories of children becoming frightened of the rain. Homes have lost their value, and land is subsiding in several places. 'Can you imagine bringing your family up in waste?' asked one resident. 'After working all your life, you gotta lived up in it? Retire in it?'[1]

A town of around 5,000 predominantly Black residents, Centreville has long been neglected by state authorities. The utility, activists claim, has ignored the residents. In the summer of 2021, they filed a lawsuit against the sewer authority and the local state, demanding repairs and proper investment in the system. One prominent activist who has campaigned on sewage and poverty across the United States, Catherine Flowers, described the town's sanitation conditions as 'one of the worst I have seen'. Nicole Nelson, of Equity Legal Services, insists that here sanitation is 'absolutely a class and race issue'.[2]

The city's mayor claimed the task was beyond the scope of the city's small budget and would require federal support. Yet the plan that was put forward for federal funding involved no consultation with residents or groups and did not go anywhere near far enough. As elsewhere, residents have often been left cleaning up the mess of and maintaining the systems themselves. Flowers has documented cases of open sewage across urban and rural America and sees the problem as one of race and class: 'The final monument to the Confederacy'.[3]

This is a politics that extends to water too. In the summer of 2022, for example, 150,000 mainly Black residents in Jackson, Mississippi, went without water when the treatment centre flooded. Even supplies of bottled water ran out. Critics pointed out that wealthier, predominantly white suburbs had newer infrastructure, while Jackson has languished with ageing and poorly maintained systems for decades.

At stake here is the question that has haunted this book: who gets what where, when, how, and why? At the heart of the idea of sanitation as a network is the question of the distribution of sanitation resources. As places like Centreville so vividly reveal, this distribution within a city, or across a region or country, is typically uneven, deeply unequal, and often highly politicised. Some places in the city suffer from too little infrastructure and too much waste while other sites and people are prioritised. There is an often powerful set of political, economic, and cultural drivers shaping those distributions.

There are four closely interrelated distributions that play vital roles in the relationship between sanitation and the right to citylife: money, land and housing, utilities, and communities. What I'm interested in here is how resources are allocated and how responsibility is understood in the sanitation crisis. This includes the role of the state and its changing relationship to the private sector and communities. Throughout this chapter, I will try to develop arguments that work not with the city we would ideally wish for but with the city as we find it, which sets out a course guided by a focus on the right to citylife. I end with an argument for urban sanitation forums as one route to institu-tionalising better sanitation planning and delivery.

It may sound obvious, but the sanitation crisis – and the deci-sions, processes, and events that contour it – is only ever happening some*where*. Yet the answer to the problem of geog-raphy does not lie in attempting to ensure homogeneity across urban space, even though the standardisation of conditions can seem a straightforward response. While there needs to be a commitment to good sanitation provisions across the city, from the home to the bus station and public square, sanitation solu-tions also must be flexible enough to respond to the social heterogeneity we find in cities and to the specific needs and limits of different contexts. 'Sanitation for all' is a universal; the route to it is not.

Getting the allocations of resources 'right' is not only a huge challenge, it is also a moving target. Cities do not stand still, and neither does the range of issues caught up with sanitation. This complexity poses a challenge for sanitation control and delivery. It demands that we deal with the 'mess' and unpredictability of cities and the unequal power relations that shape them. Unfor-tunately, because it is a lot of work, getting allocations right depends on a geographically nuanced approach that works with the differences of the city as we find them, rather than in spite of them. It is a vast task.

But it is doable – and not as financially expensive as we might think, particularly when the focus shifts from 'costs' to 'invest-ment', including the generation of human, ecological, and economic gains over the long term. Insofar as the right to citylife hangs on a politics of allocation, that politics connects state disinvestment and cultural marginalisation to ideologies of the market, expectations placed on residents, and the stuff of urban living (land, homes, infrastructure, wastes, and so on). It is a politics, like the right to citylife itself, that is rarely if ever settled.

The machinic city?

What makes sanitation successful at the city scale, given that 'success' must be about a degree of flexibility and diversity in provisions? We know from existing research that coordination and investment at the city level is important.[4] Without this, it is difficult to see how cities can combine capital-intensive provisions such as sewerage, drainage, and waste treatment with appropriate localised toilet and water provisions and maintenance systems. Likewise, we know that when regulations on minimum standards are enforced, costs are transparently accounted for, and maintenance actually occurs in practice, success can follow. All of this requires a clear institutional framework that is enforced and widely understood.

There is an inherited tradition of modernist thinking that imagines the city as a kind of machine. In this view, there are levers that can be put to work to make change happen. The political task of allocating resources becomes one of honing the machine, applying it to the problems, and watching to make sure it operates effectively, maybe doing the odd bit of tinkering. The levers include the state and its various departments at the national, regional, and local scale, as well as how it works with the private sector, civil society groups, international donors, and so on. Here, there are vexed debates around the relative roles, responsibilities, and politics of the private sector, utilities, communities, and civil society groups in provisions across the city.[5] This is a linear, billiard-ball view of the city, a clunky conception of change as A leading to B and C. Distribution becomes an effect of the machine.

Alternatively, we might begin with a messier view of the city – one that grapples with change at the city level by staying with the reality of disorder, unpredictability, changeability, and multiplicity. Some urbanists have described this view as 'seeing like a city', a neat phrase that places us in the inevitable complexity of urban life and how that textures much of what we try to get done.[6] In this view, cities are spaces of multiple actors and interests: of public and private authorities, power brokers and alliances, embedded histories and agendas, happenstance and contingencies. The state itself, including city government, is no monolith, but a set of political parties, bureaucratic actors, inherited routines, changing agendas, improvised arrangements, disparate forms of knowledge, and checks and balances, all of which might be moving in all kinds of directions and with varying degrees of strategy.

Getting things done often requires all manner of compromises, rethinks, and improvisations. The stubborn materiality and social complexity of the city can mean that the best-laid plans often need elaborate translation before, and especially when, they hit the ground. Infrastructure needs rerouting past properties or roads or public objections. Financial disbursements get caught up amid other local priorities and agendas. Recalcitrant parties, officials, or residents subvert plans or pull them in new directions for all kinds of reasons. If we could zoom out and look at the city as an entity, what we would see is not a machine but an ongoing bricolage of coalescing, fragmenting, and changing actors, agendas, and objectives. Not a machine, but perhaps so many little machines – part social, part technical – with their own logics and forms of operating, variously connected and disjointed. This is the city not just of blueprints and models but of workarounds, redirects, and nonlinear change.

In any case, why would a 'roll out' from the machine even be desirable? However frustrating the 'mess' of cities, especially large cities, might be, that mess is partly how the democratic realm takes force.[7] Difference, conflict, objections, alliance building, and so on are expressions of the diversity of people and agendas at work in a city at any one time. It's not always pretty to look at, but they can't, and often shouldn't, be stepped around. Of course, it is not quite as simple as this implies, because not all actors or agendas have equal voice and force in urban change. In the past few decades, in most cities most of the time it is the private sector and the profit imperative that has trumped the concerns and voices of many ordinary citizens and organisations, especially those living on the urban margins.

So, the question of the allocation of sanitation resources involves dealing not just with the disarray and muddle but with their unequal nature, sorting through which agendas to endorse or promote and which to avoid, fight, or reorient. It is, in other words, not simply a question of how we understand and approach the city but how we fight its political inequalities. And this is assuming that the city government wants to deliver decent sanitation across the city. While many do, there are planners who simply do not prioritise sanitation, or who prioritise it in narrow ways. In many contexts, planners and policymakers in cities are still dominated by men, for example, who may not 'see' or prioritise the experiences and needs of women and girls. Getting women into positions at the heart of urban planning itself remains a significant fight in many cities, let alone seeing agendas and concerns being pushed through. As Sue Parnell and Edgar Pieterse put it in relation to their work in Cape Town, 'you need to be "seen by the state" before benefitting from it.'[8]

Political will, and the personnel at city government, matter to how distributions and redistributions take shape. But will is not enough on its own. One Water Aid report on how states and municipalities have created successful change in sanitation identifies four factors.[9] First, substantial support from the very top of government. Second, clear goals and activities across the relevant bureaucratic structures, tailored to cultural contexts. In Malaysia, for example, local officials held weekly prayers while sitting next to maps of sanitation coverage and discussed how to address interdepartmental differences. Third, the autonomy of implementers at the local level to adapt to contingent challenges and opportunities and flexible use of finances. This includes enrolling local groups. In South Korea, for example, teachers agreed to monitor helminth infections as a proxy for improving sanitation conditions. And fourth, a culture of 'course correction', in which problems in design, implementation, bureaucratic setbacks or other bottlenecks might be acknowledged, discussed, and resolved.

This focus on culture, autonomy, and course correction is really an argument for a better understanding of the *urban*: its material form, its social densities and heterogeneities, its jostling formal and informal political authorities, its inequalities and vulnerabilities, and so on. Rather than a pessimistic view, attending to the mess, and the inequalities in voice in the urban cacophony, takes us closer to a workable set of positions. It locates change in the city as we find it, rather than the one we might wish for.

I am not quite saying here that the mess is always to be protected. There are limits to this view of the city, and it can't be an excuse for justifying dysfunctional and just plain badly organised governance. Some of the mess does need tidying up and to become more machinic in how it functions. For example, one of the challenges in allocating resources is that state responsibility for sanitation often sits at different levels. Some parts of the equation, such as community toilets, are with the municipality, others such as drainage with the regional or national state. Different groups within relevant departments, ranging from water engineers to social welfare officers, may not coordinate their efforts when they need to be. The sectoral and siloed policy processes on water and sanitation have worsened health conditions. In Mali, for example, sanitation governance includes five central government ministries working with public and private utilities, municipalities, and civil society groups.[10] This is not unusual.

Nonetheless, as a general state of affairs the workaround city is here to stay. How, then, to shift the workaround city in the right direction? At the heart of this question is turning sanitation into a *central political agenda in urban policy and planning*. This means framing sanitation, as Shilpi Srivastava and colleagues have argued, 'as a health and urban planning emergency', and I would position the right to citylife as a response. While a focus on crisis is necessary, it is not itself sufficient. There has to be a positive vision and agenda for action. Citywide planning is essential if sanitation is to be delivered universally, but only if that larger view includes the sanitation network rather than, say, a focus on building toilets or on hygiene education alone.[11]

There is lots of evidence for the success of mainstreaming sanitation in policy and planning leadership. In a study of three cities that are performing relatively well with sanitation – Kumasi in Ghana, San Fernando in the Philippines, and Visakhapatnam in India – Water Aid identified four key drivers of progress: sanitation 'champions' at the municipal level; national political support; economic investment; and collaborations between different groups ranging from donors and multilateral and bilateral agencies to local and international NGOs and universities.

In all three cases, clear leadership with the power to coordinate relevant groups and roles was important, whether from the mayor's office or key municipal officials. Otherwise, it becomes very difficult to leverage resources, form and maintain partnerships within the state and between the state and other relevant actors, or to commit to a strong programme of monitoring and maintenance.[12] Indeed, it is increasingly common to hear arguments for city mayors as the route to delivering coordinated change in cities. Here, the story typically goes that tackling deep, thorny problems like sanitation demands an office that is empowered to make cross-sectoral decisions effecting multiple parts of the sanitation network.

In his arguments for building 'happier' cities, economist Charles Montgomery discusses the highly popularised story of the former mayor of Bogota, Enrique Penalosa, and his campaign to promote pedestrianisation, cycling, public transport, infrastructure, and public space. He argues that 'visionary mayors' are a crucial ingredient in transforming the city's hardware and urban experience.[13] Much is made, for better or worse, of the impact of mayors on cities. During the COVID-19 pandemic, *The Economist* argued that mayors would be key to driving economic recovery in cities.

Mayoral leadership matters, but it is a risky strategy to place too much faith in a single individual and office to effect change. Arguments for the strong mayor carry with them the historical image of the heroic individual, typically male, and easily bring us back to the misleading image of city-level change as delivered through the levers of municipal machinery. Sanitation 'champions' and dedicated offices are vital to developing a committed citywide strategy for sanitation. But for this to work in the longer term, it has to be developed through meaningful understanding of and involvement with the city's different groups and organisations, especially the poor and marginalised who suffer most from inadequate sanitation.

As Sheela Patel and the team at SPARC, an influential NGO in Mumbai, have argued based on two decades of developing sanitation, this means creating the time to develop choices and consensus based on reliable local data and residential participation on the design and delivery of programmes and interventions.[14] Residents and local organisations on the ground need to sign up to at least enough of the agenda for it work, and getting to that point requires negotiation and compromise that establishes clear objectives. It also means working with a range of groups, not just one civil society organisation that the state believes 'represents' the voice of the marginalised but in fact simply mirrors the state's preferred agenda.

During the COVID-19 crisis, a wide range of municipal departments and civil society groups were often forced to work better together. For Razanakombana Rakotonavalona Allyre, director of water, sanitation and hygiene for the Urban Commune of Antananarivo (CUA), Madagascar, the crisis 'helped us to strengthen the collaboration between departments within CUA': 'I am so happy to see wider communication on hygiene, the COVID-19 crisis is providing great momentum around handwashing. I have worked to promote handwashing for many years now and realise how powerful communication is. Many people now know what a handwashing station is.'[15] There is evidence, too, that when a diversity of 'stakeholders' in urban sanitation work effectively together, a wider pool of skills and experience becomes available.[16]

The approach to city-level distribution must remain rooted in the inevitability of the disorder and improvisation that cities generate. The challenge here is to ensure that it is not more powerful groups – whether residents, private companies, NGOs, or political parties – that dictate the changes, while less powerful groups find that they are denied voice in the planning, policy, and implementation processes. It is even worse if the latter groups find, too, that resources are channelled disproportionately into wealthier areas (a theme I return to below) or that the less desirable aspects of sanitation delivery – waste treatment plants, for instance – are shunted onto their neighbourhoods. Remaining with the mess means that the city government must ensure that, as much as is reasonably possible, there are transparent and equitable processes of consultation, participation, consensus building, and conflict resolution. Easier said than done.

Of course, organisations working together across sectors does not itself mean that greater resources are allocated to sanitation, let alone those in need, though it can help. With this in mind, I turn now to the question of money.

Meeting the costs

Estimating the economic cost of the global sanitation crisis is not a straightforward task. In any given city, sanitation provision might be overestimated, particularly given that systems can fall into disrepair, while the numbers of people in need can be underestimated because poor and marginalised residents are sometimes not documented and counted. Costing is further complicated by uncertainties and variability in projected costs, including in the lifespan and maintenance of infrastructure. In cities, there is the added cost of building structures in dense, built-up spaces where there can be intense pressure on land and complex arrangements to work around. Nonetheless, there have been some relatively reliable and careful global costings. One produced by the World Bank puts the global costs of meeting the water, sanitation, and hygiene Sustainable Development Goals (SDGs) by 2030 at US$114 billion per year.[17]

However large that number might seem, it is more than US$100 billion less than the US$223 billion that that World Resources Institute estimates that the global sanitation crisis costs every year as a result of the impacts on health and lost productivity and wages.[18] That's before we factor in other potential economic gains resulting from people pursuing new opportunities that are currently difficult for them to even consider, or from people simply being able to participate in everyday life in the city.

The maths are not difficult, and the numbers are far from insurmountable. US$114 billion per year is dwarfed, for example, by the $US2.3 trillion that the US government spent in its initial response alone to the COVID-19 pandemic in March 2020, and far less, too, than the US$459 billion the UK spent on its pandemic response during the two years that followed the outbreak (though the UK government still found it justifiable to cut its aid budget from 0.7 percent to 0.5 percent, including an 80 percent funding cut for water, sanitation, and hygiene projects).[19] When governments declare a crisis, whether it is COVID-19 or the 2008 financial crisis, it is remarkable how quickly the economic calculus can shift.

Meeting the costs of the global sanitation crisis does not require anything like those COVID-19 levels of spending, but what we continue to see is nowhere near the kind of financial response that is needed. The World Bank estimates that the sanitation proportion of the larger water, sanitation, and hygiene (WASH) bill is 69 percent and that meeting the stipulations demands 'significantly greater spending' than current levels, not just on access but also on operations and maintenance, especially so in the most 'off-track countries', which are mainly in sub-Saharan Africa and South Asia.[20] The Bank argues that these costs should be met in part by greater tax revenues from the private sector, recognising the longer-term economic gains of sanitation for all.

Fine, but one simple step that would make a huge difference would be writing off the debts of lower-income countries. The World Bank and IMF-led G20 Debt Service Suspension Initiative could be expanded and deepened. The poorest countries in the world pay $45 billion to creditors each year, almost 40 percent of the sum estimated per year for WASH investment. According to one estimate, that leaves more than forty countries paying more on debt than on health.[21]

We need to be mindful, too, of how we are weighing up costs over the longer term. Sewers may seem expensive in the short-term but will save in the long run, both in avoiding replacing defunct provisions and in the health and economic positives they bring. We lack reliable systematic data comparing the relative costs of systems in different contexts, though there is extensive research on the economics of distinct systems in particular sites.[22] But we are even more uncertain about the potential savings over the longer run by investing now, save to say that they will be huge.

Part of the reason it is difficult to arrive at reliable data on costs is that those that do exist often do not factor in the costs of servicing or treatment, much less those resulting from the impacts of contamination when maintenance is not provided. Costs may also shift in relation to changing levels of local residential densities. To arrive at meaningfully accurate city costs, any estimation must factor in three elements: the larger sanitation chain, from toilets to collection, treatment and maintenance; the intersections of necessary infrastructures and services, such as water, electricity, and hygiene promotion; and the local conditions at delivery, including the physical landscape and densities.

In any case, governments frequently baulk at the costs, and too often, the poorest in the city are forced to pay for their own sanitation. The cost to individuals of providing makeshift sanitation is not easy to calculate. The nature of improvised toilets – including their material construction, where they are built, and whether they are connected to sewers or septic tanks – varies considerably, as does the cost of maintenance. A rudimentary wood and corrugated metal structure with a cloth covering and no connection to a septic tank or sewer will cost less than a concrete structure that is connected – which itself can be US$16 in Maputo and $23 in Mumbai – but may end up costing more to maintain. In Karachi, a household might pay US$165 for a private septic tank, and the tank itself requires emptying and other maintenance costs.

Communal septic tanks are typically cheaper in household contributions than individual tanks, especially in dense areas. In Dhaka, communal septic tanks can cost between five and twenty families a total of US$711. Emptying a pit latrine safely in poorer neighbourhoods in Kampala can cost residents 8 percent of their average income, and some feel forced to empty untreated waste nearby. In Colombo, paying for a sewer connection might be as much as 300 percent of the monthly income of poorer groups, making it all but impossible without substantial state support. In Maputo, residents can pay as much as thirteen times for privately provided water than those who have direct access to publicly provided piped water.[23]

Residents who own and feel secure in their home may be more prepared to invest than those – the majority of the urban poor – who lack security or who rent. Some landlords extract fees for structures, some won't even provide permission; some write fees for emptying pits and tanks into rental contracts, others charge recurring and sometimes changeable fees. In neighbourhoods that are located on vulnerable grounds that flood during the monsoon or which are subject to landslides, residents have to pay for sanitation again and again. What all of this means is that residents even within one neighbourhood can end up paying wildly different amounts for sanitation, once we factor in the toilet, the waste, the water, and the maintenance, and very often more than wealthier residents in the same city.

At the same time, sanitation can generate income in different ways through small-scale sanitation entrepreneurs. A growing number of companies are seeking to find new sources of profit from 'bottom of the pyramid' groups of the urban poor, often in ways that deepen social cleavages between those who can afford to pay and those who can't. The chase is firmly underway for 'sanicorns' who capitalise on what the Toilet Board Coalition – a private-sector platform that includes powerful actors who have been involved in water and water privatisation, such as Veolia, alongside Unilever, Tata, and others – calls a 'market opportunity'.[24] The Coalition estimated that the Indian sanitation economy alone was worth around US$60 billion in 2021.

Stories of new sanitation innovations are common and increasing globally, from students at the University of Cape Town creating bricks made from human urine to 'smart toilets' or mobile inflatable temporary septic tanks.[25] Alongside this innovation is its accomplice – an intensifying set of marketing campaigns – using strategies such as knocking door-to-door with leaflets in attempts to gain leads and conversions, to recruiting trusted local individuals such as grocery store owners in poor neighbourhoods and paying them to market products to their customers. London-based non-profit group Water and Sanitation for the Urban Poor (WSUP), for example, markets financially viable sanitation provisions and asks, in one case from Bangladesh, how to market the 'unmarketable' in places 'where many are unwilling to pay for sanitation'.[26]

To put this emerging world of small-scale sanitation economies in context, it is helpful to think through what entrepreneurs and markets can and can't do for the urban poor. There is a vital qualitative distinction in, for example, residents charging local businesses for biogas and investing the profit in a community social space or using desludging technologies (usually for septic tanks) to create earning opportunities versus companies charging adults and children to use toilets or access water in the poorest neighbourhoods. There is a difference between profiteering and generating a livelihood.[27]

Figure 11. Desludging truck, Nepal. Source Dave Robbins, CC BY-SA 2.0.

In cash-strapped urban contexts in which there are long histories of residents piecing together social economies around infrastructure, it is counterproductive to take a wholesale anti–private sector position. Instead, the more complex but appropriate question is to ask which kind of private involvement and where, how, and for whom. The state is the fundamental guarantor of the right to citylife, but that does not mean rejecting the myriad small-scale world of private enterprise on ideological grounds. Doing so not only misreads what is and has in many places always been going on, it potentially harms urban worlds (I return to the private sector below).

There is a great deal of evidence showing that the cost of delivering sanitation is offset by the money saved in health care and better attendance at work and school.[28] It is a common refrain of city and national governments that they lack the capital to deliver sanitation for all. The claim is typically that the real cost of urban sanitation systems lies not in the infrastructures and associated services and administration alone – although these themselves are sometimes viewed as too expensive – but in the disruption and compensation impacted by closed transport routes, impacted businesses, displaced homes, and reconstruction.

Sanitation improvements are, to be sure, financially and practically challenging, and there are city governments, particularly in smaller cities, that genuinely lack the financial resources and which cannot see routes to raising it.[29] Part of the answer lies in the sections that follow – with land and housing, utilities, and forums, for instance – but it also lies in ensuring, as I argued at the start of the chapter, that sanitation is given the political and spending priority it needs at city and national level and that local states work meaningfully with local organisations across the city to work out strategies in place.

Land as sanitation politics

Cities under capitalism are divided, carved up, controlled, commodified, gated, and gentrified. Land and housing are at the heart of this. New upmarket apartment blocks in the central areas of Mumbai or Phnom Penh may intensify vertical densities in some areas while pushing lower-income residents into poorer areas. While global real estate makes up 60 percent of the world's assets, 75 percent of which is in housing, growing numbers of people watch runaway capital development as they scrape by in often poorly provisioned neighbourhoods. There is substantial evidence that more equally distributed land creates more equal societies and sustained economic growth. Yet, land inequalities are growing globally, from peri-urban 'land grabs' by private actors to deepening inequalities caused by land commodification and rising housing and rent costs.[30]

Land presents all kinds of challenges for sanitation, from marshy soils that make construction difficult to lingering manufacturing contaminants in brownfield sites and watercourses. Poorer neighbourhoods might be located on peripheral land vulnerable to hazards, from landslides and flooding to exposure to industrial wastes, often more exposed to the impacts of climate change than other parts of the city. Dense areas may have little space for constructing new sanitation interventions and may be difficult to reach with sewer or water pipe extensions.

Then there is what land costs mean for constructing public toilets. In October 2022 in San Francisco, the world's most expensive city to build in, a single small public toilet destined for a public square in the Noe Valley neighbourhood generated controversy when the project costs were put at $1.7 million. 'Our restroom building costs are consistent with the inflationary pressures on all San Francisco public works projects,' said Phil Ginsburg, the recreation and parks department's general manager. The city is not alone. In New York it costs between $3 and $5 million to construct standalone public toilets in parks.[31] Costs can be $1.3 million in Hong Kong, and $400,000 in Mumbai.

Little wonder that for some activists, the urban sanitation crisis is primarily a crisis of land. Rather than seeking out slithers of land to build sanitation systems that are vulnerable to breaking down and which often involve long queues of people at peak times, reliable sanitation and water might best be pursued through radical reforms to the distribution of land and housing, alongside better regulation of the costs. In this view, sanitation would not only be a standalone set of interventions, whether public toilets or toilets in homes, but would be largely addressed through better housing that brings better sanitation with it.

There is no doubt that land and housing reform must be a part of the sanitation solution in many contexts. Land reform in Colombia decreased the number of households living in overcrowded conditions with inadequate sanitation, water, and electricity.[32] Dharm Joshi, an activist in Nepal, has argued that the COVID-19 crisis starkly revealed the close intersections between landlessness and water and food shortages.[33] The provision of land and land titles in places like Kathmandu are an important part of the longer-term solution. Housing inequalities are most starkly expressed in Africa, and despite some improvements almost half of urban Africans are estimated to be living in what is often called 'unimproved housing'. Here, poor sanitation is the most common expression of housing deprivation and the single most urgent challenge.[34] As sub-Saharan Africa continues to urbanise, we are seeing the mushrooming of elite housing and commercial complexes alongside some of the poorest neighbourhoods in the world.

One of the reasons there has been such a significant growth of 'backyard dwellings' in South African cities, where residents rent makeshift shacks within the grounds of other residents, or of 'rooftop slums' of subdivided housing in cities like Hong Kong, is because the poor are restricted to deeply historically segregated land allocation systems.[35] There is a profound need for a process of long-term redistribution that dispenses with the short-termist reactionary politics of 'migrant invaders' and which seeks to address the lingering land, housing, and infrastructure inequalities of systems like apartheid and other land enclosure legacies.

In neighbourhoods with too little space to build sanitation or where there are environmental risks such as flooding or landslides that cannot be resolved, it may be that what's needed is building new housing in a nearby location and that good sanitation is provided with that housing. Obviously this is not a straightforward process. To do this, existing housing has to be demolished, and people are often temporarily housed elsewhere. There are plenty of cases in which those residents, who typically lack the kind of voice and power of wealthier residents, never see the new house.[36] Or the new house is located in an entirely different location, making people's jobs impossible or difficult and disrupting schooling. In the process of being in transit, the new housing is sometimes reallocated along political lines and networks. The housing itself may not be much better and may not suit residential socialities and economies especially well. In a review of the Government of India's Basic Services for the Urban Poor (BSUP) programme across eleven cities, there was a lack of genuine participation of the urban poor, a tendency to favour demolition and redevelopment over upgrading, little care over questions of tenure, and a focus on outputs over quality.[37]

Rather than see their neighbourhoods demolished, residents generally want to remain where they live but to see the area improved and consolidated.[38] It is usually better to work with what is already there, and to genuinely involve residents in that process from start to finish, than to rehouse. But one of the challenges in making any kind of sanitation intervention is security of tenure, and state definitions of legal occupation are pivotal. Poorer neighbourhoods often lack secure land tenure. In areas where the state refuses to recognise the inhabitants, residents are either invisible in official planning and sanitation delivery or are regarded with hostility as 'invaders'. Even gaining official tenure is no guarantee of sanitation provision from the state, which may prioritise other areas of the city for electoral or other political reasons. The process is typically slow and bureaucratic, and tenure is sometimes removed later, either for political reasons or because of subsequent legal challenges by groups who want to see the site put to another use.[39] In Morogoro, Tanzania, residents were issued two-year residence permits, but there was no long-term tenure security and so sanitation investments were stalled.[40]

While campaigns for tenure are crucial for more progressive urbanism, it is important to be mindful of the political trappings and shortcomings for both housing and sanitation. Often, residents work with civil society groups to obtain not just tenure, but proof of residence that can be used to claim inclusion in government provisions. For example, the social movement Slum/ Shack Dwellers International (SDI), operating in more than thirty countries, has used community mapping and documentation to establish proof of residence in efforts to persuade local and national states to provide services and infrastructure. Similarly, in Bangladesh, where 3.5 million people live in informal neighbourhoods in Dhaka, Habitat for Humanity International increased access to safe shelter through participatory upgrading, community action planning, neighbourhood mapping, and capacity building.[41]

The neighbourhood picture here, though, is often complex and the process of building housing security needs a nuanced geographical approach. Owner-occupiers, landlords, and tenants may live side by side, creating complex patterns of conditions and access to infrastructure and services. Precarious renters sometimes live in structures with multiple and opaque residency – for example the 'backyarders' in South African cities or those in subdivided homes from Hong Kong to Delhi – and can suffer the worst sanitation conditions while having little ability to appeal to sometimes exploitative landlords. In South Africa, backyarders may find that the on-site toilet is available only to the landlord or is prohibitively expensive. In Pikine-Dakar in Senegal, 77 percent of tenant households share sanitation facilities with other households, compared to 17 percent of owner-occupiers.[42] There is, too, a gender dimension at work, where women are less likely to be named as tenants or property owners and in some cases actively prohibited from doing so.[43] A politics of tenure security and improved sanitation conditions demand, then, an understanding of the different housing conditions at play, rather than a simplified imaginary that everyone is in the same boat.

The politics of land ownership can put a brake on sanitation improvement. In Antananarivo, Madagascar, a plan to deliver wastewater treatment to low-income peripheral neighbourhoods came up against contested claims about who owns the land. The result was a two-year delay until a decree was issued stating that the land was publicly owned.[44] Progressive municipalities sometimes find they are slowed and caught up in a politics of landlordism. In some cases, including in Antananarivo, landlords who refuse to meet sanitation standards are fined, backed up by a mayoral decree. In other cases, municipalities have acted as brokers between landlords and community groups, proposing memoranda of understanding that set out how costs are to be shared for provision and maintenance. There has been mixed success in these schemes – it is notoriously difficult to get every-one on side – but the lessons from cities like Nairobi that have attempted this indicate that a combination of 'carrot and stick' approaches are needed when working with landlords.[45]

In situations where people lack secure tenure and perhaps have the threat of demolition hanging over them, it is not sur-prising to find that they are sometimes reluctant to invest the time and money in sanitation. Prindex, a joint initiative of the Global Land Alliance and the Overseas Development Insti-tute, reports that around a quarter of residents in Uganda, Honduras, Morocco, and Côte d'Ivoire feel tenure insecurity. When residents do invest in sanitation, such as self-built latrines or water connections, their rent is sometimes increased by landlords. And changes in real estate markets may lead to increased rents so that sanitation becomes unaffordable.[46]

Sanitation campaigners have long argued for clear state-led processes for tackling land and housing politics. In addition to land redistribution, housing investment, and building, this includes area-based interventions: identifying the tenure mix of the area, setting up a framework for dialogue between different relevant groups, ensuring there is a clear carrot and stick approach to landlords, and requiring service providers to follow approaches that work for lower-income groups, regard-less of their legality.[47] This approach offers a starting point for mapping out a larger process in a set of entrenched and difficult power relations between and within groups. It offers, too, a direction that does not necessarily require entirely new housing, a position that can inadvertently serve as an excuse for states not to provide decent sanitation on the basis that people will eventually move into a structure with in-built sanitation at some point down the line.

More broadly, it is clearly important to tackle head on the inequalities that shape exclusive real estate economies and drive out those on lower incomes from large swathes of the city. There are encouraging examples here. In Berlin, which in 2018 had one of the fastest growing property and rental markets in

Europe, the five-year freeze on increasingly expensive rents was one example of halting patterns of urban change that tend towards exclusion. Municipalities, including Berlin and Barcelona, have also sought to limit the impact of companies like Airbnb on rising rent and housing and construction costs.

If these decisions emerge from the municipality, other changes to urban investment necessarily demand action from the national or federal state. Redistribution – including higher taxes on wealth, inheritance, and upper-income earners – will be necessary to fund public interventions and set fiscal rules and mechanisms for investment in better housing, infrastructure, and services.[48] San Fernando in the Philippines instigated a new sanitation tax to pay for wastewater treatment. Tackling the role of land in relation to sanitation demands strategies focused on consolidation and improvement *in place* alongside a focus on the larger political economies and cultures of land and housing *in the city more generally*, including patterns of redistribution and investment, as well as controls on construction costs for housing or toilet blocks in central areas. Investment in sanitation and the provision of tenure security will often have to be accompanied by rent and housing cost controls so that people can continue to afford to live in their homes.

But the urgency of the sanitation crisis cannot be put on hold while an ambitious programme of radical land redistribution is attained. The vested interests of the city make such a political programme's chances low at best, even if it is important to keep those ambitions and debates on the urban table. In most cases, the political strategy on land, housing, and sanitation is likely to be best pursued through a focus on tenure security, rent freezes, and adequate provisioning of space, infrastructure, and services. What this amounts to is a spatial politics of care and an investment in the everyday world of sanitation rooted in an understanding of social diversity focused on provision, repair, maintenance, and improvement that works to enable citylife.

There are cases of historical success in this area. In Surabaya, Indonesia, for example, the Kampung Improvement Program, which ran between 1969 and 1998, involved participatory on-site upgrading of poor neighbourhoods. Residents, and community data, were at the centre of decision-making and incremental but significant upgrade work, including public toilets, waste management, drainage improvements, paved foot-paths, and better provisions in schools.[49] Prioritising on-site gradual improvement has often proven successful. But rather than delimit this politics to the house, I want to move now to consider those agencies responsible for water and sanitation delivery, and here utilities – organisations I've discussed only in passing so far – are vital actors.

Utilising institutions

The growing role of the private sector in delivering and manag-ing fundamental social and environmental goods like water has become one of the most controversial issues in city politics, international development, and environmental change.[50] The past few decades have seen a vast experiment in the privatisation of infrastructural services, from electricity and transport to water and sanitation, whether through outright privatisation or variations of public–private partnership or private-sector participation.

While most water and sanitation utilities remain state owned and run, the past thirty years have witnessed an expansion of interest by some of the world's largest multinationals in water ownership and operation, including Enron, Vivendi, and Bechtel, alongside a growing ethos of marketisation and com-mercialisation. Karen Bakker has tracked how the world's water crisis has become an increasingly urban question, with the size, densities, growth, and economies of scale in cities attracting growing private investment into water.

Water is both a human right and, as Bakker has argued, a 'frontier for capitalism'. There has been an economic and polit-ical 'speculation on thirst' by hegemonic groups, especially at moments of water scarcity and crisis.[51]

Most countries still rely on state-owned enterprises to deliver most of their infrastructure, including in the poorest countries where it can be difficult to provide financial guarantees to private investors and operators. However, there has been a larger neoliberal shift that has ideologically positioned private actors as necessary, more efficient, and more effective. The World Bank has been a prominent driver.[52] The consequences include exclusionary price hikes and growing polarisation. Water and sanitation represent one of the areas in which this has been most pronounced, sometimes through aid 'conditionalities' that demand private-sector involvement.

What complicates this, however, is that the commitment to involving the private sector has existed far more as an aspiration than an actual tangible outcome. A survey of 174 countries in 2018 found that 90 percent had adopted some form of public–private partnership, but only 22 percent had managed to then generate that private investment – likely due to the high input costs and low fiscal recovery rates. Over the past decade, then, a broad contradiction has played out in that the discourse, ethos, and presence of the private sector in water and sanitation has deepened, while the actual number of public–private partnerships in practice has actually decreased.[53] And so we often see halfway-house positions. This includes an array of contractual arrangements, from management contracts in which a private company will assume responsibility for operation and maintenance (an example would be Johannesburg), to more partial contracting arrangements in which private companies take on part or all of the tariff as revenue, or where control and risk is distributed jointly across a host of companies.[54] Utilities often remain public but take on a more commercial ethos and practice. These models work in different ways across the world. Sometimes they end up being too expensive for the poor and cater to wealthier neighbourhoods. In other cases, provided there is a genuine commitment to cross-subsidise poorer and excluded areas, they can work well.[55]

The task of water and sanitation utilities, individually or collectively, is to serve the city, but they often inherit practices, ways of operating, or legal restrictions that exclude poorer neighbourhoods. Utilities are often accustomed to serving particular voices and vested interests, and they lack incentives to prioritise the urban poor. At the same time, they face an increasingly metaphysical crisis given that in cities all over the world, more and more public utilities are being run as, or partially or completely sold off to, private companies. These shifts, however partial they might be in practice, are accompanied by vociferous debate and conflicts over escalating costs for users and the nature of public goods and rights. If this trajectory of privatisation has applied to water more than sanitation, sanitation has not been immune to these processes, and of course the cost of water directly impacts sanitation conditions.

Privatisation is not just the sale of assets but the wider range of activities through which the private sector enters into the control, ownership, provision, and maintenance of water and sanitation. This includes management, contracts, consulting, and partnerships with the public sector. Bakker has differentiated forms of market involvement. While commercialisation is the *incorporation* of market-derived business models, and marketisation the *creation* of markets for exchange, privatisation is the *transfer* of ownership or management to companies – with sanitation, the first two have applied far more than the third.[56] I do not include here the large array of small-scale private operators and entrepreneurs – removing waste, providing water, cleaning or managing local toilet structures, and so on – who, in many cities, have always been part of the delivery of water and sanitation, especially to poorer neighbourhoods.

It is important to recognise, too, that the categories of 'public' and 'private' are often blurred in practice, given that in many cities there has always been a diverse set of actors and forms through which water and sanitation have been met. In fact, many people connect across these different forms even in the duration of a single day, and some of them are partly public and 'free' – for example, they might involve water or sewage pipes – and partly private and commodified, such as a group clearing the septic tank or the company running the water tankers.[57] There is a spectrum of arrangements in water and sanitation across, and often also within, different cities. The idea of 'public' is neither fixed nor universally shared. Decades of neoliberalism have both eroded it as a concept and practice and made it more deeply contested. Bakker writes instead of 'degrees of "publicness" '.[58]

There are signs that the pro-privatisation neoliberal ethos is beginning to lose traction. Cases of failed or failing privatisation, or of private operators charging high costs to residents, have led to a growing questioning in national and global debates. Uruguay amended its Constitution in 2004 to outlaw the private provision of water, and Ecuador prohibited private investment in electricity in 2008. Complex arrangements of private actors have been replaced by single nationalised systems, as Mali has done in relation to electricity when privatised experiments were found to exclude some of the country's poorest regions. In Delhi, efforts to privatise water failed in the face of protests about potential tariff increases and accusations of corruption in the granting of contracts. One study in 2020 found that, across the globe, privately run projects have been increasingly cancelled or 'distressed', reaching a peak in the early 2000s. In the wake of the 2008 financial crisis some cities – Paris and Marseilles, for example – re-municipalised water.[59]

Private operators have often depended on state subsidies or found that the only way to generate the necessary surplus to extend infrastructure networks is to increase costs or engage in 'cream skimming' from more profitable areas or groups. There are cases where private operators appear to perform better than public ones in the same country, but where the better performance turns out to be because private actors are targeting more profitable areas while public utilities struggle to meet needs in other places.

Private firms tend to introduce a wider range of technologies, including the often-controversial practice of tracking usage for charging through meters, but they typically operate with less staff to respond to local needs and emerging concerns. In South Africa, for example, a so-called 'culture of non-payment' of water charges in townships led many municipalities to install prepaid meters that self-disconnect when payment isn't made. In Johannesburg, pseudo-privatised utility Johannesburg Water – a private firm in which the state retains shares – became an agent of neoliberal 'cost recovery' and disciplinary power as well as a provocation in the politicisation of the post-apartheid urban condition.[60]

At the same time, there are cases where the perceived success of the private sector builds its own momentum. In Accra, Ghana, some in wealthier neighbourhoods on the urban periphery have given up on unreliable public piped water supplies and instead use more costly but more reliable private suppliers, thereby further denuding the funds available for public provisioning.[61] The historical trend in Accra towards the integration of infra-structures like water across the city has been reversed, creating an increasingly fragmented system that serves different classes and exacerbates existing urban inequalities. While private net-works paid for by wealthier residents can sometimes themselves provide options for lower-income residents to access, and which are therefore partially subsidised by those on higher incomes, that is not a reliable or uniform tendency.

Moreover, the risk of increased fragmentation is that utilities have progressively less capital to invest in extending or main-taining networks to poorer groups and areas, making it more likely that they entrench 'cost-recovery' policies. Under cost-recovery arrangements, utilities might provide the main pipes but residents have to find the money to pay for and maintain connections to their houses, either in addition to or as part of water charges. The consequence can be that poorer areas and groups are increasingly dependent on sometimes expensive market providers or 'water mafias'. Across Ghana and beyond, the absence or limited presence of public utilities in many areas has meant that there is a sometimes fierce politics around who gets to run and profit from cost-recovery arrangements in water and sanitation.

In her work on toilet politics in Ghana, Brenda Chaflin argues that what she calls the 'right to shit' must include the right to use human waste as a resource with value, including the right not to be financially exploited through the introduction of fee-paying toilets via privatisation. Chaflin describes how toilet privatisation in the city of Tema generated a considerable and consistent economy for those who were positioned to capitalise on it: 'Open 18 hours a day, 365 days a year and attracting 25 customers an hour (and upwards of 100 patrons during the morning rush) . . . a public toilet could easily generate upwards of 18,000 Ghana cedi in revenue over the course of a year.'[62]

For residents who are part of utility networks, not only do they often find themselves cast as 'customers' rather than 'citizens', the question of who runs the utility has increasingly lacked accountability. For example, the privatisation of water supply in the UK in the late 1980s and 1990s led to a series of complex sell-offs and the financialisation of household supply, largely benefiting investors rather than citizens. The privatisation of the largest water company in the UK, Thames Water, which was purchased by a German group and then later an Australian bank, the Macquarie Group, left customers with little say in who owns the water, how it might be priced, or where their money goes. The opaque nature of water and sanitation ownership and responsibility is accompanied by a financialisation of risk. Customers increasingly find themselves in obscure risk-taking financial arrangements, while their experience of the service falls from corporate view.[63] State regulators have been missing in action or weak in their responses.

Meanwhile, many of the poorest in cities have never had anything approaching regular access to utility-provided water and sanitation.[64] In the United States, one in five residents are not provided by utility networks, meaning people rely on septic tanks of varying quality and cost.[65] Most of these residents are poor and Black. As Kartik Chandran, an environmental engineer, says, 'it's like they don't exist'. In urban Africa, decent incentives for utilities to better serve low-income households are often non-existent, and there may be no measurable targets, monitorable data, or consequences for failure.[66] Incentives might include setting or changing subsidies and financial targets that are focused on poorer groups and neighbourhoods, but what's needed are clear legal requirements and consequences.

To be sure, government subsidies can play a role in incentivising utilities to extend provisions to areas they conventionally deem less profitable and reducing or waiving costs to poorer residents. There have been examples of this working well, such as in eThekwini in South Africa.[67] But there also needs to be a dose of realism around how well utilities perform. While utilities can be fined for not meeting agreed targets, some utilities carry large debts and may lack capacity, and so simply pointing fingers at utilities is not always the best route to resolving a fragmented set of provisions.

The COVID-19 pandemic reduced the funds coming into utilities through user charges from residents or businesses, or via state subsidies, as well as through stalled projects that might have improved or extended services. In the summer of 2020, for example, a financial analysis of three water service providers in Kenya identified an urgent need for US$1.4 million just to continue operations for the subsequent six months, and in the US water and wastewater utilities anticipated a massive US$27 billion shortfall.[68] This was also obviously before the global economic impacts of inflation and recession catalysed by Russia's war in Ukraine. The capacity of utilities to deliver to marginal neighbourhoods and groups is more likely to be enhanced if they work with state and civil society actors in legally enforceable frameworks, rather than being scapegoated.

In most African cities, utilities play a limited role in serving the poorest homes, especially in sub-Saharan Africa – in some places, as low as 2 percent. Water provision by utilities in poorer neighbourhoods often takes the form of public standpipes, which may be out of the way or might not provide enough for a day's need. This means that residents often end up paying more to access private water tankers or small-scale providers. Raising money to extend provisions might require charging wealthier groups more to subsidise extensions in provision and/or lower rates for poorer neighbourhoods. A flat rate, which is common among utilities, ends up excluding the poorest and benefiting the richest. Similarly, income from larger cities can be used to subsidise water provisions to smaller cities, as is common in much of West Africa. In Côte d'Ivoire, water utility SODECI provides water to more than 500 towns, only a very small group of which generate a surplus. [69]

While there are, rightly, significant concerns about the role of private actors in providing fundamentally public goods like water and sanitation in both the short and longer term, the evidence suggests that in relation to *access* at least, the key issue is less who runs the system and more how the system is governed and with what aims.[70] There are some cases where introducing public–private partnerships has led to an extension of piped water to poorer homes, including in African cities.[71] However, the evidence that the growing role for private actors has made water and sanitation *less affordable* is stronger, and there is little evidence that attracting private finance has led to a more general distribution of affordable water and sanitation across cities. In addition, to satisfy private investors, utilities often stress efficiency and seek to aggregate performance benchmarks rather than focus on who gets what where, turning water and sanitation into 'technocratic exercises' rather than 'social policy domains'.[72]

In Brazil, the National Sanitation Information System has been collecting data on water and sanitation utilities since 1995, using a proliferation of indicators – eighty-four and counting – which measure just about everything except whether the poorest and most marginalised are actually getting water. Such systems of measurement are replicated elsewhere, including globally through the International Benchmarking Network for Water and Sanitation Utilities. One of the tendencies is to measure gains in cost recovery from users to fund maintenance and operations, and some utilities that do well on that measure do less well in meeting poorer residents' needs. The Addis Ababa Water and Sewerage Authority in Ethiopia might rank highly in UN accounting on 'universal' access to water, but in poor neighbourhoods it is either non-existent or only present in the form of public fountains of varying quality.

One of the key political questions is how and where to use and extend state subsidies to utilities. The record globally is not good. Subsidies tend to not be well targeted and can even entrench existing inequalities. Most utilities, be they public, private, or hybrid, have some form of subsidy. The World Bank's International Benchmarking Network for Water and Sanitation Utilities, for example, has identified 86 percent of 1,589 utilities as having subsidies (that is, only 14 percent generate the necessary revenue to cover their costs). Most subsidies end up going to wealthier residents, with only relatively small amounts reaching the poorest. Subsidies tend to be used to support those who are already networked and sewered for water and sanitation.[73]

According to one estimate, subsidies for water and sanitation in much of the world, excluding China and India, amount to between US$289 and $353 billion per year, and the figure is higher if the costs of infrastructure expansion and environmental impacts are added. This estimate is between two and three times the US$114 billion per year that the World Bank estimates is needed to meet the 2030 SDG of safely managed water and sanitation for all. A lot of money, and yet it represents between just 0.05 and 2.4 percent of global GDP, with poorer countries closer to the 2.4 percent.[74] Subsidies are not only often poorly targeted, there are not enough of them. There is typically an absence of transparency as to their allocation, too, and they are not well designed and monitored.

So, not cheap, but not impossible sums of money for many – not all – countries and cities. The profound human importance of decent water and sanitation, and the economic, environmental, and social returns that investment generates in the longer term, makes a powerful case for increasing utility subsidies. But there must be far greater focus on expansion to poorer and marginalised places and groups. Tackling affordability in a way that enables a genuine provision of water and sanitation for all demands a refocusing of state and international development subsidies into those areas most in need.

Often, local states, from Bharatpur in Nepal to Centreville in the United States, will need financial support from the national state and sometimes international agencies, and winning that support can take years of activist struggle. Financially struggling utilities might adopt strategies of 'blending' funding from matching funds (such as extractive industry taxes), solidarity levies (surtaxes on consumer items or industries), and global philanthropy (such as the Gates Foundation), with a strong focus on meaningful impact on poverty and inequality.[75] The resources are there provided sanitation is given the central priority and understanding it deserves.

The central focus must be on access, delivery, and affordability, measured against those most in need, with a careful attention to where and how money is spent and targeted. For the poorest, water and sanitation ought to be subsidised and free, not a source of constant worry and calculation over meeting bills for fundamental provisions. Where possible, basic goods like water and sanitation should be owned, run, and delivered by public utilities with a clear mandate for universal provision, funded through taxation and higher rates for businesses and wealthier residents.

Even when the frameworks are in place and working well, though, we cannot assume that delivery will remain fair and equitable. Provisioning is always political, and the nature of that politics can change over time. Decisions on spending can be influenced by political parties who may be hostile to groups and neighbourhoods outside their electoral base. States and municipalities sometimes become caught up in legal disputes, typically ethically blinkered, about whether a neighbourhood deemed 'illegal' by the state should qualify for provisions. And yet at other times, the 'community' is positioned by the state as the solution to the crisis.

From community to forum

Alongside the discursive shift to private-sector participation in sanitation in recent decades is that other neoliberal buzzword: *decentralisation*. There has been a massive increase in the numbers of small-scale, community-based provisions, from local businesses and entrepreneurs to co-operative and small public–private partnerships. Some, of course, are not new and have been in action for as long as cities themselves. Typically, these are of a different order from the examples described above.[76] There has also been a growing emphasis on partnership between the state, donors, and civil society organisations, with increasing talk of 'co-producing' knowledge, policy, and planning.

While the rhetoric of community partnership is welcome, in practice it is too often little more than rhetoric or, worse, a thinly disguised effort to offload state responsibilities to already over-burdened poorer people. International development agencies have argued that effective sanitation provision in low-income neighbourhoods must centre on 'community mobilisation' and seek to 'create support and ownership' within neighbourhoods.[77] This global context resonates with a wider turn towards 'best practice' in international development, from actors like the World Bank to local NGOs, where a discourse of 'community empowerment' or 'participatory citizenship' sometimes positions residents, and not states, as responsible for the deeply laborious work of attending to infrastructure.

In her research on waste infrastructure in Dakar, Senegal, Rosalind Fredericks shows how urban governments and NGOs subjected residents, especially women, to 'dirty-labor burdens' in the name of building 'community' and 'neighbourhood' waste systems that tapped into local knowledge and rhythms, to ostensibly develop 'gender empowerment'.[78] She describes one NGO project in which women were enrolled to use 'traditional' sanitation systems like horse-drawn carts to collect garbage from their neighbours, working several times a week for a small fee. Not only did this reinforce local ethnic power relations by working with one group over others, it entrenched gendered discourses of women as responsible for cleanliness, exposed women to risk and disease, and led to tensions over fees between collectors and residents.[79]

A discourse of community empowerment and control is used here in different ways: first, by local states to offload budgetary cuts and austerity onto communities, and, second, by NGOs to sustain their role and funding. Women were left, argues Fredericks, 'to literally pick up the pieces of a degrading infrastructure as the neighbourhood's new "housekeepers" ' and told it was 'empowerment'.[80] These are precisely some of the social differences and power relations that are often hidden by the term 'community'. For all the advantages of NGOs and community organisations, they do not always represent the community or its best interests.

The underbelly of the 'community solution' rhetoric is blame, exploitation, and abandonment. Take, for example, the ongoing crisis of sanitation, race, and class in Alabama. Here, ageing septic tanks spill into streets, homes, and fields. *E. coli*, hookworm, faecal coliform, respiratory problems, and gastrointestinal illness play havoc with people's health and leave them exhausted. There are residents who take medicines to treat sewage-incurred illnesses because it's cheaper than paying for septic tank costs. And yet in 2018, Sherry Bradley of the Alabama Department of Public Health described the situation this way: 'If you've got sewage on the ground, it's your fault you're dumping sewage on the ground. I was raised poor, but we were proud. We were clean'.[81]

She later said she was quoted out of context, but this points to a larger history of blaming the poorest and seeking to justify leaving them to get on with sorting sanitation themselves.

Residents can be fined for not having functional septic tank systems – as much as $500 in Alabama – while installing a new system can cost $20,000, well beyond the capacity of most. In one case, the Alabama Department of Public Health sought to arrest a twenty-seven-year-old single mother who lived in a mobile home with her autistic child for not adequately maintaining her septic system. In 2011, a Report of the UN's Special Rapporteur on the Human Right to Safe Drinking Water and Sanitation explicitly mentioned conditions in Alabama, noting that in predominantly poor, Black Lowndes County, half the on-site septic tank systems were failing and the majority of residents lacked adequate human waste collection systems.[82] Yet, in a process with a much longer history than the neoliberal turn, elements of the state actively blame the poor, devolve responsibility to communities, and withhold improved sanitation.

These, then, are deeply political matters – not simply questions of getting the right governance balance between state and non-state 'stakeholders'. Rather than shift the burden of delivery onto residents, there are three directions that matter for the role of communities in the right to citylife. First, there needs to be genuine commitment to include local people in the planning, design, and delivery of appropriate and flexible sanitation facilities. Local needs, aspirations, and differences in bodies and subjectivities matter to the success of sanitation systems, as do issues such as the type of technology used. This demands some understanding of local contexts and conditions.

There is a challenge here in ensuring that the representative voices of local areas reflect the social heterogeneity of the place and do not become dominated by particular groups (typically established men) who hold relative formal and informal power. This means designing participatory processes and forums that reach out across the community. Genuine participation in state planning and delivery systems is a vital part of realising the right to citylife, but loading the labour and operation onto already burdened and often vulnerable residents, who are short on resources and time, goes in precisely the wrong direction.

Second, there has to be a clear framework that locates responsibility for sanitation delivery and maintenance not with the 'community' but with designated institutions. This framework might include private-sector and civil society actors, as well as utilities and municipalities, and these groups will involve residents and community structures. What matters most here is ensuring that the bulk of infrastructural, technical, regulatory, and operational work is taken on by institutions that have capacity to perform in sustained ways. Those frameworks need to have the legal and regulatory clarity to be usable as a source of appeal should systems go astray.

In short, strong notes of caution and care are necessary against discourses and strategies that support community solutions, alongside a clarity on exactly what is meant by 'community' in a given context. These are, to be sure, often contested debates and they can be laborious too, which is why adopting clear frameworks matters. The political route forward is not one of redistributing sanitation labour onto residents, but of placing their perceptions and experiences at the centre of the wider resource allocation of sanitation in the city.

Third, we cannot underestimate the vital work of activism, research, and supportive policy actors in drawing attention to the plight of residents who are variously blamed, abandoned, or exploited in the name of the community solution. As US activist Catherine Flowers has put it, after years of campaigning on sewage in the US in her struggles for poor, Black residents, once the private worlds of sanitation poverty are exposed, even the powerful can have trouble ignoring it. Flowers has helped turn sanitation inequality into a national issue in the US and had some success in bringing federal money to often ignored parts of Alabama. Struggles like those she is involved in are powerful reminders that mainstream discourses, economic priorities, and governance approaches can be challenged and that the sanitation crisis can be seen anew.

How, then, might local people's involvement in sanitation planning and delivery be institutionalised in a progressive way? One compelling route here is the urban sanitation forum. The forum is an old idea in the city. In ancient Rome, it was a central space for gatherings, large enough to hold the city's crowds, replete with imposing building and monuments to state power. It was a site of assembly, bringing different groups together to address urban challenges and priorities. Today, forums take all kinds of forms, both online and offline, from one-off consultation events on a particular policy or online discussion platforms run by local authorities to citizen juries that deliberate on specific thorny urban problems or participatory budgeting that sets neighbourhood and citywide spending priorities. Cities need to learn again and again the sanitation needs, priorities, and aspirations of their different residents and to bring that into the heart of planning and policy in a meaningful way. The forum is one mechanism for delivering that.

At their best, urban sanitation forums shift us away from the old model of sanitation experts at the centre who adjudicate on what works where, why and for whom, without descending into a naive or opportunistic community solutionism. They would bring an expanding range of perspectives together from across the city, functioning as platforms for disagreement, conflict resolution, and holding those in power to account. They might operate at a neighbourhood or city level, and their conclusions would lead to meaningful changes in policy and budget.

But the challenges for building effective forums are considerable. Take development aid money, for example. At the moment, global urban development funds typically go to national governments and not to city governments or to civil society organisations that can be better connected to the places and communities in need. As Jorge Hardoy, David Satterthwaite, and others have long argued, global development funds that operate through government aid, development banks (the World Bank, the Asian or African Development Banks, the European

Bank for Reconstruction and Development, etc.), or the UN system are typically dispersed as large funds for big projects via state authorities, and often with tight financial rules of accountability that can restrict activity.[83]

For all the talk in recent decades by governments and international agencies of 'decentralisation', 'partnership', 'participation', 'empowerment', and 'co-production' with residents, it is difficult to make the case that institutions are, in practice, significantly shaped by the perspectives of the poor and marginalised. When operating successfully, the forum provides what Edgar Pieterse calls an 'effective countervailing institution'.[84] Effective sanitation forums would be guided not by appeals to a machinic city but by the messy city as we find it. Here, four central principles are especially important: *listening, long-termism, a networked view,* and *an openness to politics.*

First, listening. The history of urban sanitation is littered with failures caused by not listening to the diversity of views and experiences. As I argued in Chapter 5 on protests, marginalised and excluded residents are sometimes forced to extremes in order to be heard, including in the unpredictable and volatile act of using human waste as a political weapon. Listening matters – but who to listen to? This is not a straightforward question. There are actors in national and local states, ranging from planning and infrastructure to finance and environment, and there are NGOs, community-based organisations, social movements, private companies small and large, think tanks and universities, all of which have stakes in urban sanitation and something to offer. Then there is the question of representation – why this group and not another, and whose agenda is being silenced or furthered when this community leader or state official is involved and another not?

It makes sense to begin by including established organisations, such as community groups and social movements working either on sanitation or focused on a particular area in which a forum is being set up. But if there is a genuine commitment to listening, then there should be a range of participants in the forum – not just the usual suspects – reflecting the social and economic heterogeneities of a place. This requires care, time, and accountability, with opportunities for people to contest selection and transparent mechanisms of appeal and decision-making.

There are limits, of course. For a start, not everyone wants or has the time to commit, and it is never possible to get 'fully' representative forums. But box-ticking is not really the point. The point is a purposeful effort to engage with social plurality, with the 'mess' of the city. It matters too that the right to be able to become involved in decision-making and to participate over the long term is genuinely available and open.

The circumstances and nature of listening matters. Is the listening conducted with a spirit of attention, generosity, and openness to the possibility of views and positions changing? Listening demands a commitment to seeing where it takes us, not as a precursor to expounding a pre-given set of positions or manifesto.[85] For elites, it has as much to do with inhabiting silence as it does with speaking. The history of urban sanitation is very often structured with experts or powerful groups talking and residents and community groups listening. The relations around the 'table' and in the 'room' need to be upturned, and it is the policy, planning, and municipal officials of the urban world who need to listen the hardest. The power relations cannot be simply wished away or manufactured out of existence, but it often helps if the 'room' shifts from the offices of local governments to community buildings, streets, and homes, where power relations are at least a little unsettled and people might feel more at ease talking – and listening.

Listening demands careful attention to place and social heterogeneity. This is listening as a politics of pluralism. As William Connolly has argued, pluralism can be both 'deep' and 'multidimensional'.[86] Deep pluralism is a recognition that the position a given participant holds is held earnestly and with commitment, but also that it is received as just one view, which others present may not share. Multidimensional pluralism

follows on and is a commitment from the start by all participants that differences – for example, in gender, race, ethnicity,
age, language, religion, values and interpretations of problems,
needs and solutions, and so on – should not be skirted or
ignored, but actively sought, expressed, and discussed. Rather
than seeking to whittle differences down into singular views,
the challenge here is to build consensus while keeping a hold of
the differences.

Second, an effective forum should focus not just on the
urgency of the moment but on the long term. Without long-
termism, it is too easy for decisions on spending and investment
to be caught up in immediate budgetary cycles and policy preoccupations, and so more difficult commitments like extending
a sewer or planning for future urbanisation and climate change
can end up shunted out of the evaluation of the possible. Given
the importance of maintenance and repair in sanitation,
short-termism is also likely to lead to familiar stories of breakdown, blockage, and failing provisions.

If its agenda is long term, then the forum is a useful institutional fit for the expanding and dynamic quality of the right to
citylife. Forums ought to be spaces where the right to citylife is
continually reframed and remade: targets fulfilled, new ones
emergent, setbacks addressed, different ideas debated, and so
on. This is the necessary paradox of the right to citylife: always
out of reach, but always an indispensable aim nonetheless.

A keyword for long-term success is 'co-production'. The
term has become something of a buzzword in international
development, but in essence it refers to an explicit political
strategy of developing collaborative relations between the
state, civil society groups, and residents. For groups like Slum/
Shack Dwellers International (SDI), for example, co-production
has meant shared responsibilities for managing budgets and
has helped foster strong relationships between low- and mid-
level city officials and the leaders of NGO and community-based
organisations. In the process, SDI has learnt more about
how planning and policy processes operate and how they

might be challenged in ways that sharpen their own political competencies.[87]

Other examples include the Asian Coalition for Community Action, which has funded upgrading projects for housing, infrastructure, and services, or the Urban Poor Fund International, which has supported improvements and tenure initiatives. These funds are sometimes raised through community contributions, which is a hard ask on financially pressed residents, and at other times through external donor support and sometimes augmented by government funding (especially if there is a track record of established success), or some combination of those.

There are successful cases where local community funds have enabled long-term processes of upgrading that are embedded in community groups and aspirations. For example, the Muungano Alliance in Nairobi brings together community organisations, social movements, and an NGO linked to SDI to run an urban poor fund called the Akiba Mashinani Trust (AMT). AMT is funded by community savings, donor funds, and bank loans and operates across Kenya to provide financial and technical support for urban upgrading of housing, infrastructure, and services, including sanitation. Between 2009 and 2016, AMT committed over US$1.7 million in grants and loans to community-led upgrading projects.[88] These cases demonstrate the potential of forums to manage and disperse funds, and to grow from what are often neighbourhood-based movements into citywide and even nationwide umbrella organisations for local forums.

Some of the most impressive experiments with urban forums over time have taken place in Brazil in the post-dictatorship embrace of participatory democracy by social movements and the Partido dos Trabalhadores (PT, the Workers' Party). The most high-profile case was in Porto Alegre, where there was mass participation, elements of redistribution, and a balanced budget. Through a set of neighbourhood-based deliberative forums on the city's budget priorities, residents debated and voted on a variety of municipal policies and positions. Participation was two-tiered, involving both individuals and community organisations. Meetings began in March, when delegates were elected to represent specific neighbourhoods, and the previous year's projects and budgets were discussed.

In the months that followed, these regional areas met to discuss local and citywide priorities and to examine thematic areas like health or education. Finally, delegates came together at the regional plenary to discuss local priorities and to vote to elect councillors – whose term was limited to two years – to serve on the Municipal Council of the Budget. Between 1992 and 1995, the housing department offered housing assistance to 28,862 families (the number was 1,714 for 1986–88), while the number of functioning public municipal schools significantly increased. There were substantial improvements in water and sanitation, too.[89]

Participatory budgeting is just one model of the forum, combining as it does representative and deliberative urban democracy. Other forums might be smaller, even if their remit remains wide, and few forums need or can realistically expect mass participation. What this period from Brazil illustrates is the potential of effective forums to shift the direction of urban planning and investment over the longer term, as well as the value of really committing to listening in a sustained, meaningful way, with clear mechanisms organising dialogue and decision-making. Forums will also change over time, moving through periods of consultation on a particular issue – sanitation technology, for instance – to periods of deeper listening – for example, on provisions for children or in transport settings – to periods of monitoring and maintenance, to moments of policy lobbying or campaigning on budgets, and so on.

Third, at the level of the city in particular, forums would typically have a broad remit, reflecting a networked view of sanitation. In practice, this means occasionally stepping back from the pressures and foci of the moment – more toilets here, better drainage here, greater space for gender and disability in sanitation policy, and so forth – to identify whether the uneven and unequal spatialities of sanitation across the urban realm are really being addressed. A broad focus for the forum includes both the multiple nature of sanitation – education, livelihood, travel, and disease as much as pipes and toilets – and the geographies of the city, from home and street to workplace, public square, outflows, and treatment sites. Building toilets in a low-income neighbourhood with historically inadequate sanitation is a good thing, but if women and disabled users feel they can't use them, or if the toilets lack adequate drainage, water, or electricity, or deposit waste untreated into the local environment, then the benefits might be quickly undone. Forums need particularly careful attention to gender inequalities and the voice of women and girls in their constitution and operation, given the historical centrality of gender across sanitation concerns.

Fourth, and finally, to be adequately situated in the mess of the urban world, the forum must recognise the unavoidably political nature of sanitation. Forums that turn into talk-shops with no clear route to influence policy, or which are restricted to technical questions or the path of least resistance, are not likely to succeed in the long run. Sanitation is political. Rather than avoid it, the politics of land, housing, gender, race, budgeting, stigmatisation, health, education, work, death, and more need to be given the space to be heard and listened to in a spirit of learning and reflection. Consensus borne from ignoring or skipping around the politics of the city is likely to quickly run aground on disengagement and alienation. In the setting of priorities, there will always be wins and losses, compromises, disagreements, trade-offs and appeals, and if faith is to remain in the forum then priorities must be arrived at in a transparent way that is explained and which can be publicly contested.

In short, urban sanitation forums are mostly likely to deliver when they are long-term commitments that reflect the heterogeneity of the city, operate with a broad and flexible remit, and are given real ability to influence policy and investment priorities by a publicly committed state. Ideally they would have their own budgets to disperse and be able receive funds from national authorities and global development agencies and banks. All of which is easy to say, but a huge struggle to institute in many cities. Placing the right to citylife, as an urban meta-frame, at the centre of the forum is a good place to begin. The right to citylife can be a focal point around which to rally and gather, to transform the direction of urban sanitation provisions, and to build a city in which people not only survive but thrive.

7

Conclusion

The COVID-19 pandemic placed sanitation at the heart of the experience of living in cities. The city became a vast exercise in sanitising people and space as, quite suddenly, many of us became obsessive about hygiene. Walk into a store, wash your hands. Press a button for the traffic lights, elevator or doorbell, or use an ATM, wash your hands. Don't shake hands, don't leave the house without hand sanitiser, don't stand too close, do wipe down surfaces often and thoroughly. There were people washing groceries when they brought them home. People became wary of public toilets when they were out in the city – though, worse, they were often closed, at least in the initial lockdowns. The very air around us, particularly in dense areas of cities, was now a source of potential infection and disease. Sanitation was mainstreamed in ways that it hadn't been, in many cities, for at least a century. And there were disturbing cases from China, India, and elsewhere of migrant workers being sprayed by government officials to 'decontaminate' them.

The United Nations has argued that the rapid changes in society brought on by the pandemic showed the potential for the 'near-overnight transformation that is needed to confront our most urgent threats', noting too that previous pandemics, such as the 1918 flu outbreak, catalysed the expansion of sewage, parks, and housing regulation to reduce overcrowding.[1] Was the pandemic, then, a turning point for sanitation inequality? Has it resulted in meaningful change for the near 1 billion people living in cities with inadequate or no sanitation?

Sadly, for all the well-meaning debate, the substantive answer is no.

The immediate impact of the pandemic was to make sanitation conditions worse, not better. Public toilets were closed off, as was access to sanitation in school and workplaces in many cases. The poorest had less access to soap, hand sanitisers, masks, and other personal protective equipment, often increasing the risk of viral spread.[2] When they became sick, they typically had reduced access to already stretched or threadbare health care systems. Spending on sanitation improvements and expansions was shelved, undermining provisions in the medium term. City and national budgets were squeezed by the economic hit. Millions of urbanites were pushed into extreme poverty, yet they were often the very people struggling to keep cities ticking: delivery drivers, transport staff, janitors, cleaners, small shop workers, nurses, garbage collectors, sanitation staff, and more.

The pandemic triggered an economic response consisting of trillions of dollars, the invention of new vaccines, and radical changes in governance and lifestyle that were previously nigh on unthinkable. Given the central role of sanitation in all of it, it should really shock us to see that we have emerged from the pandemic entirely without a new urgency and investment in tackling the global sanitation crisis. The pandemic ought to have been a rallying call for change. But the sanitation story I have told in this book remains largely hidden from, or at least marginal to, mainstream public and political views. Millions are still condemned to struggle each day just to fulfil a basic bodily need, with all the implications I have explored across the book. Ageing sanitation infrastructure across the urban world continues to be neglected. The working conditions of sanitation staff often remain abhorrent. Rivers, lakes, and coasts remain contaminated. But should we really be surprised?

It is easier to imagine the end of the world than the end of capitalism – so goes the phrase attributed to Fredric Jameson, elaborated by Mark Fisher in his book, *Capitalist Realism*. If that is indeed the case, then we are perfectly capable of putting the sanitation crisis out of mind. Fisher's argument was not just that capitalism had become global, that it subsumes everything into itself to leave billions 'trudging through the ruins and relics', but that it had become increasingly difficult even to imagine an alternative to it.[3] For some, the pandemic response was itself a triumph of capitalism. British prime minister Boris Johnson is rumoured to have argued that it was capitalism – indeed, 'greed' – that came up with the vaccine solutions (never mind that it was scientists at Oxford University that created the AstraZeneca vaccine and that huge amounts of public money and infrastructure were used to secure and distribute vaccines).

The pandemic could have catalysed a new centrality for sanitation inequality. Instead, the impetus has generally been to return as quickly as possible to business as usual. It is a version of the narrative of the 2021 climate crisis film, *Don't Look Up*, in which politics and culture conspire to evade confronting the impending destruction of a meteor by encouraging people to simply look away from it. The important difference, of course, is that most middle-class and elite urbanites can insulate themselves from the hardships of the sanitation crisis. As the film implies, it is not only that there is just so much else to be distracted by, but that our cultures, political structures, and economic configurations work so persistently to return attention to business as usual.

Rather than affirmative sanitation that would promote the right to citylife, too often we continue to see destructive sanitation that 'cleans' the city by displacing the poor, sometimes violently and often without compensation. In early 2021, for example, just as some were hoping that the pandemic might be kickstarting a new chapter in urban sanitation politics, the Karachi Metropolitan Corporation (KMC) began marking up houses and shops in the lower-income Manzoor Colony for a massive demolition programme. The aim was to widen and clean the *nullah* – watercourse – that carries sewage to the sea, and so the decision was made to remove the occupants, thereby protecting neighbourhoods to the north from flooding.[4] The nullah had in fact once been a healthy river, but it is now clogged with solid and human waste, and rather than improve it by identifying the actual sources of waste and supporting the residents, the rumours were that the plan is to clear the area for real estate developers.

The urban sanitation story is one of increasingly rampant inequality. In the summer of 2022 in India, anti–manual scavenging group Safai Karamchari Andolan (SKA) ran a seventy-five-day campaign protesting the deaths of sanitation workers in sewers and septic tanks. The campaign, called 'Stop Killing Us', demanded recognition, better provisions, compensation, and adequate support for alternative livelihoods. All of this is provided legally, but in practice it barely exists (see Chapter 2). The *Times of India* reported the death of fifty-seven workers between 15 August 2021, Indian Independence Day, and spring 2022, yet social justice minister Ramdas Athawale initially claimed there had been no deaths over five years, only later retracting the comment to note that there had been some deaths through accidents. The campaign moved across Indian cities, with workers and activists holding 'Stop Killing Us' banners, chanting, and delivering speeches. Still, they were often met with what SKA leader Bezwada Wilson called a 'deafening silence'.

Add to these cases the more familiar stories of infrastructure disinvestment in cities across the world and of municipalities and states failing to prioritise sanitation investment. There are exceptions and positive cases, which I've discussed in the book, but this is a context that can leave you wondering: what will it take? How is it possible to shift the direction when there are such deeply embedded and often scandalous forms of sanitation inequality, political violence, and neglect? What are the drivers that might push affirmative sanitation? And if a global pandemic doesn't instigate a new prioritisation of sanitation, then what might?

Legal changes are vital, but they are often not enough. Ask manual scavengers in India risking their lives and health cleaning blocked toilets, drains, tanks, and sewers whether the fact that it is illegal has supported them out of these awful labour conditions. A legal right won't necessarily change the minds of those who would exclude residents or workers because of prejudices based on race, ethnicity, or caste, or who would discriminate against disabled or homeless groups. Legal provisions are necessary but not sufficient for the right to citylife.

But, there are reasons to keep faith. There are at least four drivers, each of which, albeit in small and specific ways, have nudged the affirmative sanitation agenda further along and will continue to do so: *precedent setting, mediatised events, urban activism,* and *the ecological crisis.*

First, precedent setting. One example here is the work of SDI, an international movement of NGOs and community federations which I have previously mentioned. SDI has often talked about the importance of precedent setting in establishing and promoting their work with residents, governments, and the media. One of SDI's strategies has been to build their own community toilet blocks in poor neighbourhoods, working with residents and other groups, and to use that as an example that might pull local politicians into a dialogue around new frameworks for change. Their work has been resourced through community savings, donor contributions, and state funding. This model has had some significant successes in South Asia and in parts of Africa, including through what SDI calls 'toilet festivals' that mark the opening of community-built facilities with celebratory events that raise awareness and promote dialogue with municipal staff and politicians.[5]

This strategy of putting the capacities and skills of the urban poor on display can be a powerful starting point, and the act of building a precedent provides a basis from which to develop a record and reputation that local and national government can see and respond to. It also opens an opportunity for organised civil society groups to begin conversing with government on their own terms, or to change existing conversations, and sometimes to do so in their own neighbourhoods. It troubles existing power relations and questions whose knowledge counts, where expertise lies, and how capacity might be developed. It can help form effective partnerships between the state, civil society, and residents around a shared sanitation mission. At the same time, there is always the risk in this kind of strategy that the state will attempt to offload responsibility and labour onto the urban poor, dressing up 'partnership' to mask a partial withdrawal from its obligations. It does not have to be that way, however, and this risk is not a reason not to pursue this route – all politics is risk, after all, to one degree or another. SDI organisations are established and savvy enough to resist state exploitation, and in some cities – Mumbai and Nairobi, for instance – they have helped set up effective versions of the kinds of urban forums I described in the previous chapter.[6]

There are other examples of precedent-setting, including by local governments. The Kampung Improvement Program in Indonesia or the 2,000 kilometres of predominantly small sewer pipes connecting 300,000 homes built in Salvador, Brazil, between 1996 and 2004, both mentioned in previous chapters, are examples. There are other cases I have discussed in the book, such as the work of the Orangi Pilot Project in Karachi. Ethiopia and India have made substantial sanitation improvements less through new technologies and approaches and instead by giving sanitation greater government priority and budgetary capacity – these two set precedents more globally, even though they are not without their debates and controversies. In many of these cases, political and economic prioritisation was given to sanitation and living conditions in particular areas, or even city-wide, and marked material improvements followed, even if often only slowly. They took years of pressure from activist and civil society groups, along with building alliances with local and national government officials.

Second, mediatised events. Sometimes, a particular moment can unexpectedly capture public and political attention in ways that drive change. In the United States, the 2005 Restroom Access Act, also known as 'Ally's Law', requires employers to make employee toilets available to any member of the public with certain medical conditions. This includes, for example, people with Crohn's disease, ulcerative colitis, and ostomies – conditions that require frequent and/or urgent toilet access. The catalyst for the act was the experience of a fourteen-year-old girl, Ally Bain, from Illinois.

She has Crohn's disease and was shopping with her mother when she began to experience intense abdominal pain. Knowing she had at most minutes to get to a toilet, she asked a clothing store to use their toilet. She was crying and doubled over in pain yet was told that the store toilets were not for public use and that she should walk to the nearest facility. She then had an accident in the store. She and her family took the story to the state legislature, which ultimately led to the governor of Illinois signing the act into law in 2005 (other states have since followed). What's notable here is how one moment has become a referent point for campaigners and officials across the US and beyond – there is a campaign in New Zealand, for instance – which carries emotive appeal and gathers media attention in ways that numbers and data so often don't. Mediatised events are not isolated, of course, but typically align with campaigns and agendas already in play. They can act as catalysts.

Third, urban activism. It is likely that both short- and long-term protest and campaigning will increase in the years to come rather than subside, as more and more urbanites find they are struggling with profoundly inadequate sanitation systems. The role of activism is vital in pushing debates, pressuring states, and keeping publics alive to the stakes of the sanitation struggle. Activism names everyday exploitations and inequalities, raises awareness, and provokes a response from different political and public fora. This includes, as I discussed in Chapter 5, activists who use human waste as a political tool, a particularly risky politics for sure that works to generate shock and which connects despair, the body, and the senses.

There are all kinds of other examples, too. We might think of campaigns resisting the removal of drains or water pipes, those demanding better management of septic tanks, or others supporting sanitation workers, such as the SKA group. In the UK, it was the committed work of campaigners in different parts of the country that led the government to eventually set up the Changing Places fund for toilets that are accessible to people with a range of disabilities and medical conditions as well as carers who need to change children and adults. These different campaigns and actions drive understanding, pressure, and agendas for change. As with precedent-setting and mediatised events, they raise awareness through mainstream and social media and can play a vital role in creating momentum.

Finally, fourth, the ecological crisis. Our understanding of the connections between sanitation and climate change are deepening, and city and national governments, along with international agencies, have begun to act on those links. Efforts to make cities more resilient and adaptive, or to mitigate the impacts, are increasingly placing the vulnerabilities of the urban poor and the inequalities of urbanisation on their agenda. The climate crisis will demand responses that have profound consequences for sanitation. The problem is that we see responses not only of affirmative sanitation but of destructive sanitation, pushing the poorest onto peripheral land, for example. In highlighting this as a fourth driver for the right to citylife, I am very aware of the risks that it could just as likely go in the other direction. The first three drivers – precedent setting, mediatised events, and activism – will be vital in pushing climate responses towards affirmative interventions.

While I've mentioned four drivers of affirmative sanitation here, the route to the right to citylife is varied, unpredictable, and intensely political. Responding to the urgency demands radical shifts in focus, spending, and long-term planning, whether through urban sanitation forums or other routes. The crisis is not some abstraction. It is being lived *now*, as people wake in the morning, go to school or work, take the bus or train, visit the local market, or move through the neighbourhood in the evening. It is present in physical exhaustion, illness, disease, harassment,

and violence. It ruins education, health, jobs, and family relationships. It is at work in moments of social shame and desperate
protest. It is seeping into soils, rivers, food, and water supplies.

Now, then, is time to get onto the sanitation battlefield. Those
of us concerned with cities or inequality are called on to act,
write, reach out, collaborate, support, teach, and campaign
with the aim that children no longer die in the thousands each
year in impoverished neighbourhoods for lack of a decent toilet,
that people are not excluded simply because they are female,
disabled, old, or of a particular caste, race, ethnicity, or religion,
that they are not subjected to abuse for a want of decent toilet
provision, that our ageing and failing sanitation infrastructures
no longer spew wastes into farms, rivers, and coasts.

Cities and countries need sanitation strategies. As much as
the right to citylife can't be addressed through the law alone, it
is remarkable that cities as big and wealthy as London do not
have either legal requirements to provide decent public toilets or
even a strategy for access to them. Not having a strategy leaves
cities undermining equality by further discriminating against
already marginalised groups, especially those on lower incomes
or with disabilities or certain illnesses and diseases. Not having
a strategy is tantamount to ignoring the devastating health
consequences – physical and mental – that unfold every day as
vulnerable residents try to make their way in the city.

As I've been trying to say, all kinds of residents, from pregnant women and nighttime workers to homeless people and bus
and delivery drivers, can suffer the consequences. We are all
affected. Not just because we've all found ourselves wondering
where on earth the nearest toilet is in the city at some point or
other, but because most people will hit points in their lives when
they are much more dependent on sanitation provision. The 'loo
leash' may then become a daily reality rather than an abstract
category or something for other people. Chances are that all of
us know of someone struggling with the physical and mental
consequences of feeling like they can't go out, or spend much
time outdoors – and for what?

There are some relatively easy wins to start with. Requiring new developments in cities, especially larger developments, to provide quality public toilets, is often cheaper and more practical than providing new toilets in already dense, busy areas, even if in the longer run that is what is needed. Reopening existing closed public toilets, which dot urban landscapes across the globe, and ensuring proper maintenance, is another relatively easy win. So too is ensuring maintenance of those that are open but which people are reluctant to use because of their condition. Large city centre businesses could be required to open their toilets to the public, with clear advertising of a 'no need to pay' commitment. And there could be far better online and offline maps and signage to those public toilets that do exist.

The harder wins are those cultural shifts in social power: a sanitation revolution that places free quality public sanitation access and treatment at the heart of urban thinking and government, with budgetary commitments adequate not just to toilet provision but to maintenance and to waste removal and treatment.

A commitment to the right to citylife demands a networked view of sanitation. In practice, this means that the roving telescope sometimes must roam across the network, investigating downstream impacts and conditions or as new concerns emerge. Cities, after all, do not stand still, and the urbanisation of sanitation is a dynamic, growing world. Given that sanitation spills over into all kinds of different domains, from work and school to subsidies for utilities or the emergence of novel viruses on urban peripheries, cities need to learn a range of what we might think of as *sanitation literacies*.

Take the microbial domain. As I argued in Chapter 4, urbanisation transforms microbial and animal worlds over time in ways that leave some people and places more vulnerable than others. The telescope has to be continually zooming in and out in and beyond the city, from peri-urban agriculture to at-risk overcrowded homes or areas where animal husbandry needs greater attention and investment. Another example is a politics of restoring the body as both a material and a cultural politics.

Bodies that are breastfeeding, menstruating, ageing, disabled in different ways, ill, or differently sized mean that we have been, or perhaps more accurately ought to have been, collectively 'learning' the body and its sanitation needs again and again, from city to city, and building a politics from there.

Restoration and care are keywords for a new urban sanitation imagination. And as I argued in Chapter 3, these terms apply not just to bodies but to things, to the material substrate without which sanitation cannot exist and function. The new urban imagination that I am pointing to here needs to think through the politics of the fragmented pipe, drain, tank, and sewer *together*, and here the guiding principles ought to be predictability, capacity, and connection. Whatever system is used, residents must be able to predict it will work over the long run, rather than be forced into ongoing maintenance or risky and laborious improvisations. This means, too, working with the city as we find it rather than as we might wish it to be, steering coordination and integration by dealing head on with the disordered, volatile, provisional, contradictory, and unruly nature of urban governing, politics, and space.

The right to citylife is, inevitably, an expanding horizon. At a minimum, we can work towards the top-level categorisation of service levels in the WHO-UNICEF Joint Monitoring Programme – 'safely managed, improved facilities' – which is sanitation where wastes are safely disposed in situ or transported and treated off-site. An important aim, but as I have been arguing, affirmative sanitation that promotes the right to citylife is much more than this. There needs to be a committed citywide vision with political and budgetary support; frameworks for clear and genuine participation of residents in planning; universalism of provisions for all residents regardless of status, location, housing type, or background; and a spatial agenda that extends sanitation in all domains across the city as a whole – in and around the home and neighbourhood, in public places and transit stations, in workplaces, prisons, schools, colleges and universities, and so on.

The right to citylife ought to be a rallying cry of anyone anywhere who cares about cities, urban poverty, and the scandal of vast inequalities. The human, economic, and ecological costs of not acting are nothing short of catastrophic. The rewards of meaningfully addressing this crisis, though, are incalculable, measured not only in toilets and pipes, or in budgets for sewers and the spreadsheets of utilities, but in lives not only protected from death, illness, injury, and attack but *more fully lived*, in cities more abundantly inhabited, and in aspirations that have the chance to be realised.

Acknowledgements

First, a big thank you to those with whom I have discussed the book or themes within it over the years: Steve Graham, Vanesa Castan Broto, Emma Ormerod, Hanna Ruszczyk, Vicky Habermehl, Jon Silver, Simon Marvin, Alex Vasudevan, Stephen Legg, Ben Anderson, Jen Bagelman, Noam Leshem, Léonie Newhouse, Gavin Bridge, Mike Crang, Rachel Colls, Jonny Darling, Marijn Nieuwenhuis, Jeremy Schmidt, Helen Wilson, Harriet Bulkeley, Louise Amoore, Ritwika Basu, Sally Cawood, Kristian Saguin, David Satterthwaite, Mary Lawhon, Ash Amin, AbdouMaliq Simone, and Michele Lancione.

Second, I am grateful to Leo Hollis at Verso for his encouragement, patience, and wisdom throughout this process. Thanks, too, to the larger team at Verso for their support, particularly to Michal Schatz, who commented on a draft.

Third, I want to acknowledge the following funded research projects, all of which widened and deepened my understanding of urban sanitation: the Economic and Social Research Council (RES-062-23-1669) 'Everyday Sanitation' project, a Leverhulme Trust prize (PLP-2013-290), the 'Knowledge in Action for Urban Equality' Global Challenges Research Fund project (ES/PO11225/1), and the European Research Council 'DenCity' project (773209).

Across those projects, my particular thanks for their respective collaborations and inspirations to Renu Desai, Vicky Habermehl, Steve Graham, Jon Silver, Chris Yap, Ankit Kumar,

Tim Ndezi, Vanesa Castan Broto, Hung-Ying Chen, Romit Chowdhury, Priyam Tripathy, Caren Levy, Adriana Allen, Alex Frediani, Camila Cociña, Allan Lavell, Belen Desmaison, Colin Marx, Saffron Woodcraft, David Heymann, Emmanuel Osuteye, Shriya Anand, Neha Sami, Aromar Revi, Michele Acuto, Stephanie Butcher, Jorge Pna, Cassidy Johnson, Jane Rendell, Yael Padan, and Catalina Ortiz. Thank you, too, to all my colleagues at Durham Geography, and to the students who helped me see the sanitation question anew.

Fourth, I have aimed to keep discussion of already published work to a minimum and to where it exemplifies a key point, where I have drawn on small sections of published academic papers. I acknowledge the following papers and thank the reviewers, editors, and especially my collaborators: Colin McFarlane, 'Repopulating Density: COVID-19 and the Politics of Urban Value' *Urban Studies*, June 2021; Colin McFarlane, 'The Urbanization of the Sanitation Crisis: Placing Waste in the City', *Development and Change* 50, 2019, 239–62; Colin McFarlane and Jon Silver, 'The Poolitical City: "Seeing Sanitation" and Making the Urban Political in Cape Town', *Antipode* 49: 1, 2012, 125–48; Colin McFarlane, Renu Desai, and Steve Graham, 'Informal Urban Sanitation: Everyday Life, Poverty and Comparison', *Annals of the Association of American Geographers*, 104, 2014, 989–1011; and Colin McFarlane, 'The Entrepreneurial Slum: Civil Society, Mobility, and the Co-production of Urban Development', *Urban Studies* 49, 2012, 2926–47.

I've had to fit this book around other commitments, which has both delayed it but also made me all the more convinced of how important the issues it examines are to me. Rachael, Keir, and Arran have had to hear about it all for too long. They have, nonetheless, always been interested, supportive, and hugely encouraging. I hope they know how much that means to me.

Just as I was finishing the book, my dear friend and colleague Gordon MacLeod passed away. Gordon was brilliant, full of warmth and light. People loved being around him. He was an excellent urbanist, too – encyclopaedic, generous, supportive, and always interested in people and ideas. I don't know what he would have thought about this book, but I hope he would have appreciated it.

Notes

1. The Right to Citylife

1. S. Koppikar, 'Death-Trap Toilets: The Hidden Dangers of Mumbai's Poorest Slums', *Guardian*, 27 February 2017.
2. This has included research funded by the Economic and Social Research Council (RES-062-23-1669), the Leverhulme Trust (PLP-2013-290), the Global Challenges Research Fund (ES/PO11225/1), and the European Research Council (773209). I have been hugely fortunate to work with some fantastic colleagues in those projects on urban sanitation, particularly Renu Desai, Steve Graham, Jon Silver, Chris Yap, and Vicky Habermehl.
3. M. Davis, 'Planet of Slums', *New Left Review*, 26, 2004; M. Davis, *Planet of Slums*, London: Verso, 2006; UN–Habitat, *The Challenge of Slums: Global Report on Human Settlements*, 2003.
4. T. P. Caldeira, 'Peripheral Urbanization: Autoconstruction, Transversal Logics, and Politics in Cities of the Global South', *Environment and Planning D: Society and Space*, 35: 1, 2016, 3–20; James Holston, *Insurgent Citizenship*, Princeton, NJ: Princeton University Press, 2008; A. Vasudevan, *The Autonomous City: A History of Squatting*, London: Verso, 2017.
5. UN-Habitat, *Water and Sanitation in the World's Cities: Local Action for Global Goals*. Earthscan: London, 2003.
6. These books have cut across mainstream and critical urban thinking. In addition to Davis's largely Marxist-inspired polemic on growing inequalities, there has been a host of others on deepening urbanisation

and the challenges and possibilities of the city today, some of which have sold very well and influenced policy and practitioner debates. These come from a variety of perspectives and authors, but the larger point here is that there has been a growing focus on the city as a whole, including its social, economic, environmental, and political dimensions, over the past two decades. Geographer Brendan Gleeson has neatly called this the new 'urbanology' (see B. Gleeson, 'The Urban Age: Paradox and Prospect', *Urban Studies*, 49: 5, 2012, 1– 13; B. Gleeson, 'What Role for Social Science in the "Urban Age"?', *International Journal of Urban and Regional Research*, 37: 5, 2013, 1839–51). Some examples: journalist Suketu Mehta's *Maximum City*, London: Penguin, 2004; urban development practitioner Jeb Brugmann's *Welcome to the Urban Revolution*, New York: Bloomsbury, 2009; architect Jan Gehl's *Cities for People*, Washington, DC: Island Press, 2010; pro-market economist Ed Glaeser's *Triumph of the City*, London: Macmillan, 2011; journalist Doug Sanders's *Arrival City: How the Largest Migration in History Is Reshaping Our World*, Windmill Books, 2011; journalist Katherine Boo's *Behind the Beautiful Forevers*, London: Portobello Books, 2012; journalist Charles Montgomery's *Happy City*, New York: Farrar, Straus and Giroux, 2015; urban economist Richard Florida's *The New Urban Crisis*, New York: Basic Books, 2017; and former New York officials Janette Sadik-Khan and Seth Solomonow's *Street Fight*, New York: Penguin, 2017. Also important have been a range of popular films on cities and inequality, such as Fernando Meirelles's *City of God* (Miramax, 2002) and Danny Boyle's *Slumdog Millionaire* (Celador, 2008), which accompanied a growth in 'slum tourism' as organised tours brought tourists to witness poverty up close, claiming it was in the name of education rather than money, as well as art and photography on 'slum' living.

7. A. Mayne, *Slums: The History of a Global Injustice*, London: Reaktion Books, 2017.

8. World Health Organization, 'Sanitation: Key Facts', who.int, 21 March 2022; G. Butler et al., *The Impact of COVID-19 on the Water and Sanitation Sector*, International Finance Corporation, 2020; GBD, 'Estimates of the Global Regional, and National Morbidity,

Mortality, and Aetiologies of Diarrhoea in 195 Countries: A Systematic Analysis of the Global Burden of Disease Study 2016', *Lancet Infectious Diseases*, 18, 2018: 1211–18; F. Mills et al., 'Costs, Climate and Contamination: Three Drivers for Citywide Sanitation Investment Decisions', *Frontiers in Environment Science*, 8, 2020, 130; K. Mugo, S. Metcalfe, and J. Du, 'Urban Sanitation Is a Climate and Economic Issue Too', *PreventionWeb*, 19 November 2020.

9. J. Corburn and L. Riley, eds., *Slum Health: From the Cell to the Street*, Berkeley: University of California Press, 2016; K. A. Dearden et al., 'Children with Access to Improved Sanitation but Not Improved Water are at Lower Risk of Stunting Compared to Children without Access: A Cohort Study in Ethiopia, India, Peru, and Vietnam', *BMC Public Health* 17: 1, 2017, 1–19.

10. G. Öberg et al., 'Conventional Sewer Systems Are Too Time-Consuming, Costly and Inflexible to Meet the Challenges of the 21st Century', *Sustainability*, 12, 1–17.

11. World Resources Institute, 'Safe, Affordable Sanitation: A Pipe Dream for Too Many Households in the Global South', press release, 18 December 2019, wri.org.

12. M. Teshome et al., 'Sub-Saharan Africans Spend 60 Hours a Year Finding a Private Place to Defecate', *Down to Earth*, 28 August 2018.

13. Institute for Sustainable Development and International Relations, *Sanitation in Developing Cities: An Imperative for Sustainable Urban Development*, 2018; D. Satterthwaite et al., *Untreated and Unsafe: Solving the Urban Sanitation Crisis in the Global South*, Washington, DC: World Resources Institute, 2019.

14. G. Hutton and M. Varughese, 'The Costs of Meeting the 2030 Sustainable Development Goals Targets on Drinking Water, Sanitation, and Hygiene', Water and Sanitation Program: Technical Paper, Washington, DC: World Bank.

15. Teshome et al., 'Sub-Saharan Africans'; UNICEF and WHO, *Progress on Household Drinking Water, Sanitation and Hygiene 2000–2017*, New York: United Nations, 2019, 7; Butler et al., *The Impact of COVID-19 on the Water and Sanitation Sector*.

16. C. Chesler, 'How Philadelphia Will Solve the Sewage Nightmare under Its Feet', *Popular Mechanics*, 3 December 2015.

17. JMP, 'Open Defecation', WHO-UNICEF Joint Management Group, washdata.org; JMP, 'Progress on WASH in Health Care Facilities 2000–2021: Special Focus on WASH and Infection Prevention and Control', WHO-UNICEF Joint Management Group, 2022.

18. S. Lwasa and K. Owens, *Kampala: Rebuilding Public Sector Legitimacy with a New Approach to Sanitation Services*, World Resources Report Case Study, Washington, DC: World Resources Institute, 2018, wri.org.

19. C. Sutherland et al., 'Water and Sanitation Delivery in eThekwini Municipality: A Spatially Differentiated Approach', *Environment and Urbanisation*, 26: 2, 2014, 469–88; G. Espelund, 'eThekwinin waterless toilets', *Waterfront*, 2018, 3–4.

20. S. M. Balloch, ' "Where Should We Go?": Thousands Left Homeless as Karachi Clears Waterways', *Guardian*, 16 June 2021.

21. J. Doherty, *Waste Worlds: Inhabiting Kampala's Infrastructures of Disposability*, Oakland: University of California Press, 2022.

22. M. Ranganathan, 'Thinking with Flint: Racial Liberalism and the Roots of an American Water Tragedy', *Capitalism Nature Socialism*, 27: 3, 2016, 17–33.

23. WHO-UNICEF, *Progress on Drinking Water, Sanitation and Hygiene, 2017: Update and SDG Baselines*, Geneva: WHO and UNICEF, 2017.

24. JMP, 'Open Defecation', 16; Satterthwaite et al., *Untreated and Unsafe*, 5; R. Baum, J. Luh, and J. Bartram, 'Sanitation: A Global Estimate of Sewerage Connections without Treatment and the Resulting Impact on MDG Progress', *Environmental Science and Technology*, 47:4, 2013, 1994–2000.

25. Satterthwaite et al., *Untreated and Unsafe*.

26. Teshome et al., 'Sub-Saharan Africans'; J. Skinner and A. Walnycki, 'Dar es Salaam's Water Supplies Need Stronger, More Flexible Management to Meet SDG6', International Institute for Environment and Development, 2016.

27. WHO-UNICEF, *Progress on Drinking Water, Sanitation and Hygiene, 2017*; Satterthwaite et al., *Untreated and Unsafe*.

28. World Bank, *Reversals of Fortunes: Poverty and Shared Prosperity, 2020*, Washington, DC: World Bank, 2020; F. Alvaredo et al., *World Inequality Report, 2018*, Cambridge: Harvard University Press, 2018;

J. Nijman and Y. D. Wei, 'Urban Inequalities in the 21st Century Economy', *Applied Geography*, 117, 2020; United Nations Development Programme, *Human Development Report: The Next Frontier – Human Development and the Anthropocene*, New York: United Nations, 2020; C. McFarlane, *Fragments of the City: Making and Remaking Urban Worlds*, Los Angeles: University of California Press, 2021.

29. T. Vieira, 'Inequality . . . in a Photograph', *Guardian*, 29 November 2017; R. Burdett, 'Counterpoint: Designing Inequality?', *Architectural Design*, 86: 3, 2016, 136–41; A. Merrifield, *The New Urban Question*, Pluto Press: London, 2014; Mayne, *Slums*; Stephen Graham, *Vertical: The City from Satellites to Bunkers*, London: Verso Books, 2016.

30. H. Lefebvre, E. Kofman, and E. Lebas (eds.), *Writings on Cities*, Oxford: Blackwell, 1996; H. Lefebvre, *The Urban Revolution*, Minneapolis: University of Minnesota Press, 2003 [1970]; M. Purcell, 'Excavating Lefebvre: The Right to the City and Its Urban Politics of the Inhabitant', *GeoJournal* 58: 2, 2002, 99–108; A. Merrifield, *Metromarxism: A Marxist Tale of the City*, London: Routledge, 2002.

31. D. Harvey, *Social Justice in the City*, Baltimore: John Hopkins University Press, 1973; L. Hollis, *Cities Are Good For You: The Genius of the Metropolis*, London: Bloomsbury, 2014; M. Gandy, 'Planning, Anti-planning and the Infrastructure Crisis Facing Metropolitan Lagos', *Urban Studies*, 43: 2, 2006, 371–96; D. Harvey, *Rebel Cities: From the Right to the City to the Urban Revolution*, London: Verso, 2012.

32. UN-Habitat and CAF (Development Bank of Latin America), *Construction of More Equitable Cities: Public Policies for Inclusion in Latin America*, Nairobi: UN Habitat, 2004.

33. K. Maharaj, 'Bombay High Court Makes Right to Clean Toilets a Fundamental Right for Women in India', Oxford Human Rights Hub, 8 February 2016; R. Pinto, 'Right to Pee Activists Return Award as Toilets Still Unclean', *Times of India*, 9 March 2016.

34. S. Faleiro, 'For Some Voters in Mumbai, This Election's All about Toilets', *Quartz*, 1, 2014; S. Patel, 'Upgrade, Rehouse or Resettle? An Assessment of the Indian Government's Basic Services for the Urban

Poor (BSUP) Programme', *Environment and Urbanization*, 25: 1, 2013, 177–88.

35. Faleiro, 'For Some Voters in Mumbai'; C. Greed, 'Join the Queue: Including Women's Toilet Needs in Public Space', *Sociological Review*, 67: 4, 2019, 908–26.

36. M. Ranganathan, and C. Balazs, 'Water Marginalization at the Urban Fringe: Environmental Justice and Urban Political Ecology across the North-South Divide', *Urban Geography*, 36: 3, 2015, 403–23; P. Chatterjee, *The Politics of the Governed: Reflections on Popular Politics in Most of the World*, New Delhi: Permanent Black, 2004.

37. Equality is distinguished from equity in that while the former typically refers to ensuring that the same resources or opportunities are shared (e.g., everyone in the city gets the same provision of education), the latter is more explicitly focused on ensuring different people have what they need in order to survive and thrive (e.g., some neigh-bourhoods or groups may receive additional educational support so that they have similar opportunities to others). In other words, equity is usually understood as a mechanism of fairness that will lead to equality. Rights, in contrast, tend to focus less on resource alloca-tion – even though it is an inevitable corollary of a rights-based approach – and more on ensuring access to resources.

38. G. Walker and H. Bulkeley, 'Geographies of Environmental Justice', *Geoforum*, 37, 2006, 655–59; Ranganathan, 'Thinking with Flint'; Ranganathan and Balazs, 'Water Marginalization at the Urban Fringe'.

39. Walker and Bulkeley, 'Geographies of Environmental Justice'.

40. S. Chaplin, *The Politics of Sanitation in India: Cities, Services and the State*, Hyderabad: Orient BlackSwan, 2018.

41. N. Fraser, 'Recognition without Ethics?', *Theory, Culture and Society*, 18: 2–3, 2001, 21–42; S. Fainstein, *The Just City*, Ithaca: Cornell University Press, 2010; M. Davidson and K. Iveson, 'Recovering the Politics of the City: From the "Post-political City" to a "Method of Equality" for Critical Urban Geography', *Progress in Human Geography*, 39: 5, 2015, 543–59; G. Williams and E. Mawdsley, 'Postcolonial Environmental Justice: Government and Governance in India', *Geoforum*, 37, 2006, 660–70.

42. E. Soja, *Seeking Spatial Justice*, Minneapolis: University of Minnesota Press, 2010.

43. H. Molotch, 'On Not Making History: What NYU Did with the Toilet and What It Means for the World', in *Toilet: Public Restrooms and the Politics of Sharing*, ed. H. Molotch and L. Noren, New York: New York University Press, 2010, 255–72; Greed, 'Join the Queue'; S. Jewitt, 'Geographies of Shit: Spatial and Temporal Variations in Attitudes towards Human Waste', *Progress in Human Geography*, 35: 5, 2011, 608–26; C. McFarlane, R. Desai, and S. Graham, 'Informal Urban Sanitation: Everyday Life, Poverty, and Comparison, *Annals of the Association of American Geographers*, 104: 5, 2014, 989–1011; M. W. Swanson, 'The Sanitation Syndrome: Bubonic Plague and Urban Native Policy in the Cape Colony, 1900–1909', *Journal of African History*, 1977, 387–410; D. Mara, 'Sanitation: What's the Real Problem?', *IDS Bulletin*, 43: 2, 2012, 86–92; L. Fewtrell et al., 'Water, Sanitation, and Hygiene Interventions to Reduce Diarrhoea in Less Developed Countries: A Systematic Review and Meta-analysis', *Lancet Infectious Diseases*, 5: 1, 2005, 42–52; D. Satterthwaite, G. McGranahan, and D. Mitlin, *Community-Driven Development for Water and Sanitation in Urban Areas: Its Contribution to Meeting the Millennium Development Goal Targets*, Geneva: Water Supply and Sanitation Collaborative Council (WSSCC), 2005; D. Satterthwaite, D. Mitlin, and S. Bartlett, 'Editorial: Is It Possible to Reach Low-Income Urban Dwellers with Good-Quality Sanitation?', *Environment and Urbanization*, 27: 1, 2015, 3–18.

2. People

1. World Bank, *The Mumbai Slum Sanitation Programme: Partnering with Slum Communities for Sustainable Sanitation in a Megalopolis*, Water and Sanitation Programme, World Bank and Cities Alliance, 2006.

2. World Bank, *The Mumbai Slum Sanitation Programme*.

3. S. Patel and SPARC, 'The 20-Year Slum Sanitation Partnership of Mumbai and the Indian Alliance', *Environment and Urbanization*, 27: 1, 2015, 55–72.

4. P. Khanolkar, 'Mehmoodbhai: Toilet Operator', in *Bombay Brokers*, ed. L. Björkman, Durham, NC: Duke University Press, 2021; R. N. Sharma and A. Bhide, 'World Bank Funded Slum Sanitation Programme in Mumbai: Participatory Approach and Lessons Learnt', *Economic and Political Weekly*, 40: 17, 2005, 1785; C. McFarlane, 'Sanitation in Mumbai's Informal Settlements: State, "Slum" and Infrastructure', *Environment and Planning A*, 40, 2008, 88–107.

5. C. McFarlane, R. Desai, and S. Graham, 'Informal Urban Sanitation: Everyday Life, Poverty, and Comparison, *Annals of the Association of American Geographers*, 104: 5, 2014, 989–1011.

6. Age UK London, *London Loos: Public Toilets in London: The Views of Older Londoners*, September 2022, ageuk.org.uk.

7. K. K. Baker et al., 'Impact of Social Capital, Harassment of Women and Girls, and Water and Sanitation Access on Premature Birth and Low Infant Birth Weight in India', *PLoS ONE*, 13: 10, 2018, e0205345.

8. S. Kulkarni, K. O'Reilly, and S. Bhat, 'No Relief: Lived Experiences of Inadequate Sanitation Access of Poor Urban Women in India', *Gender and Development*, 25: 2, 2017, 167–83.

9. M. H. Zérah, 'Splintering Urbanism in Mumbai: Contrasting Trends in a Multilayered Society', *Geoforum*, 39: 6, 2008, 1922–32.

10. I. Chatterjee, 'How Mumbai's Poorest Neighbourhood Is Battling to Keep Coronavirus at Bay', *Conversation*, 20 May 2020; D. Mili, 'Migration and Healthcare: Access to Healthcare Services by Migrants Settled in Shivaji Nagar Slum of Mumbai, India', *Health* 2: 3, 2011, 82–5; C. Vaidya and S. Srivastva, *Mumbai Human Development Report 2009*, New Delhi: Oxford University Press, 2010.

11. V. Gidwani and R.N. Reddy, 'The Afterlives of "Waste": Notes from India for a Minor History of Capitalist Surplus', *Antipode*, 43, 5, 2011, 1625–58; L. Weinstein, 'Mumbai's Development Mafias: Globalization, Organized Crime and Land Development', *International Journal of Urban and Regional Research*, 32: 1, 2008, 22–39.

12. A. Ademas et al., 'Does Menstrual Hygiene Management and Water, Sanitation, and Hygiene Predict Reproductive Tract Infections among Reproductive Women in Urban Areas in Ethiopia?', *PLoS ONE*, 15: 8, 2020, e0237696; N. Moffat and L. Pickering, ' "Out of Order": The Double Burden of Menstrual Etiquette and the Subtle Exclusion of

Women from Public Space in Scotland', *Sociological Review*, 67: 4, 2019, 766–87; A. Burrows and S. Johnson, 'Girls' Experiences of Menarche and Menstruation', *Journal of Reproductive and Infant Psychology*, 23, 2005, 235–49; C. Quint, 'From Embodied Shame to Reclaiming the Stain: Reflections on a Career in Menstrual Activism', *Sociological Review*, 67: 4, 2019, 927–42.

13. A. Bhakta, B. Reed, and J. Fisher, 'Behind Closed Doors: The Hidden Needs of Perimenopausal Women in Ghana, in *Reproductive Geographies*, ed. M. Fannin, H. Hazen, and M. R. England, London: Routledge, 2018, 67–88; Kulkarni, O'Reilly, and Bhat, 'No Relief'; N. Iqbal, 'Why I Resent the Politics of Periods', *Guardian*, 29 November 2020, 49.

14. E. Grosz, *Volatile Bodies: Toward a Corporeal Feminism*, London: Routledge, 2020; I. M. Young, *On Female Body Experience: 'Throwing Like a Girl' and Other Essays*, Oxford: Oxford University Press, 2005; R. Longhurst, *Bodies: Exploring Fluid Boundaries*. London: Routledge, 2001.

15. C. Greed, 'Join the Queue: Including Women's Toilet Needs in Public Space', *Sociological Review*, 67: 4, 2019, 908–26.

16. L. Lowe, *No Place to Go: How Public Toilets Fail Our Private Needs*, Toronto: Coach House Books, 2018.

17. T. Soundararajan, 'India's Caste Culture Is a Rape Culture', *Daily Beast*, 6 September 2021; S. Phadke, S. Khan, and S. Ranade, *Why Loiter? Women and Risk on Mumbai Streets*, New Delhi: Penguin Books India, 2011, 82; D. Joshi, B. Fawcett, and F. Mannan, 'Health, Hygiene and Appropriate Sanitation: Experiences and Perceptions of the Urban Poor', *Environment and Urbanization*, 23: 1, 2011, 91–111; T. Rheinländer et al., 'Hygiene and Sanitation among Ethnic Minorities in Northern Vietnam: Does Government Promotion Match Community Priorities?', *Social Science and Medicine*, 71: 5, 2011, 994–1001.

18. Greed, 'Join the Queue'; S. R. Parkar, J. Fernandes, and M. G. Weiss, 'Contextualizing Mental Health: Gendered Experiences in a Mumbai Slum', *Anthropology and Medicine*, 10: 3, 2003, 291–308.

19. K. O'Reilly, 'From Toilet Insecurity to Toilet Security: Creating Safe Sanitation for Women and Girls', *WIREs Water*, 3: 1, 2016, 19–24, 22.

20. Y. Truelove and K. O'Reilly, 'Making India's Cleanest City: Sanitation, Intersectionality, and Infrastructural Violence', *Environment and Planning E: Nature and Space*, 4: 3, September 2021.

21. Water Aid, 'Celebrating 10 Years of Water and Sanitation as a Human Right, with Photographers from Around the World', wateraid.org.

22. K. Kar, 'Why Not Basics for All? Scopes and Challenges for Community-Led Total Sanitation', *IDS Bulletin*, 43: 2, 2012, 93–6; R. George, *The Big Necessity: Adventures in the World of Human Waste*, London: Portobello Books, 2008; World Health Organization, 'Sanitation: Key Facts', who.int, 21 March 2022; H. Molotch, 'Introduction: Learning from the Loo', in *Toilet: Public Restrooms and the Politics of Sharing*, ed. H. Molotch and L. Noren, New York: New York University Press, 2010, 1–20; A. Fantz, 'Lack of Soap Means Illness, Death for Millions of Children', *CNN Health*, 15 November 2011; R. F. Breiman et al., 'Population-Based Incidence of Typhoid Fever in an Urban Informal Settlement and a Rural Area in Kenya: Implications for Typhoid Vaccine Use in Africa', *PLoS One*, 7: 1, 2012.

23. S. Bartlett, 'Water, Sanitation and Urban Children: The Need to Go Beyond "Improved" Provision', *Children, Youth and Environments*, 15: 1, 2005, 115–37.

24. P. Tiwari, *Toilet Torture in Mumbai's Slums*, Mumbai: Observer Research Foundation Mumbai, 2015.

25. World Health Organization, 'Sanitation'.

26. UNICEF-WHO, *Progress on Drinking Water, Sanitation and Hygiene in Schools: Special Focus on COVID-19*, New York: UNICEF, 2020, 8; UNICEF, *Three Stories about How Clean Water Saves Kids' Lives*, 2018, unicefusa.org; JMP, 'Open Defecation', WHO-UNICEF Joint Management Group, washdata.org.

27. UNICEF-WHO, *Progress on Drinking Water*, 58; Molotch, 'Introduction: Learning from the Loo'.

28. UNICEF-WHO, *Progress on Drinking Water*.

29. UNICEF, *Three Stories*; G. McGranahan, 'Realizing the Right to Sanitation in Deprived Urban Communities: Meeting the Challenges of Collective Action, Coproduction, Affordability, and Housing Tenure', *World Development*, 68, 2015, 242–53.

30. C. Mitchell et al., ' "Why We Don't Go to School on Fridays": On Youth Participation through Photo Voice in Rural Kwazulu-Natal', *McGill Journal of Education*, 41: 3, 2006, 282.

31. Mitchell et al., ' "Why We Don't Go to School on Fridays" ', 279.

32. A. Thomas and A. Alvestegui, *Sanitation in Small Towns: Experience from Mozambique*, WASH Field Note, April 2015, UNICEF, 2015; C. B. Olayiwole, Mrs. Ezirim, and G. C. Okoro, 'Children as Agents of Sanitation and Hygiene Behaviour Change', paper presented at the 29th WEDC International Conference, Abuja, Nigeria, 22–26 September 2003; Fantz, 'Lack of Soap Means Illness'; UNICEF, *Three Stories*.

33. J. Knee et al., 'Effects of an Urban Sanitation Intervention on Childhood Enteric Infection and Diarrhea in Maputo, Mozambique: A Controlled Before-and-After Trial', eLife, 9 April 2021, elifesciences.org.

34. Knee et al., 'Effects of an Urban Sanitation Intervention', 16.

35. P. Akhilesh, 'Failing the Sanitation Worker Again', *Indian Express*, 21 September 2020; S. Cawood and A. Bhakta, 'Man or Machine? Eliminating Manual Scavenging in India and Bangladesh', *FemLab* (blog), 19 March 2021, femlab.co.

36. B. Wilson, 'Safai Karmachari Andolan: An Insider's Account (Conversation with Bezwada Wilson)', in *The Right to Sanitation in India: Critical Perspectives*, ed. P. Cullet, S. Koonan, and L. Bhullar, New Delhi: Oxford University Press, 2019, 288–90.

37. S. Khanna, 'Invisible Inequalities: An Analysis of the Safai Karmachari Andolan Case', in Cullet, Koonan, and Bhullar, *The Right to Sanitation in India*, 306.

38. Wilson, 'Safai Karmachari Andolan', 295.

39. Akhilesh, 'Failing the Sanitation Worker Again'.

40. Akhilesh, 'Failing the Sanitation Worker Again'.

41. Akhilesh, 'Failing the Sanitation Worker Again'.

42. D. Satterthwaite et al., *Untreated and Unsafe: Solving the Urban Sanitation Crisis in the Global South*, Washington, DC: World Resources Institute, 2019; M. Zaqout et al., 'Sustainable Sanitation Jobs: Prospects for Enhancing the Livelihoods of Pit-Emptiers in Bangladesh', *Third World Quarterly*, 42: 2, 2020, 329–47.

43. V. Gidwani, 'The Work of Waste: Inside India's Infra-economy,' *Transactions*, 40: 4, 2015, 575–95.

44. World Bank, *Health, Safety and Dignity of Sanitation Workers: An Initial Assessment*, Washington, DC: World Bank Group, 2019, 81; Water Aid, *Risk and Vulnerability of Sanitation and Waste Workers during COVID-19 Pandemic in Five Major Cities of Bangladesh*, June 2020, wateraid.org.

45. Water Aid, *Safety and Wellbeing of Sanitation Workers during COVID-19 in South Asia: A Rapid Assessment from Bangladesh, India, Pakistan and Nepal in Lockdown*, 2020, wateraid.org; Water Aid, *Risk and Vulnerability of Sanitation and Waste Workers*.

46. K. Allen, '5 Myths about Refugees and WASH', Sanitation and Water for All, 4 February 2020, sanitationandwaterforall.org; N. Behnke et al., 'Improving Environmental Conditions for Involuntarily Displaced Populations: Water, Sanitation, and Hygiene in Orphanages, Prisons, and Refugee and IDP Settlements', *Journal of Water Sanitation and Hygiene for Development*, 8: 4, 2018, 785–91; UNHCR, *Global Trends: Forced Displacement in 2018*, Geneva: United Nations High Commissioner for Refugees, 2019; B. Mosello et al., *Sanitation Under Stress: How Can Urban Services Respond to Acute Migration?*, London: Overseas Development Institute, 2016.

47. P. Connor, 'Nearly One in a Hundred Worldwide Are Now Displaced from Their Homes', Pew Research Centre, 3 August 2016, pew research.org; United Nations, *The Sustainable Development Goals Report 2016*, New York: United Nations, 2016; Allen, '5 Myths about Refugees and WASH'.

48. A. Betts, E. Easton-Calabria, and K. Pincock, 'Refugee-Led Responses in the Fight against COVID-19: Building Lasting Participatory Models', *Forced Migration Review*, 64, 2020, 73–6; World Health Organization, *Health of Refugees and Migrants: Practices in Addressing the Health Needs of Refugees and Migrants, WHO Region of the Americas, 2018*, June 2018; M. J. Toole and R. Bhatia, 'A Case Study of Somali Refugees in Hartisheik A Camp, Eastern Ethiopia: Health and Nutrition Profile, July 1988–June 1990', *Journal of Refugee Studies*, 5: 3–4, 1992, 313–26; C. Knowles, *Still Thinking: Refugees' Health and Healthcare in Nairobi*, British Academy, 2020, thebritishacademy.ac.uk.

49. Mosello et al., *Sanitation Under Stress*.

50. T. Barfield, 'Berlin Refugee Boss Resigns in Disgrace', *Local*, 10 December 2015.

51. M. Lancione, 'Assemblages of Care and the Analysis of Public Policies on Homelessness in Turin, Italy', *City*, 18, 2014, 25–40; M. Lancione, and C. McFarlane, 'Life at the Urban Margins: Sanitation Infra-making and the Potential of Experimental Comparison', *Environment and Planning A*, 48: 12, 2016, 2402–21.

52. J. Darling, *Systems of Suffering: Dispersal and the Denial of Asylum*, London: Pluto Press, 2022; C. McIlwaine et al., 'Feminised Urban Futures, Healthy Cities and Violence against Women and Girls: Transnational Reflections from Brazilians in London and Mare, Rio de Janeiro', in *Urban Transformations and Public Health in the Emergent City*, ed. M. Keith and A. de Sousa Silva, 55–78, Manchester: Manchester University Press, 2020.

53. Betts et al., 'Refugee-Led Responses in the Fight against COVID-19'.

54. UNHCR, *Global Strategy for Public Health: Public Health – HIV and Reproductive Health – Food Security and Nutrition – Water Sanitation and Hygiene (WASH): A UNHCR Strategy, 2014–2018*, Geneva: UNHCR, 2014.

55. J. S. Josset, 'Self-Help Project in Niger Churns Out Hygiene Products in Fight against Coronavirus', UNHCR, 18 May 2020, unhcr.org.

56. UNICEF and WHO, *Progress on Household Drinking Water, Sanitation and Hygiene 2000–2017*, New York: United Nations, 2019.

57. H. Northover, 'Beyond Political Will – How Leadershop Makes a Difference on Water and Sanitation', Oxfam blogs, 14 April 2021.

58. L. Björkman, *Pipe Politics, Contested Waters: Embedded Infra-structures of Millennial Mumbai*, Durham, NC: Duke University Press, 2015.

59. McFarlane, Desai, and Graham, 'Informal Urban Sanitation'; J. De Wit and E. Berner, 'Progressive Patronage? Municipalities, NGOs, CBOs and the Limits to Slum Dwellers' Empowerment', *Development and Change*, 40: 5, 2009, 927–47.

60. C. McFarlane and J. Silver, 'The Poolitical City: "Seeing Sanitation" and Making the Urban Political in Cape Town', *Antipode*, 49: 1, 2017, 125–14.

61. M. Morales, L. Harris, and G. Öberg, 'Citizenshit: The Right to Flush and the Urban Sanitation Imaginary', *Environment and Planning A*, 46, 2014, 2816–33.

62. S. Parnell and E. Pieterse, 'The "Right to the City": Institutional Imperatives of a Developmental State', *International Journal of Urban and Regional Research*, 34: 1, 2010, 146–62; I. Turok, 'Persistent Polarisation Post-apartheid? Progress towards Urban Integration in Cape Town', *Urban Studies*, 38: 13, 2001, 2349–77; M. Rubin, 'At the Borderlands of Informal Practices of the State: Negotiability, Porosity and Exceptionality', *Journal of Development Studies*, 54: 12, 2018, 2227–42.

63. T. M. Li, *The Will to Improve: Governmentality, Development, and the Practice of Politics*, Durham, NC: Duke University Press, 2007; Parnell and Pieterse, 'The "Right to the City"'.

64. L. Zárate, 'Pandemic Lessons, Progressive Politics: Right to the City and New Municipalism in Times of COVID-19', *Minim*, 19 May 2020; P. Vijayan, 'Challenges in the Midst of the COVID-19 Pandemic', *Economic and Political Weekly*, 55: 24, 13 June 2020.

65. George, *The Big Necessity*; R. Chambers and K. Kar, *Handbook on Community-Led Total Sanitation*, Brighton: Institute of Development Studies, 2008; B. Penner, *Bathroom*, London: Reaktion Books, 2013; S. Srivastava et al., 'Making "Shit" Everybody's Business: Co-Production in Urban Sanitation', IDS Policy Briefing 164, Brighton: Institute of Development Studies, 2019.

66. T. W. Abebe and G. T. Tucho, 'Open Defecation–Free Slippage and Its Associated Factors in Ethiopia: A Systematic Review', *Systematic Reviews*, 9, 2020, 252.

67. Oxford Poverty and Human Development Initiative, *Global Multidimensional Poverty Index 2020: Charting Pathways Out of Multidimensional Poverty – Achieving the SDGs*, 2020.

68. L. Mehta and M. Movik, *Shit Matters: The Potential of Community-Led Total Sanitation*, Rugby: Practical Action, 2012; Abebe and Tucho, 'Open Defecation–Free Slippage'.

69. Penner, *Bathroom*.

3. Things

1. P. Ackroyd, *London Under: The Secret History beneath the Streets*, London: Chatto and Windus, 2011, 78–80.

2. H. Brewis, 'Thames Is Filled with Millions of Tonnes of Sewage Each Year ... But Half of Londoners Still Think It's Safe to Swim In', *Evening Standard*, 5 August 2020.

3. C. Hentschel, 'Postcolonialising Berlin and the Fabrication of the Urban', *International Journal of Urban and Regional Research*, 2014, 79–91.

4. A. Simone, 'People as Infrastructure: Intersecting Fragments in Johannesburg', *Public Culture* 16: 3, 2004, 407–29; A. Simone, 'Ritornello: People as Infrastructure', *Urban Geography*, 42: 9, 2021, 1341–48.

5. A. Amin, 'Lively Infrastructure', *Theory, Culture and Society*, 31: 7-8, 2014, 137–61; B. Larkin, 'The Politics and Poetics of Infrastructure', *Annual Review of Anthropology*, 42, 2013, 327–43.

6. H. Lefebvre, *The Production of Space*, Oxford: Blackwell, 1991 [1974].

7. H. Molotch, 'Introduction: Learning from the Loo', in *Toilet: Public Restrooms and the Politics of Sharing*, ed. H. Molotch and L. Noren, New York: New York University Press, 2010, 1–20; B. Penner, *Bathroom*, London: Reaktion Books, 2013.

8. D. Inglis, 'Dirt and Denigration: The Faecal Imagery and Rhetorics of Abuse', *Postcolonial Studies: Culture, Politics, Economy*, 5: 2, 2002, 207–21.

9. P. Joyce, *The Rule of Freedom: Liberalism and the Modern City*, London: Verso, 2003; C. Otter, 'Cleansing and Clarifying: Technology and Perception in Nineteenth-Century London', *Journal of British Studies*, 43, 2004, 40–64; German Department for International Development, 'Access to Water and Sanitation in Sub-Saharan Africa', *Deutsche Gesellschaft für Internationale Zusammenarbeit (GIZ)*, 2019; A. Oberg, 'Problematizing Urban Shit(ting): Representing Human Waste as a Problem', *International Journal of Urban and Regional Research*, 43: 2, 2019, 377–92.

10. D. Satterthwaite et al., *Untreated and Unsafe: Solving the Urban Sanitation Crisis in the Global South*, Washington, DC: World Resources Institute, 2019, 39.

11. M. Black and B. Fawcett, *The Last Taboo: Opening the Door on the Global Sanitation Crisis*, London: Earthscan, 2008; R. Biswas, K. Arya, and S. Deshpande, 'More Toilet Infrastructures Do Not Nullify Open Defecation: A Perspective from Squatter Settlements in Megacity Mumbai', *Applied Water Science*, 10, 2020, 96.

12. S. Žižek, 'The Secret Clauses of the Liberal Utopia, *Law and Critique*, 19: 1, 2008, 1–18; Penner, *Bathroom*.

13. S. Phadke, S. Khan, and S. Ranade, *Why Loiter? Women and Risk on Mumbai Streets*, New Delhi: Penguin Books India, 2011, 82; S. Patel, 'Upgrade, Rehouse or Resettle? An Assessment of the Indian Government's Basic Services for the Urban Poor (BSUP) Programme', *Environment and Urbanization*, 25: 1, 2013, 177–88.

14. A. Keesey, 'Composting Loos Should Be the Answer to the World's Toilet Crisis', *Guardian*, 25 March 2019.

15. Penner, *Bathroom*.

16. Satterthwaite et al., *Untreated and Unsafe*; F. Mills et al., 'Costs, Climate and Contamination: Three Drivers for Citywide Sanitation Investment Decisions', *Frontiers in Environment Science*, 8, 2020, 130.

17. Penner, *Bathroom*.

18. M. Morales, L. Harris, and G. Öberg, 'Citizenshit: The Right to Flush and the Urban Sanitation Imaginary', *Environment and Planning A*, 46, 2014, 2816–33.

19. Keesey, 'Composting Loos Should Be the Answer'.

20. Keesey, 'Composting Loos Should Be the Answer'.

21. Morales et al., 'Citizenshit'.

22. M. K. Magistad, 'China's Failed Experiment with Dry Toilets', *World*, 31 May 2011; W. Shan, 'World's Biggest Eco-toilet Project Ends in Failure', *China Dialogue*, 30 July 2012.

23. I. Braverman, 'Potty Training: Nonhuman Inspection in Public Washrooms', in *Toilet: Public Restrooms and the Politics of Sharing*, ed. H. Molotch and L. Noren, New York: New York University Press, 2010, 65–86; D. Z. Bliss and Y. S. Park, 'Public Toilets in Parklands or Open Spaces in International Cities Using Geographic Information Systems', *International Urogynaecology Journal*, 31, 2020, 939–45.

24. E. Yuko, 'Where Did All the Public Bathrooms Go?', *Bloomberg*, 5 November 2021.

25. J. Steet-Porter, 'Access to a Toilet Is a Human Right – Closing Public Loos Is One Austerity Cut Too Many', *Independent*, 3 June 2016.

26. Satterthwaite et al., *Untreated and Unsafe*, 13.

27. D. Fenney, 'A Lav Affair: Do We Care Enough about Public Toilets?', *Kings Fund*, 26 April 2019; L. Jones and R. Schraer, 'Reality Check: Public Toilets Mapped', *BBC News*, 15 August 2018; L. O'Dwyer, 'Here's Why We Need to Talk about Public Toilets', *CityMetric*, 18 July 2016; C. P. Williamson, ' "Fountain", from Victorian Necessity to Modern Inconvenience: Contesting the Death of Public Toilets', *Urban Studies*, 59: 3, 2022, 641–62.

28. Age UK London, *London Loos: Public Toilets in London: The Views of Older Londoners*, September 2022, ageuk.org.uk; London Assembly Health Committee, *The Toilet Paper*, 2021.

29. Royal Society for Public Health, *Taking the Piss: The Decline of the Great British Public Toilet*, 2019, rsph.org.uk.

30. Williamson, ' "Fountain" '.

31. D. Dunnico, 'Inconvenienced: How Cuts Have Hit Public Toilets', *Red Pepper*, 1 June 2014.

32. Toilet Tales, *Around the Toilet*, aroundthetoilet.wordpress.com/toilet-tales.

33. L. Lowe, *No Place to Go: How Public Toilets Fail Our Private Needs*, Toronto: Coach House Books, 2018.

34. Toilet Tales, *Around the Toilet*.

35. P. Wiseman, 'Lifting the Lid: Disabled Toilets as Sites of Belonging and Embodied Citizenship', *Sociological Review*, 67: 4, 2019, 788–806.

36. A. Cooper et al., 'Rooms of Their Own: Public Toilets and Gendered Citizens in a New Zealand City, 1860–1940', *Gender, Place and Culture*, 7: 4, 2000, 417–33.

37. L. Pickering and P. Wiseman, 'Dirty Scholarship and Dirty Lives: Explorations in Bodies and Belonging', *Sociological Review*, 67, 4, 2019, 746–65; D. Inglis, *A Sociological History of Excretory Experience: Defecatory Manners and Toiletry Technologies*, Lewiston, NY: Edwin Mellen Press, 2001.

38. N. Robinson, 'Why Is San Francisco . . . Covered in Human Faeces?', *Guardian*, 18 April, 2018; S. Schuffman, 'How to Fix San Francisco's Poop Problem', *San Francisco Examiner*, 4 December 2019.

39. Lowe, *No Place to Go*.

40. C. Pablo, 'Potty Talk: Vancouver Eyes Portland Loo as Likely Model for Stand-Alone Washrooms in Parks', *Georgia Straight*, 27 October 2020.

41. C. Greed, 'Join the Queue: Including Women's Toilet Needs in Public Space', *Sociological Review*, 67: 4, 2019, 908–26.

42. L. Brooks, 'Closure of Public Toilets Causing Anxiety, Distress, and Frustration across UK', *Guardian*, 10 July 2020.

43. S. Chua, 'District of Squamish's Low-Rent Campground to Shut for the Winter', *Squamish Reporter*, 28 October 2020.

44. Chua, 'District of Squamish's Low-Rent Campground'.

45. N. Anselme, 'Closing the Municipal Campground Was Cruel and Shameful', *Squamish Reporter*, 12 November 2020.

46. J. Okely, *The Traveller-Gypsies*, Cambridge: Cambridge University Press, 1992.

47. C. Greed, 'Creating a Nonsexist Restroom', in Molotch and Noren, *Toilet*, 117–41; H. Molotch, 'On Not Making History: What NYU Did with the Toilet and What It Means for the World', in Molotch and Noren, *Toilet*, 255–72.

48. K. Otsuki, 'Infrastructure in Informal Settlements: Co-production of Public Services for Inclusive Governance', *Local Environment*, 21: 12, 2016, 1557–72.

49. P. Onyango and C. Rieck, *Public Toilet with Biogas Plant and Water Kiosk Naivasha, Kenya – Case Study of Sustainable Sanitation Projects*, Sustainable Sanitation Alliance (SuSanA), 2010; F. Orsini et al., 'Urban Agriculture in the Developing World: A Review', *Agronomy Sustainable Development*, 33, 2013, 695–720.

50. 'Urban Age Award in 2007', Alfred Herrhausen Gesellschaft, Deutsche Bank, 2007, ahg.db.com.

51. S. Mehta, 'Maximum Cities: Mumbai', in *Research and Responsibility: Reflections on Our Common Future*, ed. W. Krull, 149–66, Leipzig: Europaische Verlagsanstalt, 2011.

52. Y. J. Lee and T. Radcliff, 'Community Interactions and Sanitation Use by the Urban Poor: Survey Evidence from India's Slums', *Urban Studies*, 58: 4, 2021, 715–32; C. McFarlane, 'Rethinking Informality: Politics, Crisis, and the City', *Planning Theory and Practice*, 13: 1,

2012, 89–108; S. Patel and SPARC, 'The 20-Year Sanitation Partnership of Mumbai and the Indian Alliance', *Environment and Urbanization*, 27: 1, 2015, 55–72; R. Fredericks, *Garbage Citizenship: Vital Infrastructures of Labor in Dakar, Senegal*, Durham, NC: Duke University Press, 2018.

53. B. Khan, 'BMC Official Holds NGOs Responsible for Mankhurd Toilet Collapse', *DNA*, 2015.

54. S. Koppikar, 'Death-Trap Toilets: The Hidden Dangers of Mumbai's Poorest Slums', *Guardian*, 27 February 2017; R. Sagh, 'Two Killed as Bhandup Chawl's 40-Year-Old Toilet Block Collapses', *Hindu*, 28 April 2018; P. Kilonzo, 'Form Three Girl Dies after School Toilet Collapses on Her', *Star*, 21 October 2019.

55. P. Khanolkar, 'Mehmoodbhai: Toilet Operator', in *Bombay Brokers*, ed. L. Björkman, Durham, NC: Duke University Press, 2021.

56. M. Davis, *Planet of Slums*, London: Verso, 2006, 141.

57. N. Mkhize et al., 'Urine Diversion Dry Toilets in eThekwini Municipality, South Africa: Acceptance, Use and Maintenance through the Users' Eyes', *Journal of Water, Sanitation and Hygiene for Development*, 71: 1, 2017.

58. N. Majola, '"We Cannot Escape the Smell": Women Have to Clear Away Sewage before They Can Do Their Laundry', *GroundUp*, 15 April 2021; Connective Cities, 'e'Thekwini Communal Ablution Blocks for Informal Settlements', 12 December 2014, connective-cities.net.

59. A. R. George, 'On Babylonian Lavatories and Sewers', *Iraq*, 77: 75, 2015, 1–6.

60. UNICEF-WHO, *Progress on Drinking Water, Sanitation and Hygiene in Schools: Special Focus on COVID-19*, New York: UNICEF, 2020; D. Satterthwaite, A. Sverdlik, and D. Brown, 'Revealing and Responding to Multiple Health Risks in Informal Settlements in Sub-Saharan African Cities', *Journal of Urban Health*, 96: 1, 2019, 112–22.

61. A. Crawford, *The Development of New Bombay*, Bombay: Israelite Steam Press, 1908; R. Ramasubban and N. Cook, 'Spatial Patterns of Health and Mortality', in *Bombay: Metaphor for Modern India*, ed. S. Patel and A. Thorner, New Delhi: Oxford University Press, 1996, 43–169.

62. D. Waltner-Toews, *The Origin of Feces: What Excrement Tells Us about Evolution, Ecology, and a Sustainable Society*, Toronto: ECW Press, 2013.

63. G. Hawkins, 'Made to Be Wasted: PET and Topologies of Disposability', in *Accumulation: The Material Politics of Plastic*, ed. J. Gabrys, G. Hawkins, and M. Michael, New York: Routledge, 2013, 63–81.

64. G. Hawkins, *The Ethics of Waste: How We Relate to Rubbish*, London: Rowman and Littlefield, 2006.

65. L. Björkman, *Pipe Politics, Contested Waters: Embedded Infrastructures of Millennial Mumbai*, Durham, NC: Duke University Press, 2015.

66. N. Anand, 'Pressure: The PoliTechnics of Water Supply in Mumbai', *Cultural Anthropology*, 26: 4, 2011, 542–64; N. Anand, *Hydraulic City: Water and the Infrastructures of Citizenship in Mumbai*, Durham, NC: Duke University Press, 2017.

67. Black and Fawcett, *The Last Taboo*.

68. A. Hasan, 'Karachi, Informal Settlements and COVID-19', International Institute for Environment and Development blog, 6 May 2020, iied.org.

69. A. Hasan, 'The Changing Nature of the Informal Sector in Karachi as a Result of Global Restructuring and Liberalization', *Environment and Urbanization*, 14: 1, 2002, 69–78; P. Rahman, 'Exploring Urban Resilience: Violence and Infrastructure Provision in Karachi', master's thesis, Massachusetts Institute of Technology, 2012.

70. G. McGranahan and D. Mitlin, 'Learning from Sustained Success: How Community-Driven Initiatives to Improve Urban Sanitation Can Meet the Challenges', *World Development*, 87, 2016, 307–17.

71. Rahman, 'Exploring Urban Resilience'; A. Hasan, 'The Sanitation Program of the Orangi Pilot Project – Research and Training Institute, Karachi, Pakistan', in *Global Urban Poverty: Setting the Agenda*, ed. A. M. Garland, M. Massoumi, and B. A. Ruble, Washington, DC: Woodrow Wilson International Center for Scholars, 2007, 117–50.

72. Satterthwaite et al., *Untreated and Unsafe*.

73. K. Mugo, S. Metcalfe, and J. Du, 'Urban Sanitation Is a Climate and Economic Issue Too', *PreventionWeb*, 19 November 2020.

74. T. Ndezi, *Developing Pathways to Urban Sanitation Equality: A Case Study of the Simplified Sewerage Solution in Dar-Es-Salaam, Tanzania*, unpublished report, 2020.

75. C. Yap and C. McFarlane, 'Understanding and Researching Urban Extreme Poverty: A Conceptual-Methodological Approach', *Environment and Urbanization* 32: 1, 2020, 254–74; C. Yap et al., 'Sanitation Challenges in Dar es Salaam: The Potential of Simplified Sewerage Systems', *Environment and Urbanization*, 9 February 2022.

76. Satterthwaite et al., *Untreated and Unsafe*; J. C. Melo, *The Experience of Condominial Water and Sewerage System sin Brazil: Case Studies from Brasilia, Salvador and Parauapebas*, Washington, DC: World Bank, 2005; M. L. Barreto et al., 'Effect of City-wide Sanitation Programme on Reduction in Rate of Childhood Diarrhoea in Northeast Brazil: Assessment by Two Cohort Studies', *Lancet*, 370: 9599, 2007, 1622–28.

77. I. Acosta, 'Uruguay: "Dry Toilets" Provide Ecological Solution in Slums', Inter Press Service, 28 December 2009, ipsnews.net.

78. D. Satterthwaite, 'Understanding Asian Cities: A Synthesis of the Findings from Eight City Case studies', *Global Urban Development Magazine*, 4: 2, 2008, 1–24.

79. G. Öberg et al., 'Conventional Sewer Systems Are Too Time-Consuming, Costly and Inflexible to Meet the Challenges of the 21st Century', *Sustainability*, 12, 1–17.

80. Öberg et al., 'Conventional Sewer Systems'.

81. A. M. Sherpa et al., 'Vulnerability and Adaptability of Sanitation Systems to Climate Change', *Journal of Water and Climate Change*, 5: 4, 2014, 487–95.

82. L. Criqui, 'Sanitation in Developing Cities: An Imperative for Sustainable Urban Development', IDDRI blog, 20 July 2018, iddri.org.

83. Satterthwaite et al., *Untreated and Unsafe*.

84. D. Satterthwaite, 'Missing the Millennium Development Goal Targets for Water and Sanitation in Urban Areas', *Environment and Urbanization*, 28: 1, 2016, 99–118.

85. United Nations Development Programme (UNDP), *Human Development Report: The Next Frontier – Human Development and the*

Anthropocene, New York: United Nations, 2020; World Health Organization, 'Sanitation: Key Facts', who.int, 21 March 2022.

86. S. Stamatopoulou-Robbins, *Waste Siege: The Life of Infrastructure in Palestine*, Stanford, CA: Stanford University Press, 2020.

87. S. Efron et al., *The Public Health Impacts of Gaza's Water Crisis: Analysis and Policy Options*, RAND Corporation, 2018.

88. Stamatopoulou-Robbins, *Waste Siege*.

89. A. Abu Shawish and C. Wiebel, 'Gaza Children Face Acute Water and Sanitation Crisis', UNICEF, 1 September 2017, unicef.org.

90. Satterthwaite et al., *Untreated and Unsafe*.

91. J. Watts, 'Mexico City's Water Crisis – From Source to Sewer', *Guardian*, 12 November 2015.

92. S. Laville, 'Environment Agency Launches Major Investigation into Sewage', *Guardian*, 18 November 2021; S. Concoran, 'Feargal Sharkey Criticises "Hypocrisy" of Government over Sewage Vote', *Evening Standard*, 26 October 2021.

93. S. Cavill, K. Tayler, and A. Hueso, *Functionality of Wastewater Treatment Plants in Low- and Middle-Income Countries: Desk Review*, London: WaterAid, September 2019, wateraid.org; M. Yesaya and E. Tilley, 'Sludge Bomb: The Impending Sludge Emptying and Treatment Crisis in Blantyre, Malawi', *Journal of Environmental Management*, 277, 2019, 11474.

94. Satterthwaite et al., *Untreated and Unsafe*.

95. Satterthwaite et al., *Untreated and Unsafe*.

96. Satterthwaite et al., *Untreated and Unsafe*, chap. 2.

97. S. Lwasa and K. Owens, *Kampala: Rebuilding Public Sector Legitimacy with a New Approach to Sanitation Services*, World Resources Report Case Study, Washington, DC: World Resources Institute, 2018, wri.org.

98. IFRC, WASTE, Oxfam GB, and USAID, *The Emergency Sanitation Project – Phase 2 – Final Narrative Report*, International Federation of Red Cross and Red Crescent Societies, WASTE, Oxfam GB, 2019.

99. Mills et al., 'Costs, Climate and Contamination'.

100. W. Kombe, T. Ndezi, and P. Hofmann, *Water Justice City Profile: Dar es Salaam, Tanzania*, Translocal Learning for Water Justice:

Peri-urban Pathways in India, Tanzania and Bolivia report, London: Bartlett Development Planning Unit, UCL, 2015.

101. Satterthwaite et al., 'Revealing and Responding'.

102. A. Gupta et al., 'Prevalence and Risk Factors of Soil-Transmitted Helminth Infections in School Age Children (6–14 years) – A Cross-Sectional Study in an Urban Resettlement Colony of Delhi', *Indian Journal of Public Health*, 64: 4, 2020, 333–8.

103. UN-Habitat, *Addressing the Most Vulnerable First: Pro-Poor Climate Action in Informal Settlements*, Nairobi: UN-Habitat, 2018.

104. C. McFarlane, R. Desai, and S. Graham, 'Informal Urban Sanitation: Everyday Life, Poverty, and Comparison, *Annals of the Association of American Geographers*, 104: 5, 2014, 989–1011.

105. Lwasa and Owens, *Kampala*.

106. D. E. Baltazar et al., 'Comparative Analysis of Septage Management in Five Cities in the Philippines', *Eng*, 2, 2021, 12–26; P. Hawkins and I. Blackett, '5 Lessons to Manage Fecal Sludge Better', World Bank, *The Water Blog*, 19 July 2016, blogs.worldbank.org; A. Peal et al., 'Fecal Sludge Management: A Comparative Analysis of 12 Cities', *Journal of Water, Sanitation and Hygiene for Development*, 4: 4, 2014, 563.

107. A. Peal et al., *A Review of Fecal Sludge Management in 12 Cities: Annexure A.5 Dakar, Senegal*, World Bank Water and Sanitation Program, 2015.

108. S. Srivastava et al., 'Making "Shit" Everybody's Business: Co-Production in Urban Sanitation', IDS Policy Briefing 164, Brighton: Institute of Development Studies, 2019.

109. P. Hawkins and I. Blackett, 'Fecal Sludge Management Is the Elephant in the Room, but We Have Developed Tools to Help', World Bank, *The Water Blog*, 6 July 2016, blogs.worldbank.org.

110. Hawkins and Blackett, '5 Lessons to Manage Fecal Sludge Better'.

111. A. Taweesan, T. Koottatep, and C. Polprasert, 'Effective Faecal Sludge Management Measures for On-site Sanitation Systems', *Journal of Water, Sanitation and Hygiene for Development*, 5: 3, 2015, 483.

112. Lee and Radcliff, 'Community Interactions'.

113. M. Teshome et al., 'Sub-Saharan Africans Spend 60 Hours a Year Finding a Private Place to Defecate', *Down to Earth*, 28 August 2018.

114. Oberg, 'Problematizing Urban Shit(ting)'.

115. T. Srinivas, 'Flush with Success: Bathing, Defecation, Worship, and Social Change in South India', *Space and Culture*, 5: 4, 2002, 368–86; D. Chakrabarty, *Habitations of Modernity: Essays in the Wake of Subaltern Studies*, Chicago: University of Chicago Press, 2002.

116. R. Desai, C. McFarlane, and S. Graham, 'The Politics of Open Defecation: Informality, Body, and Infrastructure in Mumbai', *Antipode*, 47, 2015, 98–120; C. McFarlane and R. Desai, 'Sites of Entitlement: Claim, Negotiation and Struggle in Mumbai', *Environment and Urbanization*, 27, 2, 2015, 441–54.

117. JMP, 'Open Defecation', WHO-UNICEF Joint Management Group, washdata.org.

118. T. W. Abebe and G. T. Tucho, 'Open Defecation–Free Slippage and Its Associated Factors in Ethiopia: A Systematic Review', *Systematic Reviews*, 9, 2020, 252; N. McCarthy, '673 Million People Still Defecate Outdoors', *Statista*, 18 November 2019; B. Mosello and D. O'Leary, *How to Reduce Inequalities in Access to WASH: Urban Sanitation in Cambodia*, London: Overseas Development Institute, 2017.

119. M. Araya and T. Woldehana, 'Poverty and Inequality in Ethiopia, 1995/96–2015/16', in *The Oxford Handbook of the Ethiopian Economy*, ed. F. Cheru, C. Cramer, and A. Oqubay, Oxford: Oxford University Press, 2019; Mosello and O'Leary, *How to Reduce Inequalities in Access to WASH*; JMP, 'Open Defecation'.

120. N. M. Kiulia et al., 'Global Occurrence and Emission of Rotaviruses to Surface Waters', *Pathogens*, 4: 2, 2015, 229–55.

4. Life

1. O. Laing, 'Group Think: Why Art Loves a Crowd', *Observer*, 23 May 2021.

2. A. Amin, 'Lively Infrastructure', *Theory, Culture and Society*, 31: 7/8, 2014, 137–61.

3. I. Thacker and G. M. Sinatra, 'Visualizing the Greenhouse Effect: Restructuring Mental Models of Climate Change through a Guided Online Simulation', *Education Sciences*, 9: 1, 2019, 14; H. Bulkeley,

Accomplishing Climate Governance, Cambridge: Cambridge University Press, 2015; A. Merrifield, *The New Urban Question*, Pluto Press: London, 2014; C. Connolly, 'Managing COVID-19 on an Increasingly Urbanised Planet', *Medium*, 29 June 2020; V. Castán Broto, *Urban Energy Landscapes*, Cambridge: Cambridge University Press, 2019.

4. World Health Organization, *WHO Guidance to Protect Health from Climate Change through Health Adaptation Planning*, Geneva: World Health Organization, 2014, who.int; S. Enggist et al. (eds.), *Prisons and Health*, World Health Organization Regional Office for Europe, 2014; G. Howard et al., 'Climate Change and Water and Sanitation: Likely Impacts and Emerging Trends for Action', *Annual Review of Environment and Resources*, 41, 2016, 253–76.

5. Howard et al., 'Climate Change and Water and Sanitation'.

6. Customer Data Platform and Local Governments for Sustainability (CDP–ICLEI), '2018–2019 Full Cities Dataset', data.cdp.net.

7. P. Sippy, 'Tanzania's Dar-es-Salaam Hit by Water Shortages as Rivers Dry Up', *Al Jazeera*, 30 November 2021.

8. A. A. Scott et al., 'Temperature and Heat in Informal Settlements in Nairobi', *PLoS One*, 12: 11, 2017, e0187300.

9. Howard et al., 'Climate Change and Water and Sanitation'.

10. M. McLennan, *The Global Risks Report 2021: 16th Edition*, Switzerland: World Economic Forum, 2021; N. Thrift, *Killer Cities*, London: Sage, 2021, 27.

11. N. Smith, 'There's No Such Thing as a Natural Disaster', *Items*, 11 June 2006.

12. J. P. Borges Pedro et al., 'A Review of Sanitation Technologies for Flood-Prone Areas', *Journal of Water, Sanitation and Hygiene for Development*, 10: 3, 2020, 397–412.

13. A. M. Sherpa et al., 'Vulnerability and Adaptability of Sanitation Systems to Climate Change', *Journal of Water and Climate Change*, 5: 4, 2014, 487–95.

14. UN-Habitat, *Addressing the Most Vulnerable First: Pro-Poor Climate Action in Informal Settlements*, Nairobi: UN-Habitat, 2018.

15. A. Bahadur and D. Dodman, *Urban Climate Resilience – A Landscape Review: India, Bangladesh and Kenya*, London: International Institute for Environment and Development, 2021.

16. Borges Pedro et al., 'A Review of Sanitation Technologies'; J. Ensink et al., *Use of Untreated Wastewater in Peri-urban Agriculture in Pakistan: Risks and Opportunities*, Research Report 64, Colombo, Sri Lanka: International Water Management Institute, 2002; H. Ernstson and S. Sörlin (eds.), *Grounding Urban Natures: Histories and Futures of Urban Ecologies*, Cambridge, MA: MIT Press, 2019; CDP–ICLEI, '2018–2019 Full Cities Dataset'.

17. B. Smyth, P. Davison, and P. Brow, 'Carbon Curves for the Assessment of Embodied Carbon in the Wastewater Industry', *Water and Environmental Journal*, 31: 1, 2017, 4–11.

18. UN-Habitat, *Addressing the Most Vulnerable First*.

19. S. L. Wear et al., 'Sewage Pollution, Declining Ecosystem Health, and Cross-sector Collaboration', *Biological Conservation*, 255, 2021, 109010.

20. C. Chesler, 'How Philadelphia Will Solve the Sewage Nightmare under Its Feet', *Popular Mechanics*, 3 December 2015.

21. United Nations Development Programme, *Human Development Report: The Next Frontier – Human Development and the Anthropocene*, New York: United Nations, 2020.

22. V. Acuña, J. Comas, and L. Corominas, *Development and Testing of a Decision-Support System to Facilitate the Implementation of Nature-Based Solutions for Urban Water Sanitation*, Science for Nature and People Partnership (SNAPP) working group report, 2019, nceas.ucsb.edu.

23. K. Aronoff et al., *A Planet to Win: Why We Need a Green New Deal*, London: Verso, 2019.

24. D. Inglis, 'Dirt and Denigration: The Faecal Imagery and Rhetorics of Abuse', *Postcolonial Studies: Culture, Politics, Economy*, 5: 2, 2002, 207–21.

25. H. Ernstson and S. Sörlin (eds.), *Grounding Urban Natures: Histories and Futures of Urban Ecologies*, Cambridge, MA: MIT Press, 2019; E. Swyngedouw, *Social Power and the Urbanization of Water: Flows of Power*, Oxford: Oxford University Press, 2004; A. Loftus, 'Intervening in the Environment of the Everyday', *Geoforum*, 40: 3, 2009, 326–34; M. Gandy, 'Unintentional Landscapes', *Landscape Research*, 41: 4, 2016, 433–40.

26. K. H. Heddy, A. M. Smith, and N. A. Page, 'GEMS Extend Understanding of Childhood Diarrhoea', *Lancet*, 388, 2016, 1252–3; L. Liu et al., 'Global, Regional, and National Causes of Under-5 Mortality in 2000–15: An Updated Systematic Analysis with Implications for the Sustainable Development Goals', *Lancet*, 388: 10063, 2016, 3027–35; UNICEF, *Strategy for Water, Sanitation and Hygiene 2016–2030*, New York: UNICEF, 2016, unicef.org.

27. M. Porecha, 'In Mankhurd Slum, a Water Revolution Is Underway', *DNA*, 7 July 2015.

28. L. Pickering et al., 'Effect of a Community-Led Sanitation Intervention on Child Diarrhoea and Child Growth in Rural Mali: A Cluster-Randomised Controlled Trial', *Lancet Global Health*, 3: 11, 2015.

29. Heddy et al., 'GEMS Extend Understanding of Childhood Diarrhoea'.

30. Liu et al., 'Global, Regional, and National Causes of Under-5 Mortality'; M. Farag et al., 'Health Expenditures, Health Outcomes and the Role of Good Governance', *International Journal of Health Care Finance and Economics*, 13: 1, 2013, 33–52; G. P. M. Root, 'Sanitation, Community Environments, and Childhood Diarrhoea in Rural Zimbabwe', *Journal of Health, Population and Nutrition*, 19: 2, 2001, 73–82.

31. S. Patel, 'Upgrade, Rehouse or Resettle? An Assessment of the Indian Government's Basic Services for the Urban Poor (BSUP) Programme', *Environment and Urbanization*, 25: 1, 2013, 177–88.

32. H. Lefebvre, *The Production of Space*, Oxford: Blackwell, 1991 [1974], 197–8.

33. L. Pickering and P. Wiseman, 'Dirty Scholarship and Dirty Lives: Explorations in Bodies and Belonging', *Sociological Review*, 67, 4, 2019, 746–65; S. Ally, ' "Ooh, Eh Eh . . . Just One Small Cap Is Enough!" Servants, Detergents, and their Prosthetic Significance', *African Studies*, 72: 3, 2013, 321–52; A. McClintock, *Imperial Leather: Race, Gender, and Sexuality in the Colonial Contest*, New York: Routledge, 2013; B. Campkin, 'Placing "Matter Out of Place": *Purity and Danger* as Evidence for Architecture and Urbanism', *Architectural Theory Review*, 18: 1, 2013, 46–61; E. Swyngedouw, 'Circulations and Metabolisms: (Hybrid) Natures and (Cyborg) Cities', *Science as Culture*, 15:2, 2006, 105–21.

34. E. Grosz, *Volatile Bodies: Toward a Corporeal Feminism*, London: Routledge, 2020.

35. A. Mol, *The Body Multiple: Ontology in Medical Practice*, Durham, NC: Duke University Press, 2003.

36. D. Waltner-Toews, *The Origin of Feces: What Excrement Tells Us about Evolution, Ecology, and a Sustainable Society*, Toronto: ECW Press, 2013.

37. Waltner-Toews, *The Origin of Feces*, 23.

38. S. H. Ali and R. Keil, *Networked Disease: Emerging Infections in the Global City*, Oxford: Wiley-Blackwell, 2008; K. E. Jones et al., 'Global Trends in Emerging Infectious Diseases', *Nature*, 451: 7181, 2008, 990–3; G. Howard et al., 'Securing 2020 Vision for 2030: Climate Change and Ensuring Resilience in Water and Sanitation Services', *Journal of Water and Climate Change*, 1: 1, 2010, 2–16; R. Carroll, I. A. Wright, and J. K. Reynolds, 'Is Geochemical Contamination from Urban Development Contributing to Weed Invasions in High Conservation Value Wetlands?', Proceedings of the 9th Australian Stream Management Conference, 12–15 August 2018, Hobart, Tasmania, 673–80.

39. C. Connolly, R. Keil, and H. Ali, 'Extended Urbanisation and the Spatialities of Infectious Disease: Demographic Change, Infrastructure and Governance', *Urban Studies*, 58: 2, 2020, 258.

40. Jones et al., 'Global Trends'.

41. G. Howard et al., 'COVID-19: Urgent Actions, Critical Reflections and Future Relevance of "WaSH": Lessons for the Current and Future Pandemics', *Journal of Water and Health*, 18: 5, 2020, 613–30.

42. F. Mills et al., 'Faecal Pathogen Flows and Their Public Health Risks in Urban Environments: A Proposed Approach to Inform Sanitation Planning', *International Journal of Environmental Research and Public Health*, 15: 181, 2018.

43. Waltner-Toews, *The Origin of Feces*, 79.

44. Howard et al., 'COVID-19: Urgent Actions, Critical Reflections'.

45. Waltner-Toews, *The Origin of Feces*.

46. Waltner-Toews, *The Origin of Feces*, 66–74.

47. R. Keil, 'The Density Dilemma: There Is Always Too Much and Too Little of It', *Urban Geography*, 41: 10, 2020, 1284–93.

48. L. C. Franco, 'A Microbiological Survey of Handwashing Sinks in the Hospital Built Environment Reveals Differences in Patient Room and Healthcare Personnel Sinks', *Scientific Reports*, 10, 2020, 8234.

49. C. J. Neiderud, 'How Urbanization Affects the Epidemiology of Emerging Infectious Diseases', *Infection Ecology and Epidemiology*, 5, 24 June 2015.

50. A. V. Jung et al., 'Microbial Contamination Detection in Water Resources: Interest of Current Optical Methods, Trends and Needs in the Context of Climate Change', *International Journal of Environmental Research and Public Health*, 11: 4, 2014, 4292–310; R. V. Pouyat et al., 'Chemical, Physical, and Biological Characteristics of Urban Soils', *Urban Ecosystem Ecology*, 55, 2010, 119–52.

51. M. Alberti, 'Eco-evolutionary Dynamics in an Urbanizing Planet', *Trends in Ecology and Evolution*, 30: 2, 2015, 114–26.

52. R. Pacheco-Vega, 'Urban Wastewater Governance in Latin America: Panorama and Reflections for a Research Agenda', in *Water and Cities in Latin America: Challenges for Sustainable Development*, ed. I. Aguilar-Barajas et al., London: Routledge, 2015, 102–8.

53. R. J. Chou, 'Addressing Watercourse Sanitation in Dense, Water Pollution-Affected Urban Areas in Taiwan', *Environment and Urbanization*, 25: 2, 2013.

54. V. Antelo et al., 'First Release of the Bacterial Biobank of the Urban Environment (BBUE)', *Microbiology Resource Announcements*, 7: 16, 2018, 1201–18.

55. Alberti, 'Eco-evolutionary Dynamics'.

56. Alberti, 'Eco-evolutionary Dynamics'.

57. L. Westcott, 'Unclean Water Kills Half a Million Newborns a Year', *Newsweek*, 17 March 2015; K. A. Alexander et al., 'What Factors Might Have Led to the Emergence of Ebola in West Africa?', *PLoS: Neglected Tropical Diseases*, 4 June 2015; D. Gomez-Barroso et al., 'Spread of Ebola Virus Disease Based on the Density of Roads in East Africa', *Geospatial Health* 12: 2, 2017, 552; G. Howard and Z. White, 'Does Payment by Results Work? Lessons from a Multi-country WASH programme', *Journal of Water, Sanitation and Hygiene for Development*, 10: 4, 2020, 716–23; F. S. Mhalu, F. D. E. Mtango, and E. Msengi, 'Hospital Outbreaks of Cholera Transmitted through

Close Person-to-Person Contact', *Lancet*, 324: 8394, 1984, 82–4; O. Faye et al., 'Chains of Transmission and Control of Ebola Virus Disease in Conakry, Guinea, in 2014: An Observational Study', *Lancet Infectious Disease*, 15, 2015, 320–6.

58. J. Lazuta, 'Turn On the Taps to Defeat the Next Ebola', *Irin*, 15 June 2015; L. M. Nyamalon, 'Ebola and Sanitation', *Liberian Observer*, 5 October 2015.

59. M. Osava, 'Zika Epidemic Offers Sanitation a Chance in Brazil', Inter Press Service, 26 February 2016, ipsnews.net.

60. H. Dempster, 'Demons of Density: Delivering Water and Sanitation to the Poor', International Growth Centre blog, 25 January 2016, theigc.org; W. Cox, 'Evolving Urban Form: Dhaka', *Newgeography*, 8 August 2012; M. M. Rahman, P. J. Atkins, and C. McFarlane, 'Factors Affecting Slum Sanitation Projects in Dhaka City: Learning from the Dynamics of Social-Technological-Governance Systems', *Journal of Water, Sanitation and Hygiene for Development*, 4: 3, 2014, 346–58; C. McFarlane, R. Desai, and S. Graham, 'Informal Urban Sanitation: Everyday Life, Poverty, and Comparison, *Annals of the Association of American Geographers*, 104: 5, 2014, 989–1011; A. Hasan, 'Karachi, Informal Settlements and COVID-19', International Institute for Environment and Development blog, 6 May 2020, iied.org.

61. Dempster, 'Demons of Density'.

62. S. Hinchliffe, 'Model Evidence – The COVID-19 Case', *Somatosphere*, 31 March 2020; C. McFarlane, 'The Geographies of Urban Density: Topography, Topology, and Intensive Heterogeneity', *Progress in Human Geography*, 40, 2016, 629–48.

63. C. M. Worrell et al., 'A Cross-Sectional Study of Water, Sanitation, and Hygiene-Related Risk Factors for Soil-transmitted Helminth Infection in Urban School- and Preschool-Aged Children in Kibera, Nairobi', *PLoS ONE*, 11, 3, 2016, e0150744.

64. R. George, *The Big Necessity: Adventures in the World of Human Waste*, London: Portobello Books, 2008.

65. World Health Organization, 'Sanitation: Key Facts', who.int, 21 March 2022.

66. World Health Organization, 'Drop in Cholera Cases Worldwide, as Key Endemic Countries Report Gains in Cholera Control', news release, 19 December 2019, who.int.

67. A. Foster, 'Lebanon Cholera: "We're Afraid of Everything Now"', *BBC News*, 30 October 2022.

68. N. Al-Faour and L. Chapman, 'A Deadly Cholera Outbreak Compounds the Misery of War-Weary Syrians', *Arab News*, 4 November 2022; Foster, 'Lebanon Cholera'.

69. Mills et al., 'Faecal Pathogen Flows'.

70. Mills et al., 'Faecal Pathogen Flows'.

71. World Health Organization, *Guidelines on Sanitation and Health*, Geneva: World Health Organization, 2018.

72. F. Mills et al., 'Costs, Climate and Contamination: Three Drivers for Citywide Sanitation Investment Decisions', *Frontiers in Environment Science*, 8, 2020, 130.

73. I. Blackett, P. Hawkins, and C. Heymans, *The Missing Link in Sanitation Service Delivery: A Review of Fecal Sludge Management in 12 Cities*, Water and Sanitation Program research brief, Washington, DC: World Bank Group, 2014.

74. K. Brandes et al., *SFD Promotion Initiative: Dar es Salaam, Tanzania*, Department of Sanitation, Water and Solid Waste for Development (Sandec) at the Swiss Federal Institute of Aquatic Science and Technology (Eawag), 2015.

75. Mills et al., 'Costs, Climate and Contamination'.

76. S. J. Raj et al. 'The SaniPath Exposure Assessment Tool: A Quantitative Approach for Assessing Exposure to Fecal Contamination through Multiple Pathways in Low Resource Urban Settlements', *PLoS ONE*, 15: 6, 2020, e0234364.

77. A. R. A. Mohammadi, 'Microbial Contamination of Pipe-Network and Associated Health Risk in Kumasi, Ghana', master's thesis, Norwegian University of Life Sciences, 2013.

78. O. G. Bahcall, 'Urban Microbiome', *Nature Reviews Genetics*, 16: 4, 2015, 194–5.

79. M. Alberti, 'Invisible City Life: The Urban Microbiome', The Nature of Cities, 3 December 2014, thenatureofcities.com.

80. M. Alberti, 'Eco-evolutionary Dynamics in an Urbanizing Planet', *Trends in Ecology and Evolution*, 30: 2, 2015, 114–26.

81. K. Boo, *Behind the Beautiful Forevers*, London: Portobello Books, 2012; P. Tripathy and C. McFarlane, 'Perceptions of Atmosphere: Waste, Space, and Narratives of Work and Life in Mumbai', *Environment and Planning D: Society and Space*, 40: 4, 2022; D. Mili, 'Migration and Healthcare: Access to Healthcare Services by Migrants Settled in Shivaji Nagar Slum of Mumbai, India', *Health* 2: 3, 2011, 82–5.

82. Alberti, 'Eco-evolutionary Dynamics'.

83. A. Akinsete et al., *The Sanitation Economy Opportunity for South Africa – Sustainable Solutions for Water Security and Sanitation – A Business Perspective*, Water Research Commission, Toilet Board Coalition, 2019.

84. K. Abeysuriya et al., *Applying the WHO's Multi-barrier Approach to Faecal Sludge Reuse*, Learning Brief, Netherlands Development Organisation (SNV) and Institute for Sustainable Futures, University of Technology Sydney (ISF-UTS), 2016.

85. Waltner-Toews, *The Origin of Feces*.

86. Ali and Keil, *Networked Disease*; Connolly et al., 'Extended Urbanisation and the Spatialities of Infectious Disease'; S. Angel et al., 'The New Urban Peripheries, 1990–2014: Selected Findings from a Global Sample of Cities', Working Paper 40, Marrion Institute of Urban Management, New York University, June 2018.

87. Cuomo quoted in B. M. Rosenthal, 'Density Is New York City's Big "Enemy" in the Coronavirus Fight', *New York Times*, 23 March 2020.

88. M. W. Swanson, 'The Sanitation Syndrome: Bubonic Plague and Urban Native Policy in the Cape Colony, 1900–1909', *Journal of African History*, 1977, 387–410; C. McFarlane and J. Silver, 'The Poolitical City: "Seeing Sanitation" and Making the Urban Political in Cape Town', *Antipode*, 49: 1, 2017, 125–14; J. Garmnay and M. Richmond, 'Hygienisation, Gentrification, and Urban Displacement in Brazil', *Antipode*, 52: 1, 124–44.

89. J. Kotkin, *The Coming of Neo-feudalism: A Warning to the Global Middle Class*, New York: Encounter Books, 2020.

90. W. R. Boterman, 'Urban-Rural Polarisation in Times of the Corona Outbreak? The Early Demographic and Geographic Patterns of the SARS-COV-2 Epidemic in the Netherlands', *Tijdschrift voor Economische en Sociale Geografie*, 2020, 1–17.

91. H. Indorewala and S. Wagh, 'How Strong Is the Link between Mumbai's Slums and the Spread of the Coronavirus?', scroll.in, 20 July 2020.

92. R. Poplak, 'Where Lockdown Meets Crackdown – Government Action Is a Velvet Glove Slipped onto an Iron Fist', *Daily Maverick*, 22 April 2020.

93. Z. Tufekci, 'How Hong Kong Did It', *Atlantic*, 12 May 2020; S. Hamidi, S. Sabouri, and R. Ewing, 'Does Density Aggravate the COVID-19 Pandemic?', *Journal of the American Planning Association*, 86: 4, 2020, 495–509.

94. R. Keil, 'Infectious Disease in an Urban Society', *Medium*, 29 June 2020.

95. Connolly, 'Managing COVID-19 on an Increasingly Urbanised Planet'.

96. W. Cox, ' "Exposure Density" and the Pandemic', *New Geography*, 12 April 2020.

97. Karachi Urban Lab, 'Why COVID-19 Is an Urban Crisis', *Dawn*, 14 April 2020.

98. Hasan, 'Karachi, Informal Settlements and COVID-19'; M. Weston, 'How to Tackle Coronavirus in Slums', *Global Dashboard*, 27 March 2020; A. Wilkinson, 'Local Response in Health Emergencies: Key Considerations for Addressing the COVID-19 Pandemic in Informal Urban Settlements', *Environment and Urbanization*, 32: 2, 2020.

99. R. Cronk and J. Bartram, 'Environmental Conditions in Health Care Facilities in Low- and Middle-Income Countries: Coverage and Inequalities', *International Journal of Hygiene and Environmental Health*, 221: 3, 2018, 409–22.

100. T. Nagpal and A. Sublette, 'Unlikely Heroes: We Neglect Sanitation and Service Providers at Our Own Peril', *New Security Beat*, 17 August 2020.

101. UN-Habitat, *UN-Habitat COVID-19 Response Plan*, Nairobi, April 2020; JMP, 'Open Defecation', WHO-UNICEF Joint Management Group, washdata.org.

102. Wilkinson, 'Local Response in Health Emergencies'.

103. J. Pitter, 'Urban Density: Confronting the Distance between Desire and Disparity', *Azure*, 17 April 2020.

104. Howard et al., 'COVID-19: Urgent Actions, Critical Reflections'.

105. P. Tiwari, *Toilet Torture in Mumbai's Slums*, Mumbai: Observer Research Foundation Mumbai, 2015.

106. Food and Agricultural Organization, *World Livestock: Transforming the Livestock Sector through the Sustainable Development Goals – In Brief*, Rome: FAO, 2018.

107. M. Johnson and D. Shastri, 'Pathway to Peril', *Sentinel*, 13 July 2017; S. S. Mohakud et al., 'The Extent and Structure of Pig Rearing System in Urban and Peri-urban Areas of Guwahati', *Infection Ecology and Epidemiology*, 10: 1, 2020, 1711576.

108. P. Atkins (ed.), *Animal Cities: Beastly Urban Histories*, Surrey: Ashgate, 2012.

109. M. Barua, T. White, and D. Nally, 'Rescaling the Metabolic', *Centre for Research in the Arts, Social Sciences and Humanities*, 12 October 2020; F. Keck, *Avian Reservoirs: Virus Hunters and Birdwatchers in Chinese Sentinel Posts*, Durham, NC: Duke University Press, 2020; A. H. Kelly, F. Keck, and C. Lynteris, *The Anthropology of Epidemics*, London: Routledge, 2019; S. Hinchliffe et al., *Pathological Lives: Disease, Space and Biopolitics*, Oxford: Wiley, 2016.

110. Thrift, *Killer Cities*, 84; P. Tullis, 'Is the Next Pandemic Brewing on the Netherlands' Poultry Farms?', *Bulletin of the Atomic Scientists*, 26 September 2022.

111. T. N. Raymond et al., 'Do Open Garbage Dumps Play a Role in Canine Rabies Transmission in Biyem-Assi Health District in Cameroon?', *Infection Ecology and Epidemiology*, 5, 2015, 26055; R. Sivakumar, '57 Dogs Died in IIT-Madras Shelter over 13 Months: Govt', *New Indian Express*, 8 December 2021.

112. H. Nicholls, 'Should Cities Be for Animals Too?' *Guardian*, 14 April 2014.

113. 'Lack of Grazing Land in Cities Can't Be Excuse to Leave Cattle on Roads Says Gujarat High Court', *Times of India*, 9 April 2022.

114. H. F. Wilson, 'Seabirds in the City: Urban Futures and Fraught Coexistence', *Transactions of the Institute of British Geographers*, 47: 4, 2022, 1137–51, 1148.

115. G. Penakalapati et al., 'Exposure to Animal Faeces and Human Health: A Systematic Review and Proposed Research Priorities', *Environmental Science and Technology*, 51: 20, 2017, 11537–52.

116. M. R. Mason et al., 'Protective Practices against Zoonotic Infections among Rural and Slum Communities from South Central Chile', *BMC Public Health*, 15, 2015, 713.

117. Penakalapati et al., 'Exposure to Animal Faeces and Human Health'; Howard et al., 'COVID-19: Urgent Actions, Critical Reflections'.

118. Howard et al., 'COVID-19: Urgent Actions, Critical Reflections'; Mason et al., 'Protective Practices against Zoonotic Infections'.

119. London School of Hygiene and Tropical Medicine, 'Drones Help Scientists Understand Emerging Zoonotic Malaria', news release, 22 October 2014, lshtm.ac.uk.

120. Mason et al., 'Protective Practices against Zoonotic Infections'.

121. F. Orsini et al., 'Urban Agriculture in the Developing World: A Review', *Agronomy Sustainable Development*, 33, 2013, 695–720.

5. Protest

1. N. Donnelly, ' "Dirty" Protest in Balbriggan Cell was "Animalistic" ', *Fingal Independent*, 13 April 2015.

2. C. Borch, *The Politics of the Crowd: An Alternative History of Sociology*, Cambridge: Cambridge University Press, 2012; J. McClelland, *The Crowd and the Mob: From Plato to Canetti*, London: Routledge, 1989.

3. I. Sonak, 'Jharkhand Protests: Land Acquisition Amendments Set Aside Important Safeguards', *Down to Earth*, 5 July 2018.

4. A. Xaxa, 'If Our Poop Protest Is Considered Uncivil, Then Tell Me What Is Civil in This Country', *India Resists*, 20 March 2015, indiaresists.com.

5. Xaxa, 'If Our Poop Protest'.

6. S. Kaviraj, 'Filth and the Public Sphere: Concepts and Practices about Space in Calcutta', *Public Culture* 10: 1, 1997, 83–113.

7. J. Melvin, 'Frenchman Launches Poo Protest against Banks', *Local*, 6 March 2014; D. Cohen, 'The Power of Poo in Southern Africa', *US News*, 4 November 2013; K. LaCapria, 'Throw Blanket', *Snopes*, 2016, snopes.com.

8. B. Cruse and B. Jolly, 'Protesters "Defecated at the Feet of the Police" during Bristol Riot', *Daily Express*, 22 March 2021.

9. *Chicagoist*, 'Chicago Buys New Riot and Surveillance Gear for NATO/G8', 14 February 2012.

10. J. J. Maher, 'More Hot, Steaming Doo Doo Accord Coverage!', *Westword*, 6 August 2008.

11. M. Liboiron, 'Tactics of Waste, Dirt, and Discard in the Occupy Movement', *Social Movement Studies*, 11: 3–4, 2012, 394.

12. Liboiron, 'Tactics of Waste, Dirt, and Discard'.

13. Liboiron, 'Tactics of Waste, Dirt, and Discard', 400.

14. J. L. Miere, 'Venezuela Crisis: Protestors "Poop Bombs" Are "Biochemical Weapon", Government Says', *Newsweek*, 12 May 2017.

15. In Ezra Pound's *Cantos*, for example, the agitating 'multitudes' are portrayed as threatening the very structure of urban capitalist society and order, so much so that England was one 'great arsehole'. See D. Inglis, 'Dirt and Denigration: The Faecal Imagery and Rhetorics of Abuse', *Postcolonial Studies: Culture, Politics, Economy*, 5: 2, 2002, 207–21.

16. C. Quint, 'From Embodied Shame to Reclaiming the Stain: Reflections on a Career in Menstrual Activism', *Sociological Review*, 67: 4, 2019, 927–42; C. Bobel, *The Managed Body: Developing Girls and Menstrual Health in the Global South*, Cham: Springer, 2018.

17. L. Jones, '10 Facts about Sanitation in Malawi', The Borgen Project blog, 7 October 2020, borgenproject.org.

18. M. Douglas, *Purity and Danger: An Analysis of Concepts of Pollution and Taboo*, New York: Routledge, 2003 [1966].

19. Quint, 'From Embodied Shame to Reclaiming the Stain', 938, 942.

20. 'Guantanamo Prisoners Now Throwing Faeces, Urine, Sperm and Vomit at Guards', RT, 13 March 2015, rt.com.

21. R. Sisk, 'Gitmo Prisoners "Splash" US Guards with Urine, Faeces and Vomit', Military.com, 12 March 2015.

22. C. Lawrence and M. Smith, 'Daily Life at Guantanamo: Hunger Strikes, Sprays of Filth', CNN, 17 May 2013.

23. Lawrence and Smith, 'Daily Life at Guantanamo'.

24. M. Moffa et al., 'A Systematic Scoping Review of Hygiene Behaviors and Environmental Health Conditions in Institutional Care Settings

for Orphaned and Abandoned Children', *Science of the Total Environment*, 658, 2019, 1161–74; G. Howard et al., 'COVID-19: Urgent Actions, Critical Reflections and Future Relevance of "WaSH": Lessons for the Current and Future Pandemics', *Journal of Water and Health*, 18: 5, 2020, 613–30.

25. A. Nellis, *The Color of Justice: Racial and Ethnic Disparity in State Prisons*, Washington, DC: The Sentencing Project, 2021.

26. A. Thakur and R. Nagarajan, 'Why Minorities Have a Major Presence in Prisons', *Times of India*, 12 February 2020.

27. J. Gregory, ' "Cramped Relic": Urgent Action Needed to "Save Lives" Inside Overcrowded Pentonville Prison, Campaigners Warn', *Islington Citizen*, 19 October 2022.

28. B. Bostock, '2 Inmates at a UK Jail Were Tested for the Wuhan Coronavirus after a Prisoner Collapsed in His Cell. Here's Why Prisons Are among the Worst Places to Handle Outbreaks', *Business Insider*, 12 February 2020; D. Shallard-Brown, 'Sanitation Problems in a Panamanian Prison', Prisoners Abroad, 19 November 2018, prisonersabroad.org.uk; S. Enggist et al. (eds.), *Prisons and Health*, World Health Organization Regional Office for Europe, 2014; J. Neff and K. Blakinger, 'First Came the Pandemic, Then Came the Raw Sewage', *Marshall Project*, 30 May 2020, themarshallproject. org; National Institute for Jail Operations, 'Standard 101.03.02: Personal Hygiene Items Issued to Inmates', Legal-Based Guidelines Monthly Brief, National Institute for Jail Organizations, 2017, jail-training.org; T. M. Martin, 'The Politics of Prison Air: Breath, Smell, and Wind in Myanmar Prisons', *Punishment and Society*, 23: 4, 2021, 478–96, 87.

29. T. P. Coogan, *On the Blanket: The Inside Story of the IRA Prisoners' 'Dirty' Protest*, New York: Palgrave Macmillan, 2002 [1980], 137.

30. J. Silver, 'The Potentials of Carbon Markets for Infrastructure Investment in Sub-Saharan Urban Africa', *Current Opinion in Environmental Sustainability*, 13, 2015, 25–31; H. Bulkeley, A. Luque-Ayala, and J. Silver, 'Housing and the (Re)Configuration of Energy Provision in Cape Town and São Paulo: Making Space for a Progressive Urban Climate Politics?', *Political Geography*, 40, 2014, 25–34.

31. D. Attwell, *Rewriting Modernity: Studies in Black South African Literary History*, Athens: Ohio University Press, 2006; E. Ngara, 'Achebe as Artist: The Place and Significance of Anthills of the Savannah', *Kunapipi*, 12: 2, 1990, 14.

32. Attwell, *Rewriting Modernity*, 148.

33. M. De Waal, 'Ayanda Kota: Unapologetic ANC Apostate', *Daily Maverick*, 7 February 2012, dailymaverick.co.za.

34. A. Kota, 'SA, We Cannot Say We Are Free', *Mail and Guardian*, 6 May 2011.

35. De Waal, 'Ayanda Kota'.

36. A. Appadurai, 'Deep Democracy: Urban Governmentality and the Horizon of Politics', *Environment and Urbanization*, 13: 2, 2001, 23–43.

37. M. W. Swanson, 'The Sanitation Syndrome: Bubonic Plague and Urban Native Policy in the Cape Colony, 1900–1909', *Journal of African History*, 1977, 387–410.

38. J. Garmnay and M. Richmond, 'Hygienisation, Gentrification, and Urban Displacement in Brazil', *Antipode*, 52: 1, 124–44; B. Finn, 'Pandemic Urbanization: How South Africa's History of Labor and Disease Control Creates Its Current Disparities', presentation to the COVID-19 and Urban Density session of the Association of American Geographers Annual Meeting, online, 7–11 April 2021.

39. O. Crankshaw, 'Deindustrialization, Professionalization and Racial Inequality in Cape Town', *Urban Affairs Review*, 48: 6, 2012, 836–62.

40. S. Robins, 'The 2011 Toilet Wars in South Africa: Justice and Transition between the Exceptional and the Everyday after Apartheid', *Development and Change*, 45:3, 2014, 479–501.

41. A. von Schnitzler, 'Traveling Technologies: Infrastructure, Ethical Regimes, and the Materiality of Politics in South Africa', *Cultural Anthropology*, 28: 4, 2013, 670–93.

42. S. Robins, 'Slow Activism in Fast Times: Reflections on the Politics of Media Spectacles after Apartheid', *Journal of Southern African Studies*, 40: 1, 2014, 91–110.

43. The bucket system and its inadequacies are described in detail in L. Taing et al., 'Challenges Facing Sanitation-Provision Partnerships for Informal Settlements: A South African Case Study', *Journal of Water, Sanitation and Hygiene for Development*, 3: 2, 2013, 230–9.

44. C. McFarlane and J. Silver, 'The Poolitical City: "Seeing Sanitation" and Making the Urban Political in Cape Town', *Antipode*, 49: 1, 2017, 125–14.

45. D. R. Peterson, K. Gavua, and C. Rassool, *The Politics of Heritage in Africa: Economies, Histories, and Infrastructures*, Cambridge: Cambridge University Press, 2015.

46. P. Lahunga, 'Showdown in Dunoon over Toilet Companies', *GroundUp*, 8 September 2020, groundup.org.za.

47. Lahunga, 'Showdown in Dunoon'.

48. P. Lahunga, 'Dunoon Residents Empty Toilets on N7', *GroundUp*, 17 August 2020, groundup.org.za.

49. L. Chenwi, 'Unpacking "Progressive Realisation", Its Relation to Resources, Minimum Core and Reasonableness, and Some Methodological Considerations for Assessing Compliance', *De Jure*, 46: 3, 2013, 742–69; S. Parnell and E. Pieterse, 'The "Right to the City": Institutional Imperatives of a Developmental State', *International Journal of Urban and Regional Research*, 34: 1, 2010, 146–62.

50. V. Baxter and M. N. Mbongeni, ' "This Shit Is Political; Shit Is Real", The Politics of Sanitation, Protest, and the Neoliberal, Post-apartheid City', *Studies in Theatre and Performance*, 40:1, 2020, 72, 76.

51. C. Healy, 'South African Students in Poo Protest against Institutional Racism', *Trinity News*, 17 March 2015, trinitynews.ie.

52. K. Serino, 'Anti-racism Protestors in South Africa Use Poop to Make a Point', *Al Jazeera*, 6 April 2015.

53. Serino, 'Anti-racism Protestors'.

54. Serino, 'Anti-racism Protestors'.

6. Allocation

1. C. Smith, ' "If White People Were Still Here, This Wouldn't Happen": The Majority-Black Town Flooded with Sewage', *Guardian*, 11 February 2021; 'Flooded and Forgotten', Centreville Sewage Crisis website, floodedandforgotten.com.

2. Smith, ' "If White People Were Still Here" '.

3. E. Pilkington, 'Activist Catherine Flowers: The Poor Living amid Sewage Is "The Final Monument of the Confederacy" ', *Guardian*, 11

February, 2021; E. Lutz, ' "They Couldn't Care Less": Plan to Solve Sewage Crisis in Illinois Town Merely "A Patch" ', *Guardian*, 13 April 2021.

4. J. E. Tiberghien and A. Hueso, *A Tale of Clean Cities: Insights for Planning Urban Sanitation from Ghana, India and the Philippines – Synthesis Report*, London: WaterAid, 2016, wateraid.org.

5. M. Black and B. Fawcett, *The Last Taboo: Opening the Door on the Global Sanitation Crisis*, London: Earthscan, 2008; D. Satterthwaite and D. Mitlin, *Reducing Urban Poverty in the Global South*, London: Routledge, 2014; UN Millennium Project Task Force on Water and Sanitation, *Health, Dignity, and Development: What Will It Take?*, New York: Stockholm International Water Institute (SIWI) and United Nations Millennium Project, 2005.

6. S. Parnell and E. Pieterse, 'The "Right to the City": Institutional Imperatives of a Developmental State', *International Journal of Urban and Regional Research*, 34: 1, 2010, 146–62; A. Amin and N. Thrift, *Seeing Like a City*, Hoboken: John Wiley & Sons, 2017; W. Magnusson, *Politics of Urbanism: Seeing Like a City*, London: Routledge, 2011.

7. Magnusson, *Politics of Urbanism*.

8. Parnell and Pieterse, 'The "Right to the City" ', 153.

9. H. Northover, 'Beyond Political Will – How Leadership Makes a Difference on Water and Sanitation', *From Poverty to Power* (blog), 14 April 2021, frompoverty.oxfam.org.uk.

10. G. McGranahan, 'Realizing the Right to Sanitation in Deprived Urban Communities: Meeting the Challenges of Collective Action, Coproduction, Affordability, and Housing Tenure', *World Development*, 68, 2015, 242–53; S. Srivastava et al., 'Making "Shit" Everybody's Business: Co-Production in Urban Sanitation', IDS Policy Briefing 164, Brighton: Institute of Development Studies, 2019; E. Ostrom, 'Crossing the Great Divide: Coproduction, Synergy, and Development', *World Development*, 24: 6, 1996, 1073–87; UN-Habitat, *UN-Habitat COVID-19 Response Plan*, Nairobi, April 2020; European Communities and Water Utility Partnership, *Better Water and Sanitation for the Urban Poor: Good Practice from Sub-Saharan Africa*, Washington, DC: World Bank Group, 2003, 79.

11. Srivastava et al., 'Making "Shit" Everybody's Business', 4; F. Mills et al., 'Costs, Climate and Contamination: Three Drivers for Citywide Sanitation Investment Decisions', *Frontiers in Environment Science*, 8, 2020.

12. Tiberghien and Hueso, *A Tale of Clean Cities*.

13. C. Montgomery, 'The Secrets of the World's Happiest Cities', *Guardian*, 1 November 2013, 324.

14. S. Patel and SPARC, 'The 20-Year Sanitation Partnership of Mumbai and the Indian Alliance', *Environment and Urbanization*, 27: 1, 2015, 55–72, 63.

15. 'This Crisis Has Helped Us to Strengthen the Collaboration between Departments within the City', Water and Sanitation for the Urban Poor, 7 October 2020, wsup.com.

16. P. Newborne, J. Tucker, and K. Bayliss, *Strengthening Pro-poor Targeting of Investments by African Utilities in Urban Water and Sanitation – The Role of the International Development Association of the World Bank*, Overseas Development Institute, 2012, washmatters.wateraid.org.

17. G. Hutton, 'Can We Really Put a Price on Meeting the Global Targets on Drinking-Water and Sanitation?', World Bank, *The Water Blog*, 12 February 2016, blogs.worldbank.org; G. Hutton and M. Varughese, 'The Costs of Meeting the 2030 Sustainable Development Goals Targets on Drinking Water, Sanitation, and Hygiene', Water and Sanitation Program: Technical Paper, Washington, DC: World Bank.

18. World Resources Institute, 'Safe, Affordable Sanitation: A Pipe Dream for Too Many Households in the Global South', press release, 18 December 2019, wri.org.

19. E. Haves, 'Urban Water and Sanitation in Developing Countries: Impact of Climate Change', House of Lords Library, UK Parliament, 11 November 2021, lordslibrary.parliament.uk; D. Nair, 'COVID-19 May Cost the Global Economy $35.3 Trillion by 2025', *National*, 27 August 2020, thenationalnews.com; C. H Lizarraga, 'UK Government Spent £376 Billion on Covid Pandemic Response', *Bloomberg*, 23 June 2022.

20. Hutton, 'Can We Really Put a Price'.

21. K. Watkins and H. Fore, 'Let's Convert Unpayable Debt into Investments for Children', Save the Children blog, 19 October 2020, savethechildren.org.uk.

22. Mills et al., 'Costs, Climate and Contamination'; L. Daudey, 'The Cost of Urban Sanitation Solutions: A Literature Review', *Journal of Water, Sanitation and Hygiene for Development* 8, 2018, 176–95.

23. K. Mugo, S. Metcalfe, and J. Du, 'Urban Sanitation Is a Climate and Economic Issue Too', *PreventionWeb*, 19 November 2020; D. Satterthwaite et al., *Untreated and Unsafe: Solving the Urban Sanitation Crisis in the Global South*, Washington, DC: World Resources Institute, 2019.

24. A. Akinsete et al., *The Sanitation Economy Opportunity for South Africa – Sustainable Solutions for Water Security and Sanitation – A Business Perspective*, Water Research Commission, Toilet Board Coalition, 2019, 7.

25. R. Ratcliffe, ' "Liquid Gold": Students Make World's First Brick Out of Human Urine', *Guardian*, 25 October 2018.

26. V. Shelbert et al., *Shared Sanitation in Low-Income Urban Settlements: Evidence from Ghana, Kenya and Bangladesh*, policy brief, London: Water and Sanitation for the Urban Poor, 2021, wsup.org.

27. D. Mitlin and D. Satterthwaite, 'Addressing Deprivations in Urban Areas, in *Empowering Squatter Citizen: Local Government, Civil Society and Urban Poverty Reduction*, ed. D. Mitlin and D. Satterthwaite, London: Routledge, 2013, 266–98; C. Mulenga, 'SME Taxation in Zambia', paper presented to the International Growth Centre Workshop on Informal Sector Taxation in Zambia, Lusaka, 16 November 2011; M. Grieco, 'Living Infrastructure: Replacing Children's Labour as a Source of Sanitation Services in Ghana', *Desalination*, 248: 1–3, 2009, 485–93; A. Lusambili, ' "It Is Our Dirty Little Secret": An Ethnographic Study of the Flying Toilets in Kibera Slums, Nairobi', STEPS Working Paper 44, Brighton: STEPS Centre, 2011; T. Lloyd-Jones and C. Rakodi, *Urban Livelihoods: A People-centred Approach to Reducing Poverty*, London: Routledge, 2014.

28. Black and Fawcett, *The Last Taboo*.

29. H. A. Ruszczyk, E. Nugraham, and E. de Villiers, *Overlooked Cities: Power, Politics and Knowledge Beyond the Urban South*, London: Routledge, 2020.

30. M. C. Wegerif and A. Guereña, 'Land Inequality Trends and Drivers', *Land*, 9: 4, 2020, 101; S. Stein, *Capital City: Gentrification and the Real Estate State*, London: Verso, 2019; T. Caldeira, *City of Walls: Crime, Segregation, and Citizenship in Sao Paulo*, Berkeley: California University Press, 2000; A. Merrifield, *The New Urban Question*, Pluto Press: London, 2014; H. Lefebvre, *The Production of Space*, Oxford: Blackwell, 1991 [1974]; N. Smith, 'Gentrification, the Frontier, and the Restructuring of Urban Space', in *Readings in Urban Theory*, ed. S. Fainstein and S. Campbell, Hoboken, NJ: Wiley, 1996, 338–58; D. Harvey, *Social Justice in the City*, Baltimore: John Hopkins University Press, 1973.

31. M. Cantor, 'Loo-dicrous: San Francisco Flushed with Anger over $1.7m Public Toilet', *Guardian*, 2 October 2022.

32. J. P. Faguet, F. Sanches, and M. J. Villaveces, 'The Paradox of Land Reform, Inequality and Local Development in Colombia', working paper, London School of Economics and Political Science, 2016.

33. D. Joshi, 'COVID-19 Pandemic Exposes Housing, Food Water and Sanitation Problems in Nepal', onlinekhabar.com, 18 April 2020.

34. L. Tusting, D. Bisanzio, and G. Alabaster, 'Mapping Changes in Housing in Sub-Saharan Africa from 2000 to 2015', *Nature*, 568, 2019, 391–96.

35. Tusting et al., 'Mapping Changes in Housing'; I. Turok, 'Persistent Polarisation Post-apartheid? Progress towards Urban Integration in Cape Town', *Urban Studies*, 38: 13, 2001, 2349–77; M. Rubin, 'At the Borderlands of Informal Practices of the State: Negotiability, Porosity and Exceptionality', *Journal of Development Studies*, 54: 12, 2018, 2227–42.

36. V. Singh and A. Srivastava, 'Lost in Transit: Residents Have Given Up Hope of Ever Returning to Their Original Homes', *DNA*, 2 September 2017, dnaindia.com.

37. S. Patel, 'Upgrade, Rehouse or Resettle? An Assessment of the Indian Government's Basic Services for the Urban Poor (BSUP) Programme', *Environment and Urbanization*, 25: 1, 2013, 177–88.

38. A. Mayne, *Slums: The History of a Global Injustice*, London: Reaktion Books, 2017.

39. D. Satterthwaite, G. McGranahan, and D. Mitlin, *Community-Driven Development for Water and Sanitation in Urban Areas: Its Contribution to Meeting the Millennium Development Goal Targets*, Geneva: Water Supply and Sanitation Collaborative Council (WSSCC), 2005.

40. Homeless International, 'How Do Land Tenure Issues Affect Sanitation Provision for the Urban Poor?', Learning Brief 1, Coventry: Homeless International, 2011.

41. N. Gill, 'IHC Global at World Urban Forum 10: Property Rights, Context, and Culture', *IHC Blog*, 7 April 2020, ihcglobal.org.

42. Water and Sanitation for the Urban Poor, 'Dealing with Land Tenure and Tenancy Challenges in Water and Sanitation Services Delivery', topic brief, London: Water and Sanitation for the Urban Poor, 2013, wsup.org.

43. Wegerif and Guereña, 'Land Inequality Trends and Drivers'.

44. M. Rakotoson, 'Who Owns the Land? The Challenges of Improving Sanitation Systems in Cities', washfunders.org, 2017 (webpage retired).

45. WSUP, 'Dealing with Land Tenure'.

46. WSUP, 'Dealing with Land Tenure'.

47. WSUP, 'Dealing with Land Tenure'.

48. K. Aronoff et al., *A Planet to Win: Why We Need a Green New Deal*, London: Verso, 2019.

49. M. Hart and R. King, 'To Fix Slums, Don't Just Knock Them Down: Involve Residents in Upgrading Efforts', World Resources Institute, 13 November 2019, wri.org.

50. K. Bakker, *Privatizing Water: Governance Failure and the World's Water Crisis*, Ithaca, NY: Cornell University Press, 2010.

51. Bakker, *Privatizing Water*, 3; I. Giglioli and E. Swyngedouw, 'Let's Drink to the Great Thirst! Water and the Politics of Fractured Technonatures in Sicily', *International Journal of Urban and Regional Research*, 32: 3, 2008, 392–414.

52. Bakker, *Privatizing Water*; L. Bagnoli, S. B. Sanchez, A. Estache, and M. Vagliasindi, 'Are the Poor Better Off with Public or Private Utilities?: A Survey of the Academic Evidence on Developing Economies', ECARES Working Paper 2020–24, Université libre de Bruxelles, 2020.

53. Bagnoli et al., 'Are the Poor Better Off', 8.

54. UN-Habitat, *Water and Sanitation in the World's Cities: Local Action for Global Goals*, London: Earthscan, 2003.

55. A. Gilbert, 'Water for All: How to Combine Public Management with Commercial Practice to the Benefit of the Poor?', *Urban Studies*, 44: 8, 2007, 1559–79.

56. K. Bakker, 'The Business of Water: Market Environmentalism in the Water Sector', *Annual Review of Environment and Resources*, 39, 2014, 469–94.

57. K. Bakker, 'Constructing "Public" Water: The World Bank, Urban Water Supply, and the Biopolitics of Development', *Environment and Planning D: Society and Space*, 31, 2013, 280–300.

58. Bakker, 'Constructing "Public" Water', 286.

59. Bagnoli et al., 'Are the Poor Better Off'.

60. A. von Schnitzler, 'Democracy's Infrastructure', in *Democracy's Infrastructure*, Princeton, NJ: Princeton University Press, 2016.

61. J. Uitermark and J. Tieleman, 'From Fragmentation to Integration and Back Again: The Politics of Water Infrastructure in Accra's Peripheral Neighbourhoods', *Transactions of the Institute of British Geographers*, 46: 2, 2020, 347–62.

62. B. Chaflin, 'Public Things, Excremental Politics, and the Infrastructure of Bare Life in Ghana's City of Tema', *American Ethnologist*, 41: 1, 2014, 92–109.

63. J. Allen and M. Pryke, 'Financialising Household Water: Thames Water, MEIF, and "Ring-Fenced" Politics', *Cambridge Journal of Regions, Economy and Society*, 6, 2013, 419–39.

64. Bagnoli et al., 'Are the Poor Better Off'.

65. A. Okeowo, 'The Heavy Toll of The Black Belt's Wastewater Crisis', *New Yorker,* 30 November 2020.

66. P. Newborne and N. Mason, 'The Private Sector's Contribution to Water Management: Re-examining Corporate Purposes and Company Roles', *Water Alternatives*, 5: 3, 2012, 603.

67. A. Loftus, 'Rethinking Political Ecologies of Water', *Third World Quarterly*, 30: 5, 2009, 953–68.

68. T. Nagpal and A. Sublette, 'Unlikely Heroes: We Neglect Sanitation and Service Providers at Our Own Peril', *New Security Beat*, 17 August 2020.

69. European Communities and Water Utility Partnership, *Better Water and Sanitation for the Urban Poor*, 10.

70. Bagnoli et al., 'Are the Poor Better Off'; K. Bayliss, 'Utility Privatisation in Sub-Saharan Africa: A Case Study of Water, *Journal of Modern African Studies*, 41: 4, 2003, 507–31; Bakker, 'The Business of Water'.

71. K. Kosec, 'The Child Health Implications of Privatizing Africa's Urban Water Supply', *Journal of Health Economics*, 35, 2014, 1–19; G. Clarke, K. Kosec, and S. Wallsten, 'Has Private Participation in Water and Sewerage Improved Coverage? Empirical Evidence from Latin America', *Journal of International Development*, 21: 3, 2009, 327–61.

72. G. Y. Carolini and P. Raman, 'Why Detailing Spatial Equity Matters in Water and Sanitation Evaluations', *Journal of the American Planning Association*, 87: 1, 2020, 101–7.

73. Bagnoli et al., 'Are the Poor Better Off'; L. A. Andres et al., *Doing More with Less: Smarter Subsidies for Water Supply and Sanitation*, Washington, DC: World Bank.

74. Andres et al., *Doing More with Less*.

75. Nagpal and Sublette, 'Unlikely Heroes'.

76. Bagnoli et al., 'Are the Poor Better Off'.

77. J. D. Sachs and J. W. McArthur, 'The Millennium Project: A Plan for Meeting the Millennium Development Goals', *Lancet*, 365: 9456, 2005, 347–53.

78. R. Fredericks, *Garbage Citizenship: Vital Infrastructures of Labor in Dakar, Senegal*, Durham, NC: Duke University Press, 2018, 98.

79. See, too, M. Samson, 'Rescaling the State, Restructuring Social Relations: Local Government Transformation and Waste Management Privatization in Post-apartheid Johannesburg', *International Feminist Journal of Politics*, 10: 1, 2008, 119–43.

80. Fredericks, *Garbage Citizenship*, 120.

81. Okeowo, 'The Heavy Toll of the Black Belt's Wastewater Crisis'.

82. C. Albuquerque, *Report of the Special Rapporteur on the Human Right to Safe Drinking Water and Sanitation*, United Nations General Assembly Human Rights Council, 2011.

83. J. E. Hardoy and D. Satterthwaite, *Squatter Citizen: Life in the Urban Third World*, London: Routledge, 1989; D. Satterthwaite, 'Transforming Aid for Urban Areas', International Institute for Environment and Development blog, 4 September 2018, iied.org; D. Mitlin, S. Colenbrander, and D. Satterthwaite, 'Editorial: Finance for Community-Led Local, City and National Development', *Environment and Urbanization*, 30: 1, 3–14, 2018.

84. E. Pieterse, 'Filling the Void: An Agenda for Tackling African Urbanisation', in *Africa's Urban Revolution*, ed. S. Parnell and E. Pieterse, London: Zed Books, 2014, 213.

85. L. Bassel, *The Politics of Listening*, London: Palgrave Pivot, 2017; L. Back, *The Art of Listening*, Oxford: Berg, 2007.

86. W. Connolly, *A World of Becoming*, Durham, NC: Duke University Press, 2011, 83.

87. Satterthwaite and Mitlin, *Reducing Urban Poverty*.

88. Mitlin et al., 'Editorial: Finance for Community-Led Local, City and National Development'.

89. G. Baiocchi, 'Participation, Activism, and Politics: The Porto Alegre Experiment and Deliberative Democratic', *Theory Politics and Society* 29, 2001, 43–72; Y. Sintomer, C. Herzberg, and A. Rocke, 'Participatory Budgeting in Europe: Potentials and Challenges', *International Journal of Urban and Regional Research*, 32, 2008, 164–78; C. McFarlane, *Learning the City: Knowledge and Translocal Assemblage*, Oxford: Wiley Blackwell, 2011.

7. Conclusion

1. United Nations, 'Chapter 4 – Urbanization: Expanding Opportunities but Deepening Divides', in *World Social Report 2020*, New York: United Nations, 2020, 107–26.

2. A. Hoffman et al., 'COVID-19: A Turning Point to Further Sanitation Justice?', *Interdisciplinary Perspectives on Equality and Diversity*, 8 April 2021.

3. M. Fisher, *Capitalist Realism: Is There No Alternative?* Hampshire: Zero Books, 2009, 4.

4. M. Maher and S. Khan, 'Filthy Rich: A Karachi Sewer Operation for a Sick City', Urban Resource Centre, 19 January 2021, urckarachi.org.

5. S. Patel and SPARC, 'The 20-Year Slum Sanitation Partnership of Mumbai and the Indian Alliance', *Environment and Urbanization*, 27: 1, 2015, 55–72.

6. D. Mitlin, S. Colenbrander, and D. Satterthwaite, 'Editorial: Finance for Community-Led Local, City and National Development', *Environment and Urbanization*, 30: 1, 3–14, 2018.

Index

Page numbers in **bold** refer to figures.